HERE
THE STORY OF A
LIES
POP-UP BUILDING
LOVE

BY

FERNANDO

SANCHO

FOREWORD BY DAVID BYRNE

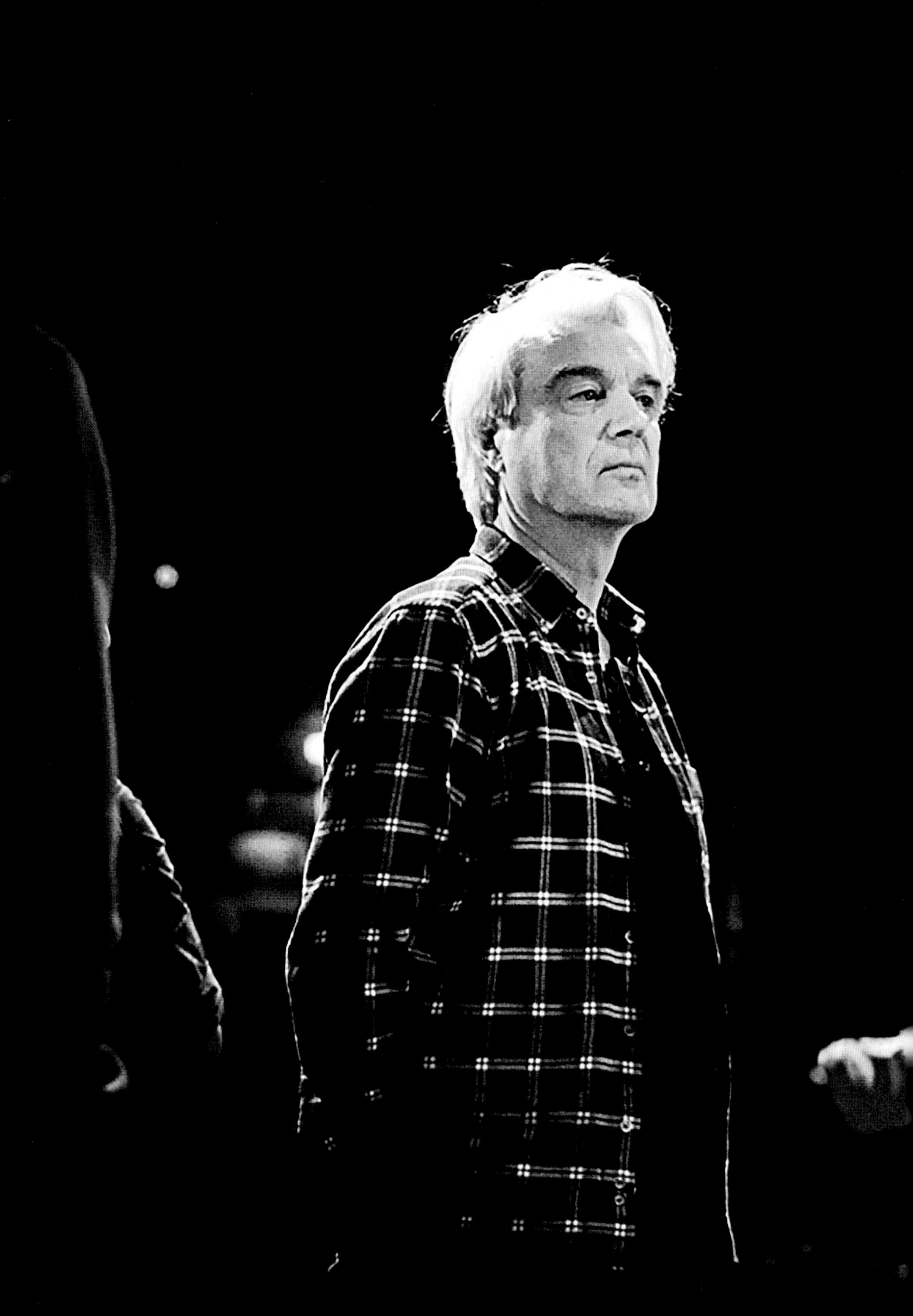

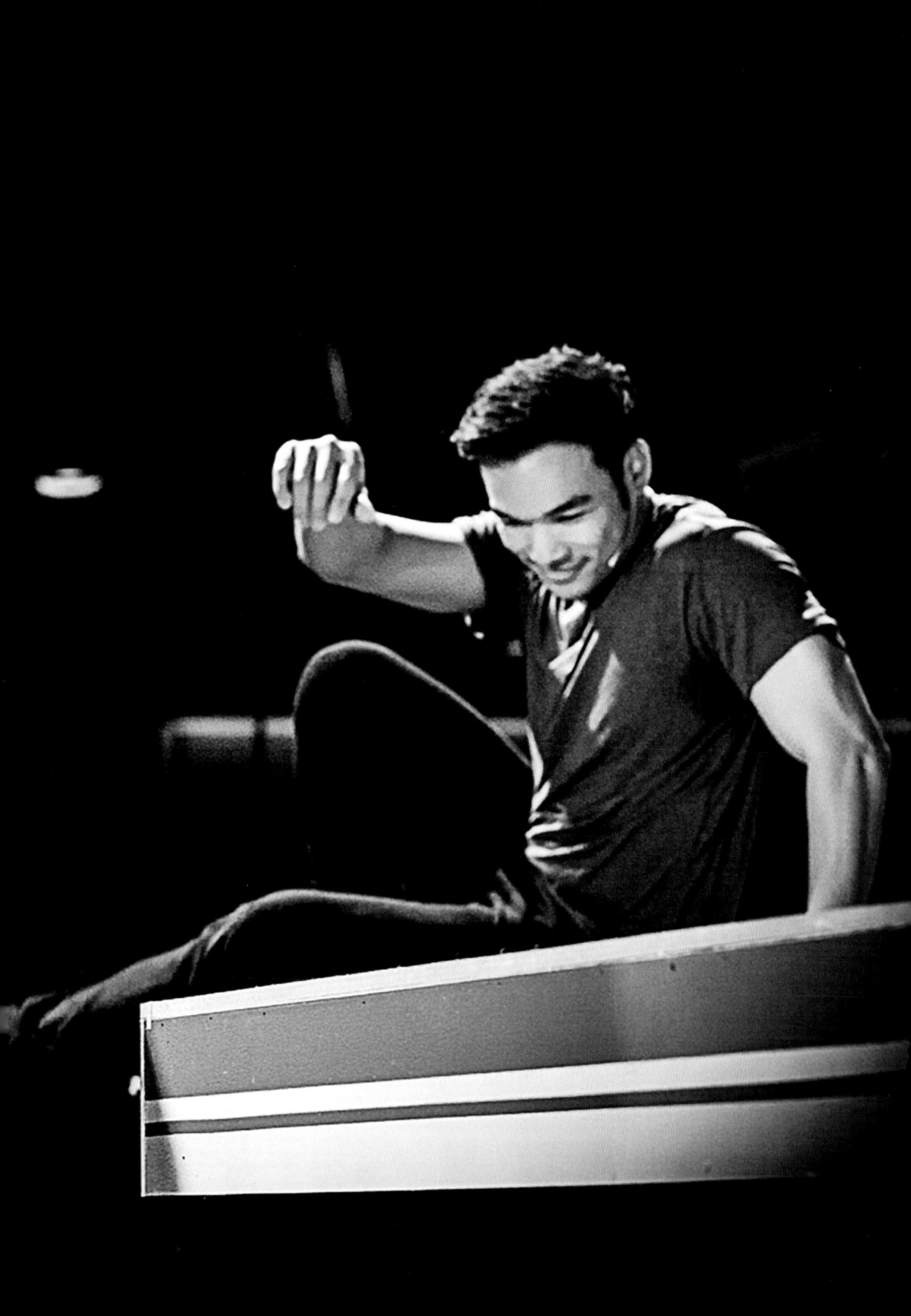

The photos of this book document the construction of the set for David Byrne's musical *Here Lies Love* in Calgary, and the installation and rehearsals for the show at the Seattle Repertory Theatre (March–June, 2017).

Photographs by
FERNANDO SANCHO

HERE LIES LOVE

Concept and lyrics by
DAVID BYRNE

Music by
DAVID BYRNE and FATBOY SLIM

Additional music by
TOM GANDEY and J PARDO

Choreographed by
ANNIE-B PARSON

Directed by
ALEX TIMBERS

Music Supervisor	Kimberly Grigsby
Music Director	Justin Levine
Scenic Designer	David Korins
Costume Designer	Clint Ramos
Hair and Wig Designer	Dave Bova
Lighting Designer	Justin Townsend
Sound Designers	M.L. Dogg, Cody Spencer
Projection Designer	Peter Nigrini

With Belinda Allyn, Renee Albulario, Mark Bautista, Melody Butiu, Debralee Daco, Jordan DeLeon, Michael Feldman, Jaygee Macapugay, Jeigh Madjus, Jonelle Margallo, Shea Renne, Conrad Ricamora, Enrico Rodriguez, Geena Quintos, Trevor Salter, Janelle Velasquez, and Tobias Christian Wong

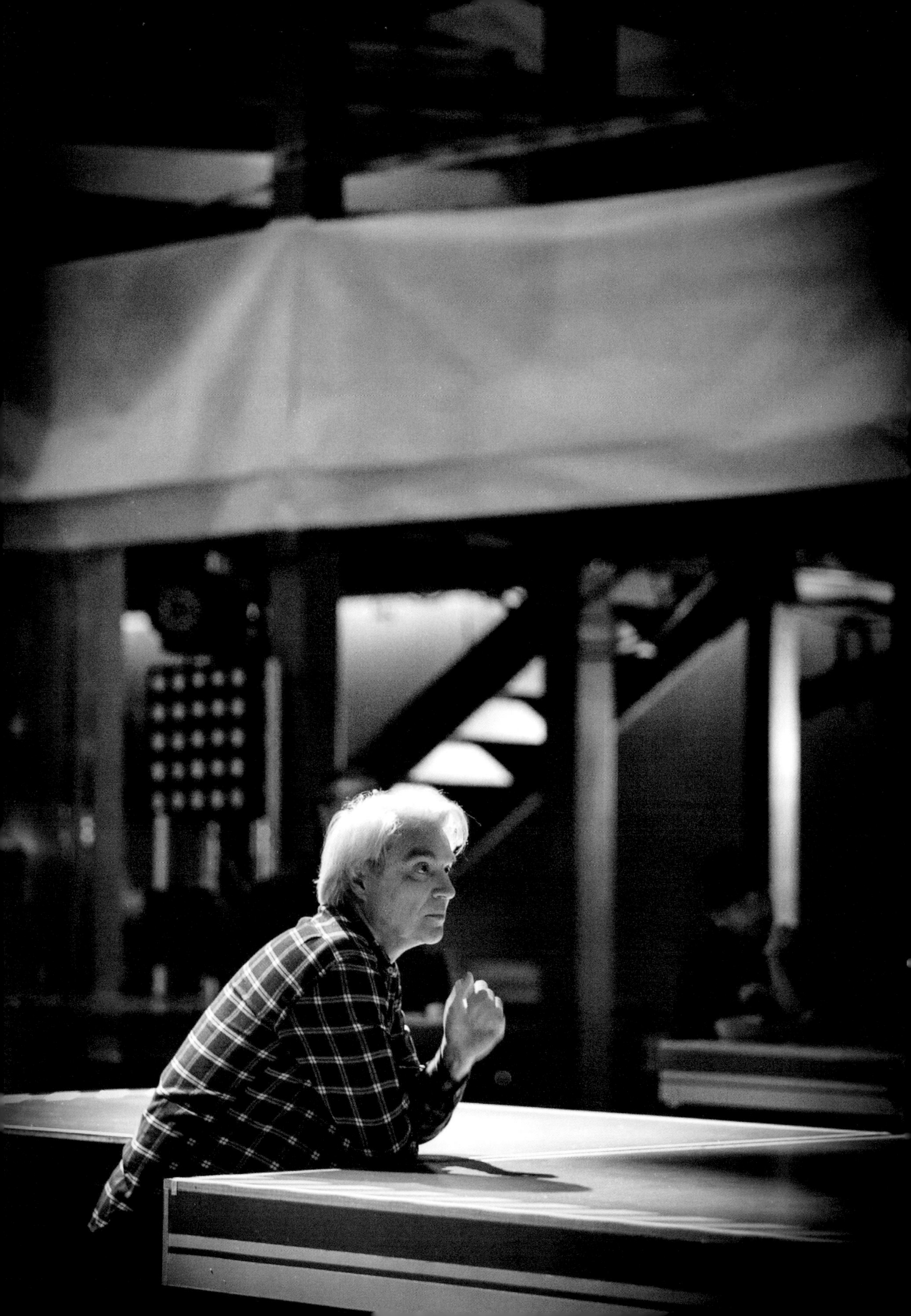

FOREWORD

HOW MANY PEOPLE DOES IT TAKE TO PUT ON A SHOW?

DAVID BYRNE

In the case of *Here Lies Love*, my immersive musical at Seattle Rep, a lot of people scattered all over the world. To document this process Fernando Sancho was given access to the construction of the set and the entire rehearsal process. His evocative photographs don't show the details of the technical process so much, but rather dive into the human engagement.

This show, about Imelda Marcos, the former First Lady of the Philippines and the revolution that ousted that dictatorship, had been previously done in open spaces in New York and London. But those kinds of spaces are limited in many other cities, so the question became: could this show be done in a conventional theater reconfigured to resemble a mega disco, which is where the action takes place? In *Here Lies Love*, the audience is on the dance floor and in observation balconies, and the action takes place mainly on small movable stages around the periphery. I conceived this to resemble performances I'd seen by singers on tiny stages in discos back in the day, and director Alex Timbers and designer David Korins expanded that idea to include

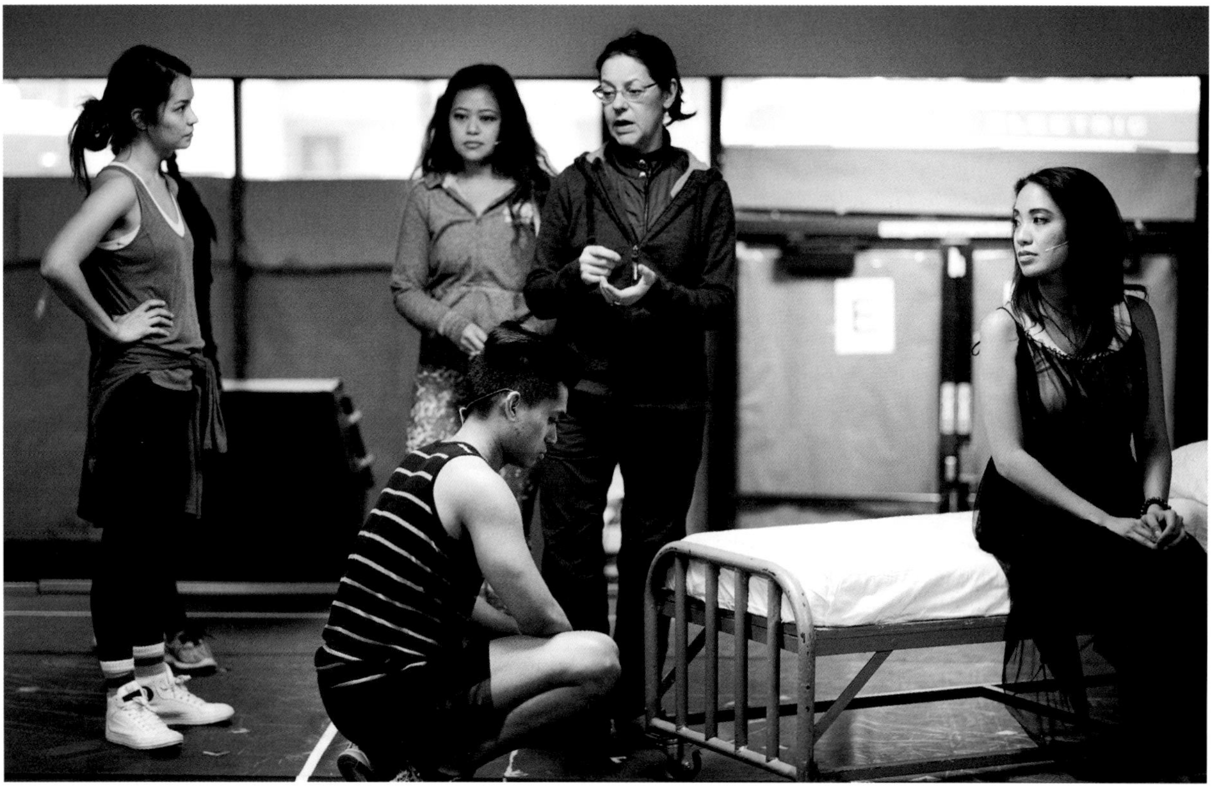

movable platforms, runways and whole stages that move. It worked—people love it and the storytelling is very clear and emotionally engaging, besides having political relevance. As a friend told me, "It's a musical for people who hate musicals."

So, Seattle Rep rose to the challenge. How would this be done? Plans were drawn up, the orchestra seats of the Bagley Wright Theatre were removed and a platform was built to effectively extend the stage out into the house. This would be the dance floor where much of the audience experiences the show. Additional seating would be in two levels of observation galleries (which also have projection surfaces on their fronts) and the existing theater balcony. Not totally unlike Studio 54, a place Imelda frequented.

That sounds a little ambitious, and given the building code requirements for a city on the fault lines, it became even more ambitious. The supports would have to be extra strong, to withstand earthquakes. Other theaters who were going to share the costs dropped out. More money needed to be raised. Fundraising events were scheduled and I attended some of them. Eventually, it came to seem doable and the project was given the go ahead.

The "set" pieces for the two levels of galleries were constructed in Calgary. Fernando went up there and documented that process—an incredible team making something the likes of which they had never made before.

Meanwhile the actors, from New York, Seattle and Manila, assembled in rehearsal spaces in New York to learn the songs and the choreography under the guidance of the original creative team—two musical directors, an assistant director, the choreographer and her assistant, production folks from Seattle and more. At least half the cast had been in previous productions, so it came back to them quickly, which sped things along, but still it's a lot to learn. No costumes, mikes or lighting yet, but still it was thrilling to see and hear.

They then moved to further rehearsals in a rather unusual rehearsal space in Seattle while the set was being installed in the theater: a former frame shop (and porno theater) downtown. After a few weeks there, I came to Seattle, as did Alex and more of the creative team, and we began tech rehearsals in the theater. Now the choreography would be on the platforms, stages and runways that make up the set. The space is larger than in previous incarnations, so there were adjustments to the movement. Gradually the lighting came in and then the sound. Teams of workers would arrive at the end of our rehearsal days and continue working on the set, the sound and the lights into the nights. The room was a round the clock hive of activity.

Fernando was there, catching those moments, and the dedication is evident on the faces of everyone who worked on this. The actors are what the audience sees, but the people shown here were in many ways just as essential to getting this unusual show up and running. It was very much a team effort. Their names may be on the program, but not being visible in the final show, they are often unsung. Fernando's images go some way to rectifying that—you still may not know all their names or what each of them did, but you can plainly see in a visceral way that these are deeply engaged people who worked behind the scenes. Without them this show would not have happened.

I am grateful to them and grateful to Fernando for capturing that on film.

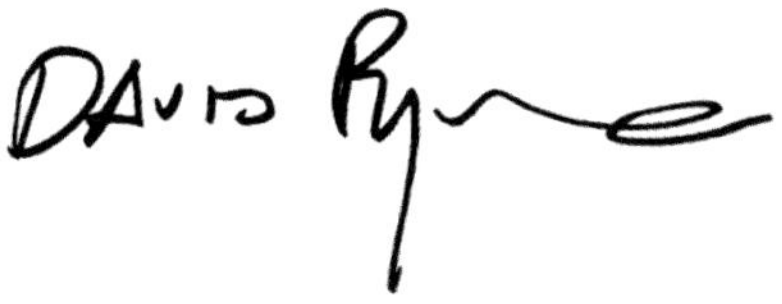

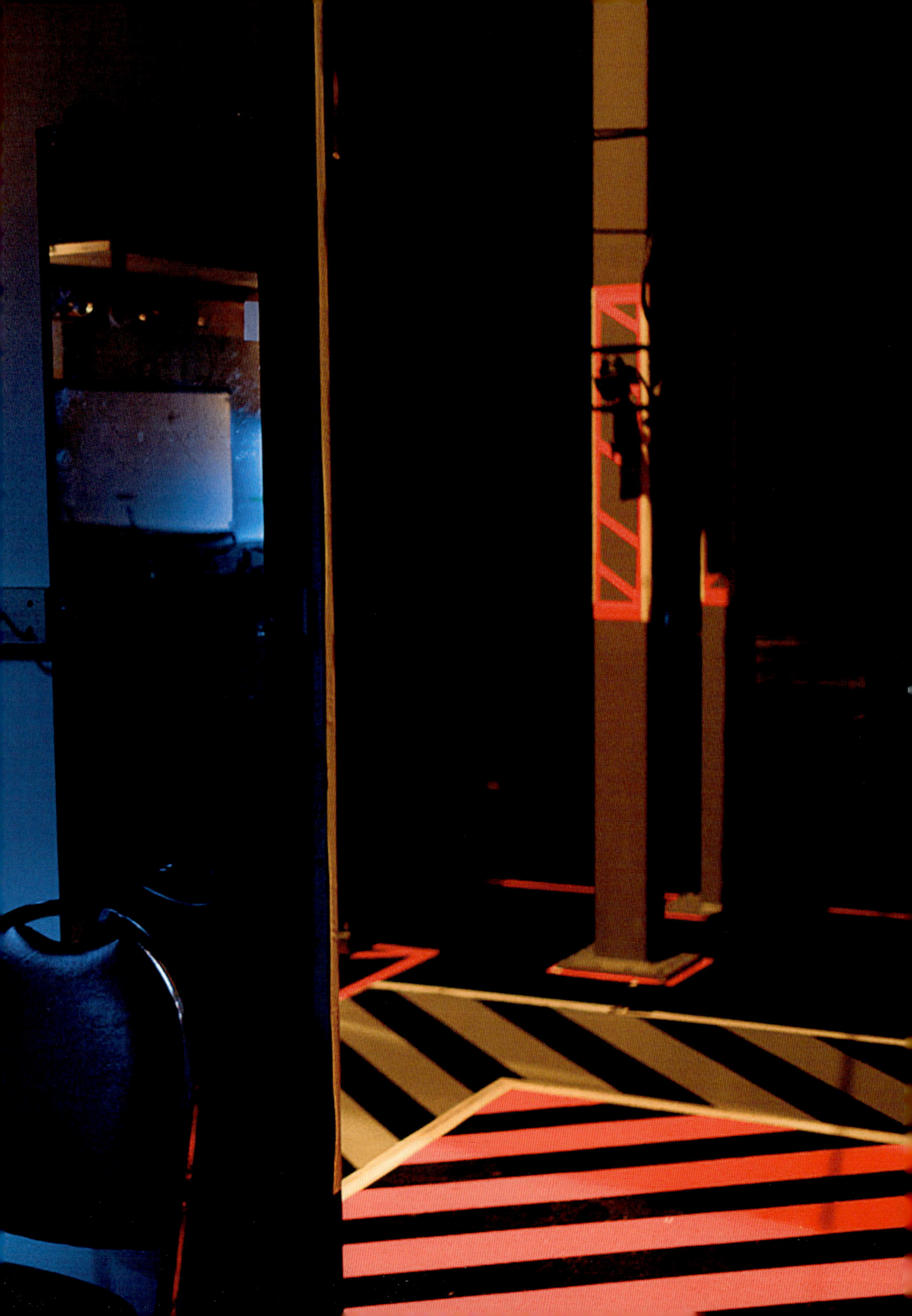

EDITOR'S NOTE

AN ARGUMENT FOR ART

BRUCE RUTLEDGE
CHIN MUSIC PRESS

An image of a disco ball in Imelda Marcos' New York City apartment sparked the imagination of David Byrne and led to his musical *Here Lies Love*. A discotheque/stage made in a cold Calgary workshop, shipped to Seattle, and loaded into the Bagley Wright Theater sparked the imagination of photographer Fernando Sancho and led to the book you hold in your hands. In this way, art begets art, and we should all be happy about that.

A play set in a disco about Imelda Marcos—you can forgive the Filipino community in Seattle for being skeptical. Of course, Seattle has a dark tie to the Marcos regime that makes it especially sensitive to any attempt at revisionist history when it comes to Ferdinand Marcos. Silme Domingo and Gene Viernes, two anti-Marcos union officers in Seattle, were gunned down in 1981 in their labor hall in Pioneer Square by a Marcos hitman. At first, the police thought it was another gang-related slaying, but court records later would implicate the Marcos regime. Two twenty-nine-year-old young men were murdered for their political beliefs by a foreign dictator on the streets of Seattle. And you want to do a play set in a disco?

But this is where the artistic sparks created something new and wonderful. For several weeks in spring 2017, the city of Seattle engaged with the play in an intimate, emotional way. Young Asians flocked to the play night after night (supported by Seattle's generous ticket discounts for youth) to see a rare version of themselves on stage. Cast members would nod and wink at the regulars. Behind the scenes, community activists met with the cast to talk about local Filipino history, about Silme and Gene, and about Uncle Bob Santos, a community leader who fought gentrification in our International District and no doubt would have been on the dance floor of the Bagley Wright Theater singing along with the cast had he not passed away in the summer of 2016.

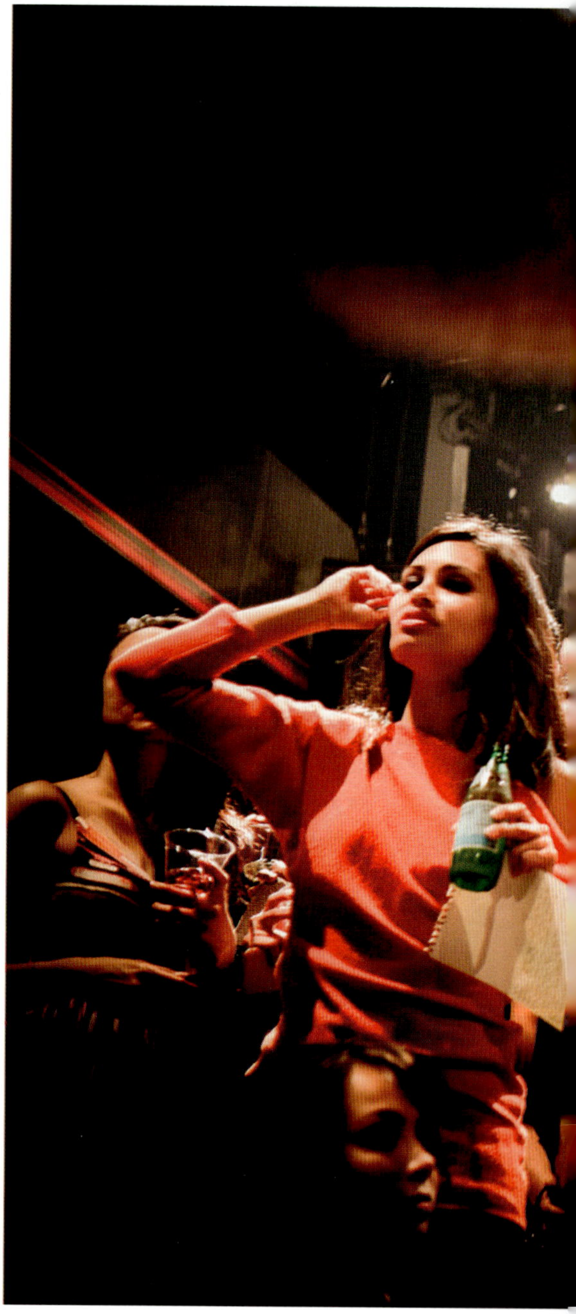

Byrne's play is no revisionist history. On the contrary, it reminds those of us old enough to remember the Marcos regime how bad it really was. The assassinations, the repression, the looting of the public trust. But it also reminds us how beautiful, if fleeting, those People Power Revolution moments were.

When *Here Lies Love* ran in Seattle in spring 2017, something special happened as the cast took the stage. I know it sounds corny, but it's true. Facades were pulled down. Difficult conversations were engaged in. Young Filipino American actors depicted the Marcoses and Benito Aquino on stage, then retired to their hotel rooms and talked about how their relatives back home could support someone as brutal and repressive as President Rodrigo Duterte. As if on cue, Duterte declared martial law in the Philippines while the play was going on. We all felt a collective chill that day. But, of course, the play must go on.

I hope *Here Lies Love* finds a new home, a new theater willing to transform itself into a discotheque, to get the crowd line dancing, and to make us think about how corrupt people come to power. But no matter the fate of the play, for several weeks in the spring of 2017, it sparked the imagination of Seattle, and I am forever grateful to David Byrne, Alex Timbers, the Seattle Rep, the cast, and Fernando Sancho for documenting these moments.

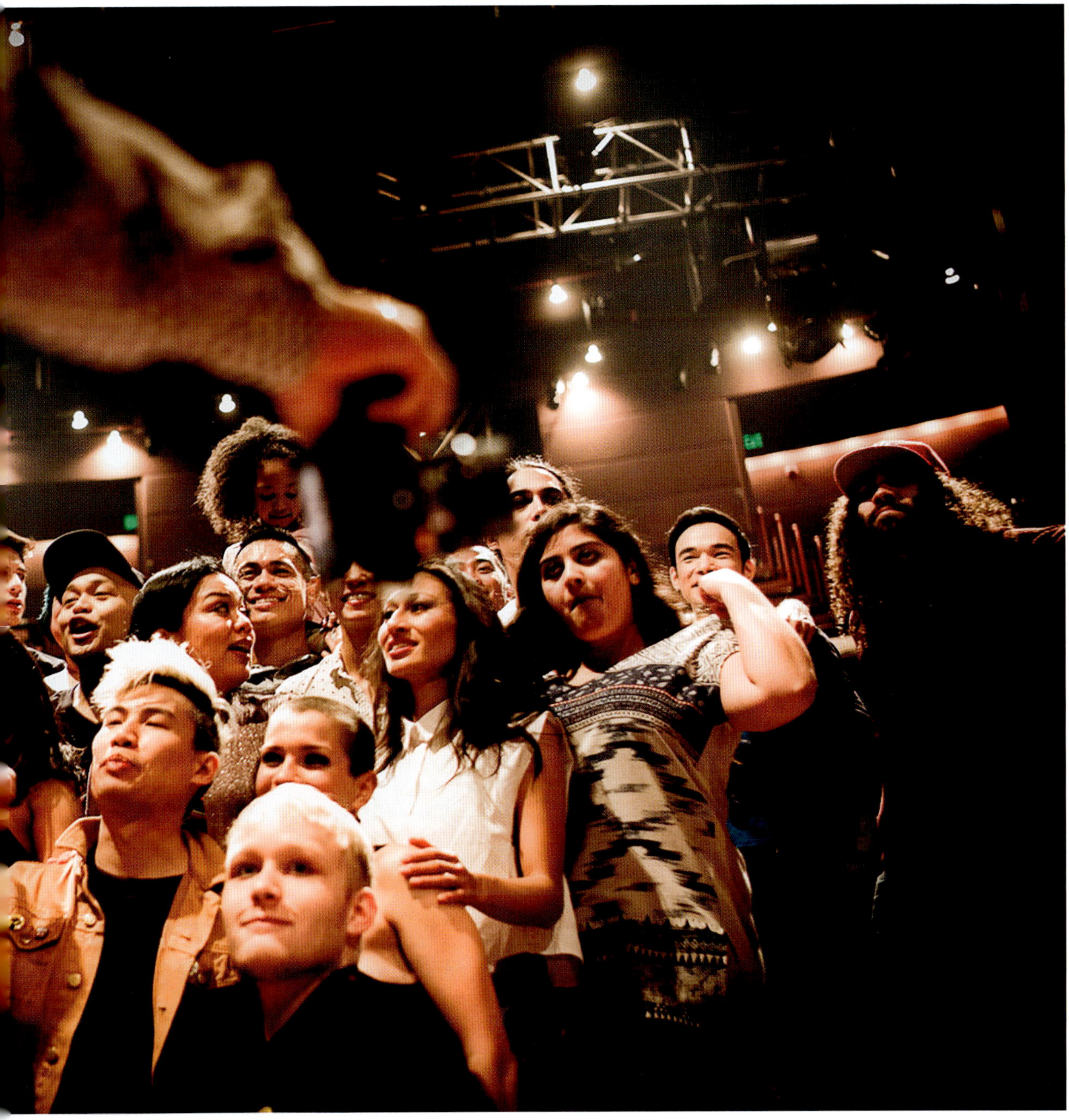

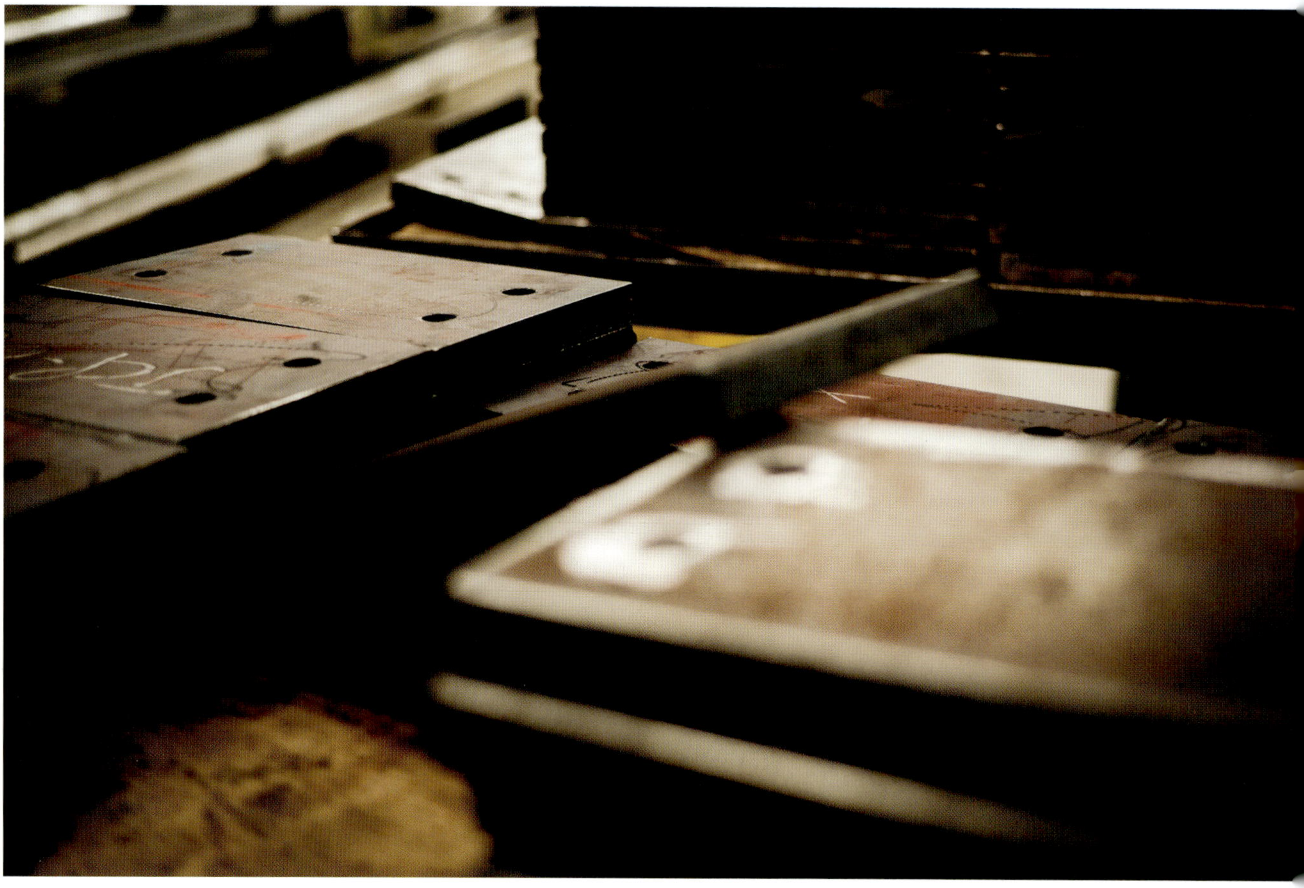

LET'S DANCE!

FERNANDO SANCHO

I am fascinated with the poetry involved in a process. We reflect our own process in whatever we do, in the constant change of our natures that are influenced by our surroundings and circumstances. Photographers act as archaeologists, constantly in search of what's behind a face or a landscape. Due to the unusual nature of my work, I have photographed empty, naked disco spaces that were closed to the public and with no music or lights. To me, it is amazing how the music played in a disco has so much in common with the design of the space. Just by looking at the space, you can almost hear the music. However, I had never before witnessed the process of putting together a disco club from scratch. When I heard that Seattle Repertory Theatre was producing David Byrne's musical *Here Lies Love*, I jumped at the opportunity to record that process. And it's been truly incredible. What I most loved about this process was the fact that everyone involved felt the absolute magic of this production, from the welder to the driver; from the architect to the designer. So, welcome to the disco! You'll listen to heart-pumping music, watch great dancers move to incredible choreography, and witness a pivotal moment in Filipino history. But the key element is that you are a part of the story. Let's dance!

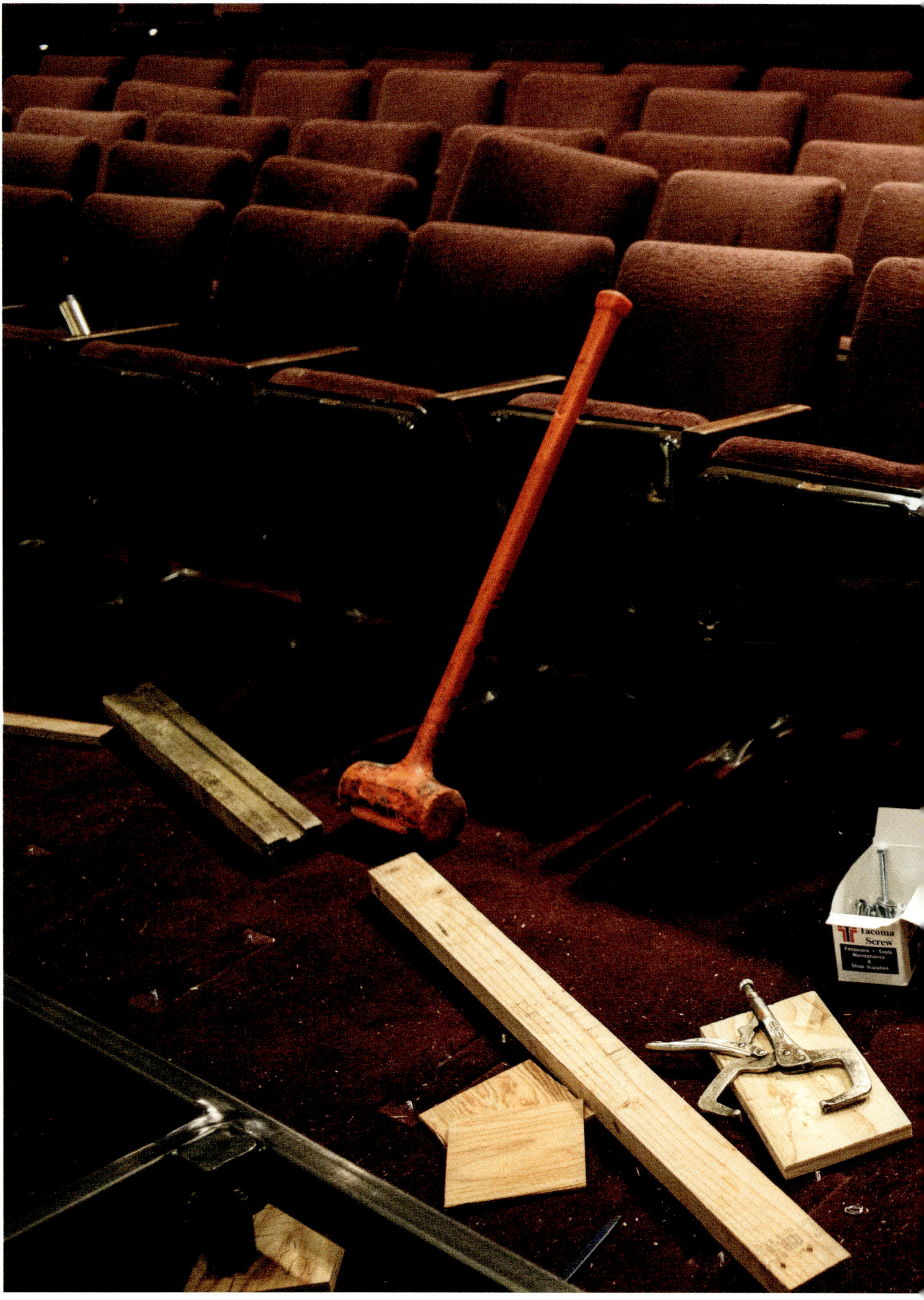
Tacoma Screw
Fasteners • Tools
Maintenance
&
Shop Supplies

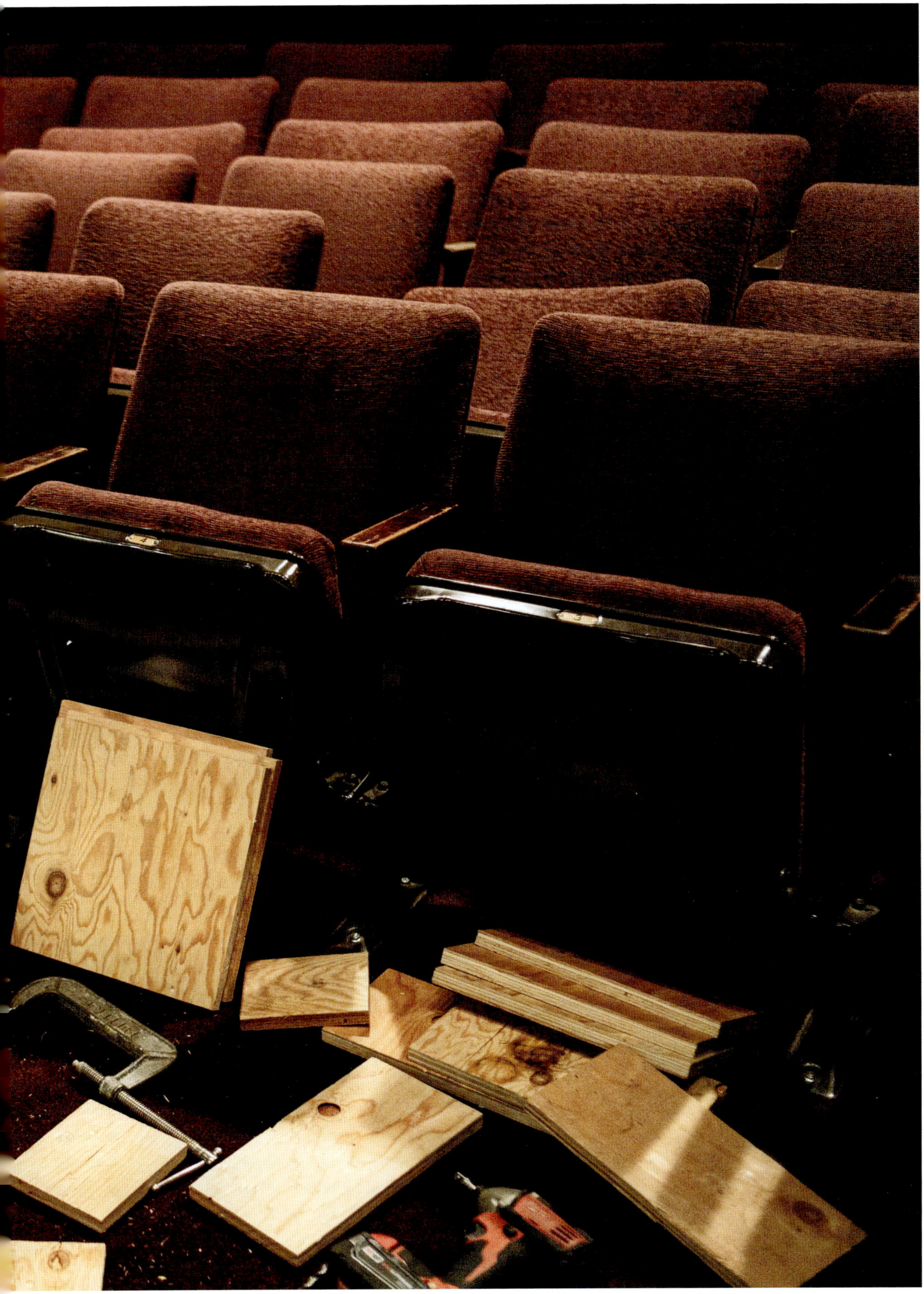

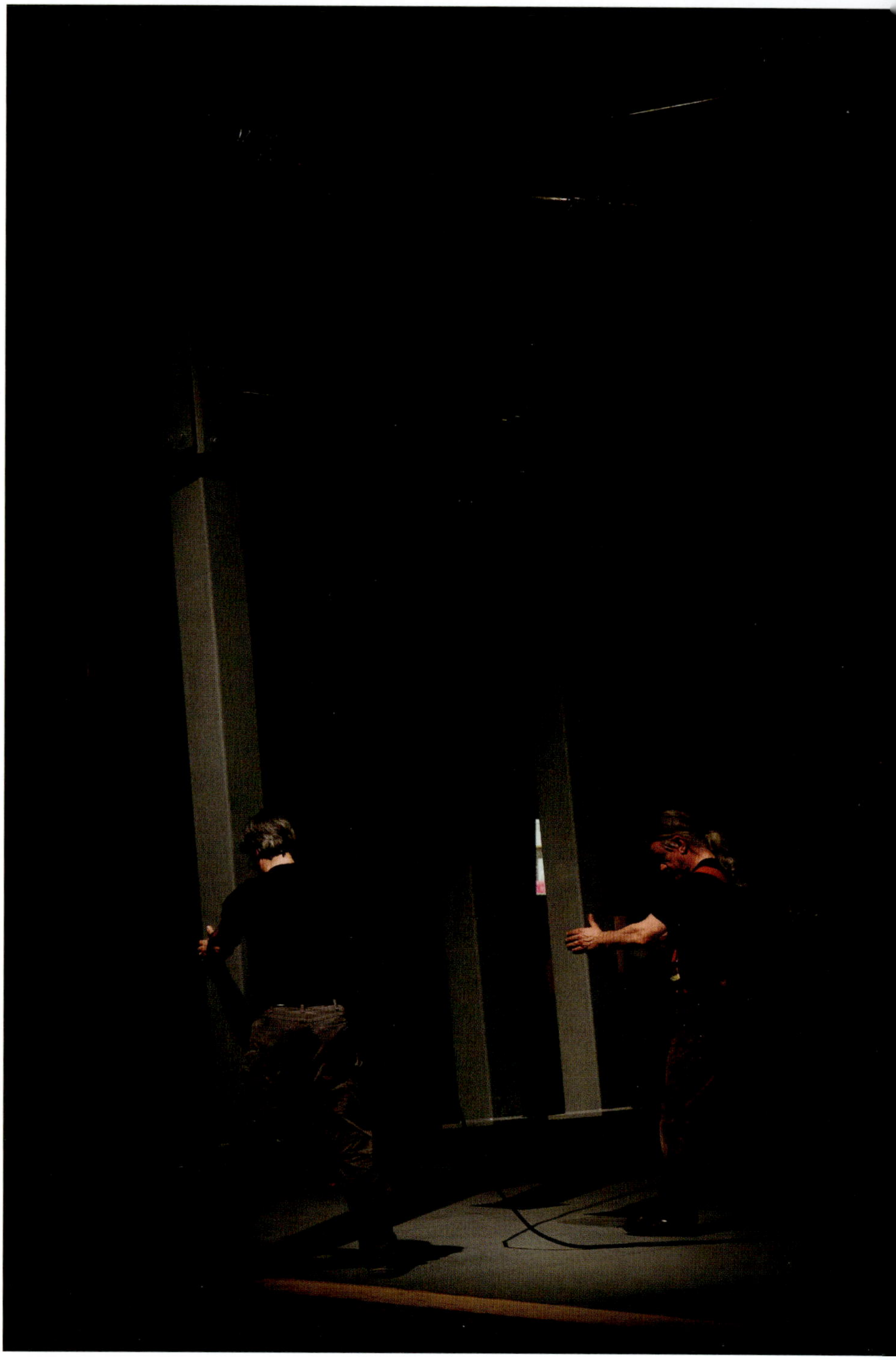

CHANGING THE WAY WE THINK ABOUT THEATRE

BRADEN ABRAHAM

By the time *Here Lies Love* arrived at Seattle Repertory Theatre in 2017, the production had already made its mark. It was the longest-running show in the history of The Public Theater where it premiered in 2014. Another critically acclaimed sold-out run followed at the National Theatre in London. The success of these productions was predicated on the daring vision of creator David Byrne, director Alex Timbers and their team of collaborators. Reunited in Seattle, they set out to adapt the original production to an even larger scale. *Here Lies Love* had yet to be attempted in a space that required this sort of transformation.

For us at Seattle Rep, it was an audacious move unlike anything we had ever attempted in our fifty-year history. Over eighteen months, we planned and transformed our 860-seat proscenium theatre into an immersive disco club. Seats were removed. The stage was built out. Giant seating towers were fabricated and trucked in from Canada as they were simply too massive to be built in our own shop.

The night of our first performance, audiences who were familiar with our theatre and who had been coming here for years, entered a space utterly transformed. Over two hundred people mingled on the floor before the show. Hundreds more filled the towers and took their seats in the balcony (the only original seating left over from before the space underwent its transformation).

This was an experience unlike any other for our audiences. They had been used to coming to the theatre to see a great story unfold—to be transported to another world either by play or musical—but they had never been literally immersed in that world as they were in *Here Lies Love*; standing and dancing on what was once the stage with the action happening all around them.

Part of what makes the show so brilliant is this feeling of total immersion; through the unique staging and music, audiences are swept up by the charismatic power of Imelda and Ferdinand Marcos and come crashing down experiencing the terrifying turn of their oppressive regime—only to be inspired as the People Power Revolution push them from power. With each surprising turn, the audience takes on a larger role within the story.

It's been a year since *Here Lies Love* closed at Seattle Rep and audiences still talk about it as an event that changed the way they think about theatre. Our space has been restored to its original configuration, but we will never look at it the same way. This production unlocked a potential in the physical space that I had only ever dreamed about, and the likes of which we had never seen, and in some ways this endeavor changed all of us at Seattle Rep. It challenged everyone involved to reach beyond the limits of their experience and draw on untapped sources of creative energy, forming new collaborative bonds with each other to make it happen. *Here Lies Love* did what all great theatrical endeavors do: instigated moments of transformation in our theatre and within us all.

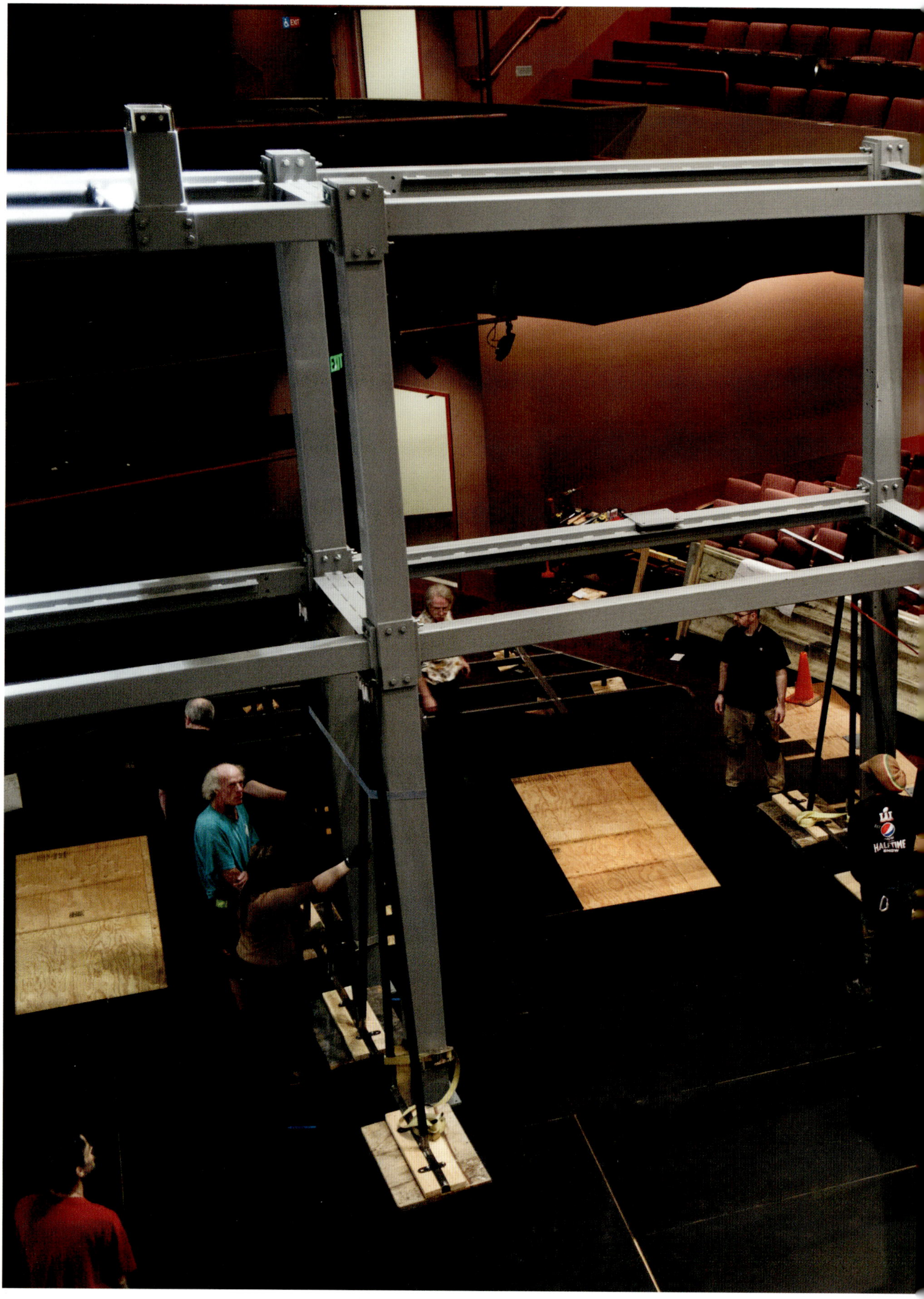
EXIT
EXIT

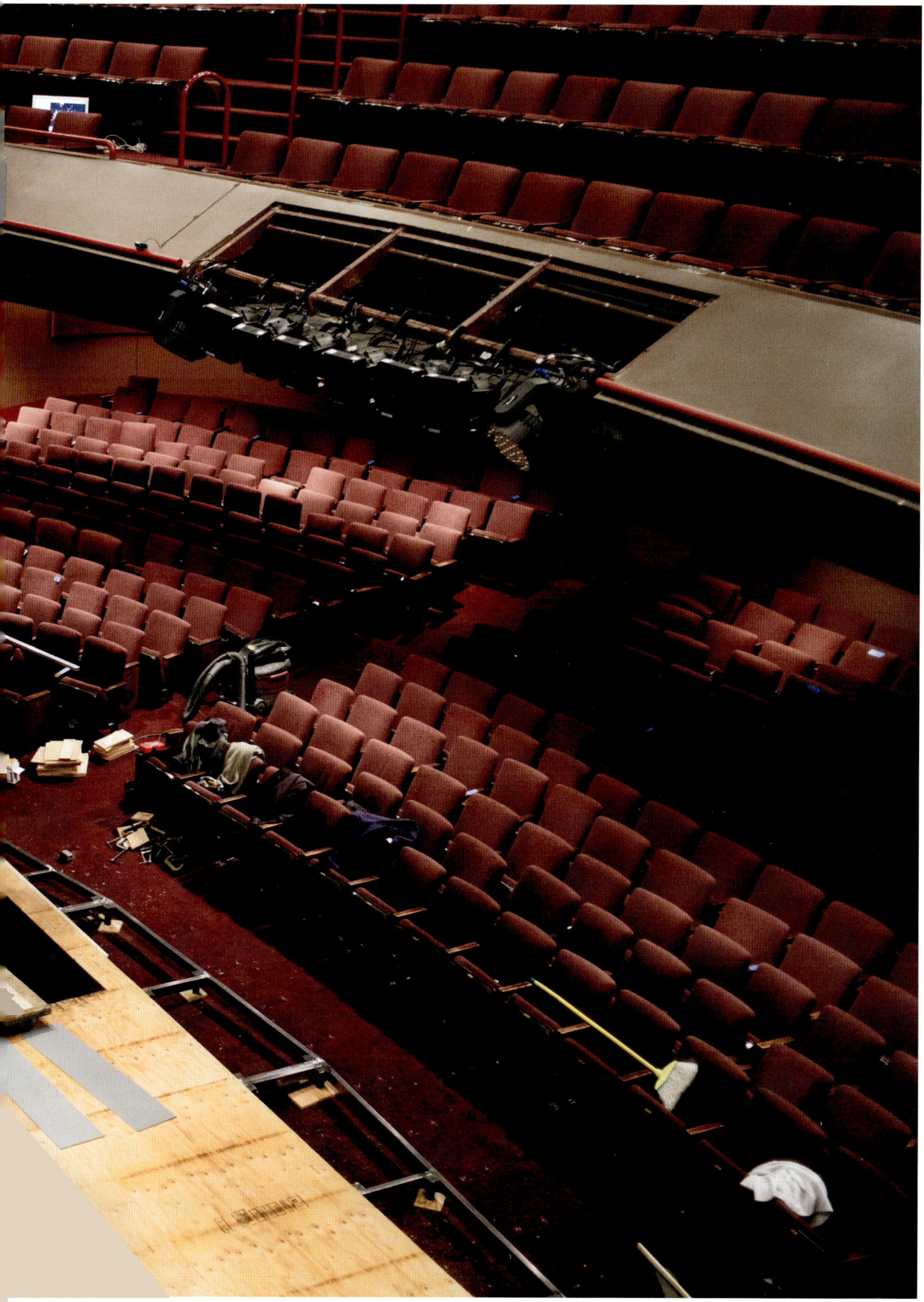

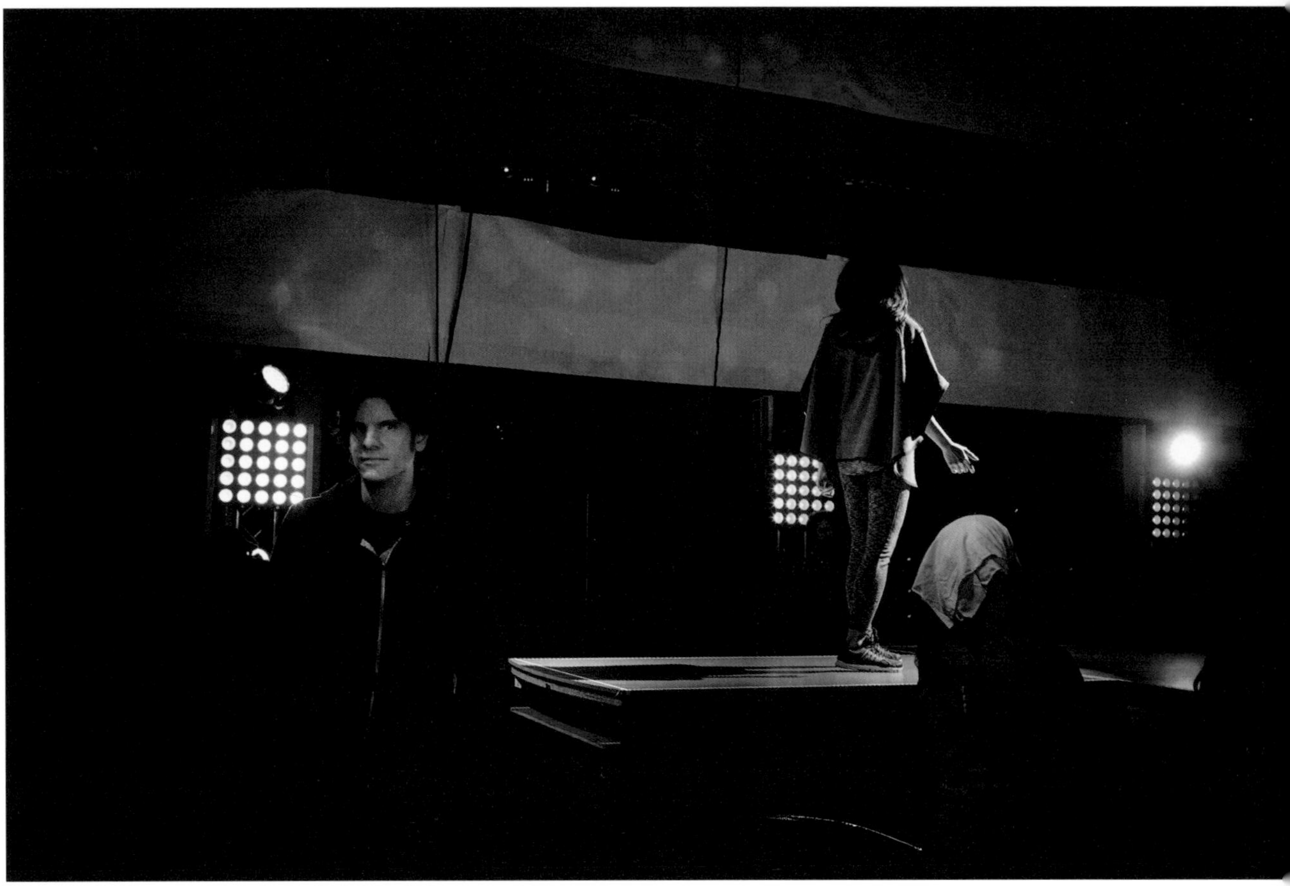

ACHIEVING AN IMMERSIVE 'COUP DE THEATRE'

ALEX TIMBERS

I first learned about *Here Lies Love* in 2009. David Byrne was meeting with Oskar Eustis, artistic director of New York's Public Theater, about adapting his same-titled concept album for the stage, and they were looking for a director.

At the time, I had a theater company that was specifically interested in taking historical subject matter and re-envisioning it in ways that felt both contemporary and accessible. So, David's notion of telling the story of Imelda Marcos through pop and club music felt intriguing and in dialogue with exactly the sort of theater I wanted to be making.

I was lucky enough soon thereafter to get the chance to "pitch" to them how I would want to approach the material and that initial pitch involved a 360-degree design with actors on platforms that reconfigured into runways and a notion of having video on all sides. David had been imagining something very similar, with the show taking place within a discotheque-like environment and so we instantly were on the same page. It was the first of many exciting and creative meetings with David and Oskar.

Over the next several years, we workshopped the show in three stages, each step focusing on a new thirty-minute chunk of the show. David's writing inspired all of us, and we began to assemble an incredible cast over these developmental stages as well as a wonderful creative team, including choreographer Annie-B Parson, music director Kim Grigsby, and set designer David Korins.

In the run up to our first full-show presentation at the museum Mass Moca in the Berkshires, we were quite worried about whether an audience would want to stand for ninety minutes and whether that would be physically exhausting for them. This idea was central to the concept, but we had never been able to test the basic premise in previous readings and workshops. Happily, those fears were quickly allayed as soon as we did the dress rehearsal and found that audiences were exhilarated and actually energized by the amount of engagement that the show desired of its attendees. At one moment, a viewer might be cast as a guest at Imelda and Ferdinand Marcos' wedding and then minutes later might be placed in the audience of an opposition party rally.

Finally, at the end, David Korins mapped out a terrific coup de theatre, where the physical relationship between the audience and the actors transformed once again in an epic gestalt shift. The show went from being all around you to becoming a proscenium show. Beyond being an exciting design moment, it cleverly physicalized the emotional moment within the narrative when the emotional plot turned on its head.

Four years after that first pitch meeting, we premiered the show at the Public Theater in Manhattan. The show received a great reception, winning many awards and extending its run multiple times. The following year, the show returned to the Public for a second engagement, and a London production premiered as well at the National Theatre.

Each of these productions was gratifying but each had operated under the premise that the show could only be performed in a large black-box-type space. We wondered: *Could the show ever be performed in a traditional proscenium theater, yet still keep the immersive design and staging that audiences so loved?*

The incredible opportunity to perform the show at Seattle Rep, the home of artistically adventurous theater programming, and within their beautiful proscenium mainstage gave us the chance to test that question.

Working closely with their creative and production staff, planning for the Seattle version took place over a year and a half as we aimed towards a spring 2017 premiere. The idea would be to platform over the orchestra seating, construct seating mezzanines on the sides, and take advantage of the theater's balcony: to expand the potential audience size significantly and make a staging that was much larger in scope than in either New York or London.

It was a tremendously happy experience collaborating with Artistic Director Braden Abraham and his kind, ambitious, and tireless team at Seattle Rep. No challenge was unbeatable, and the sprawling nature of the production seemed to inspire them at every turn. As the director of the show, it was truly an extraordinary achievement to behold what they accomplished. Seattle audiences received the show rapturously, and it was a privilege to get to perform the show for such an artistically engaged, creatively savvy crowd.

The fact that Fernando has captured the Seattle Rep production, from its very beginnings through to its opening night, with such beautiful photography is a further gift. I'm filled with joy looking through these pictures and revisiting this out-sized adventure and the wonderful, virtuosic performances that happened every night onstage—as well as everything it took to make the production possible.

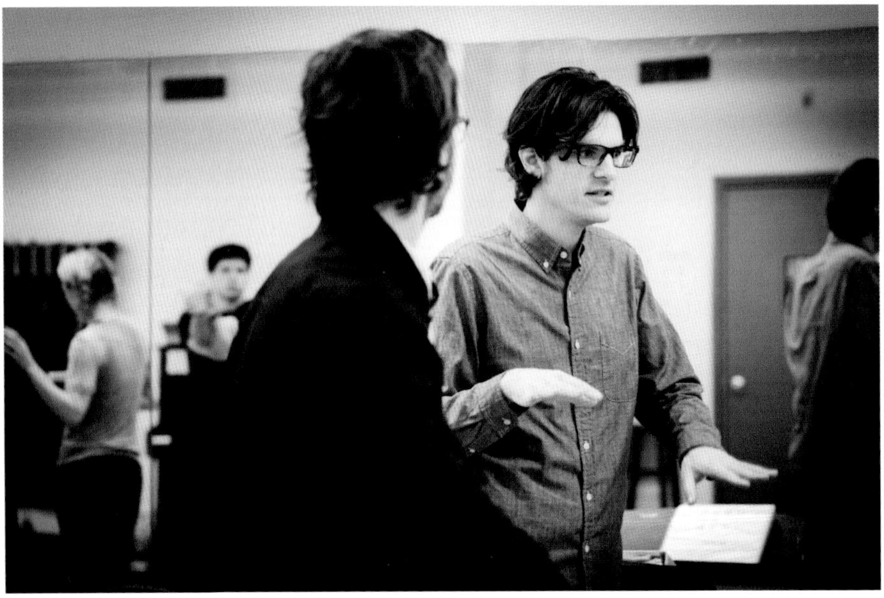

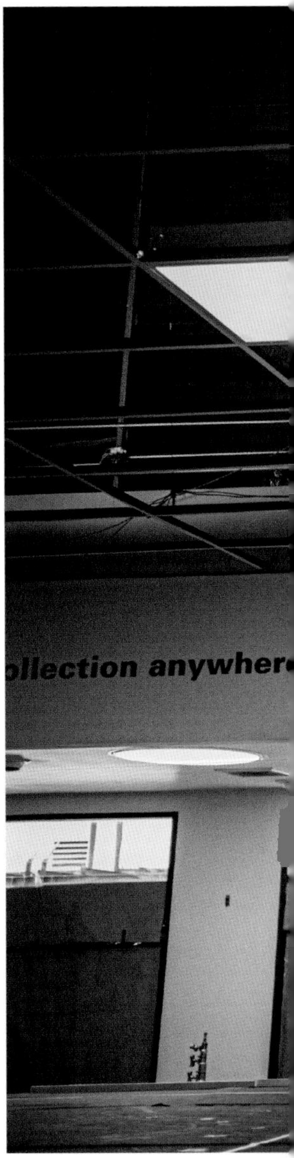

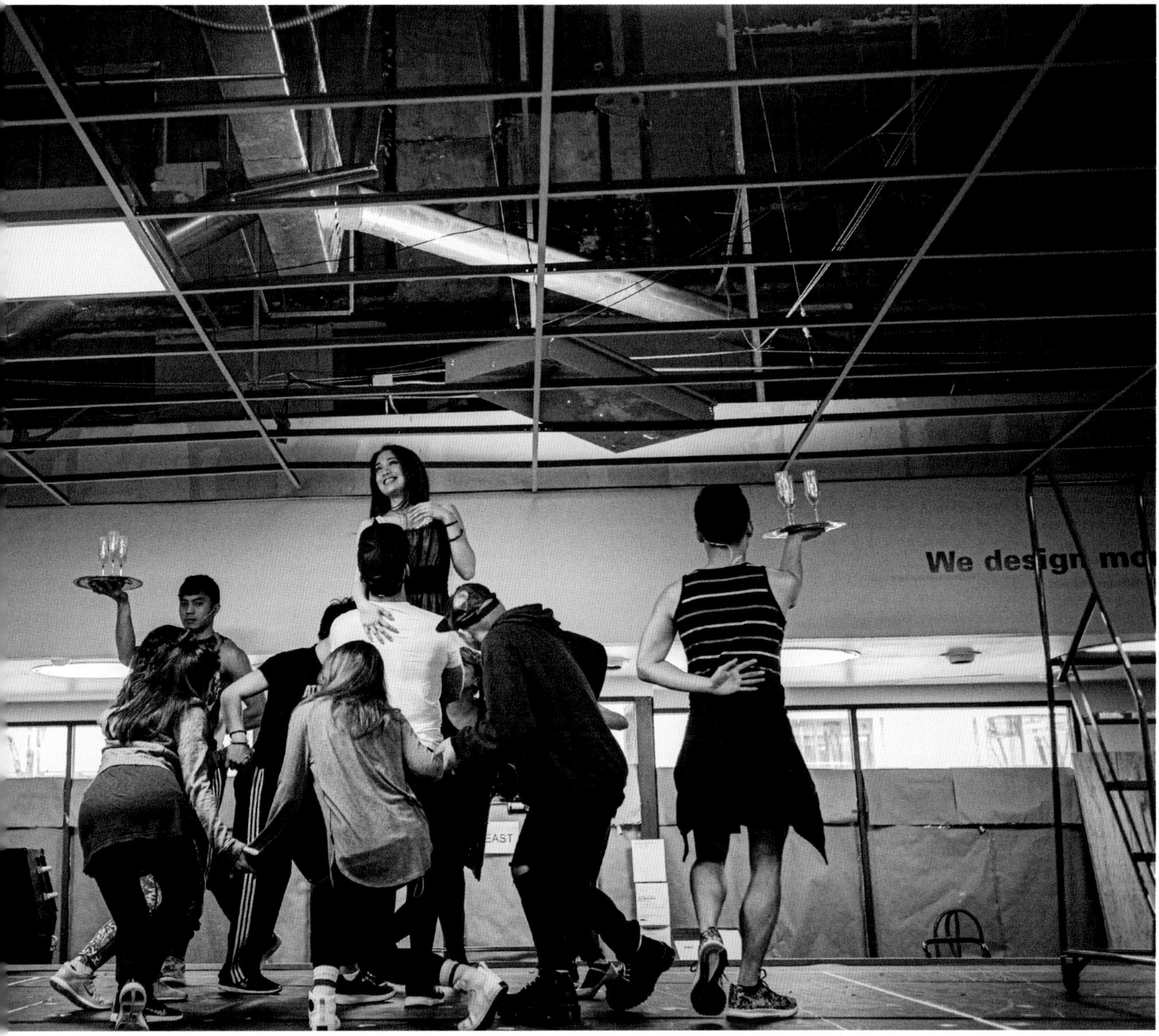
We desig

IS IT A SIN TO LOVE TOO MUCH?

IS IT A SIN TO CARE?

I DO IT ALL FOR YOU

HOW CAN IT BE UNFAIR?

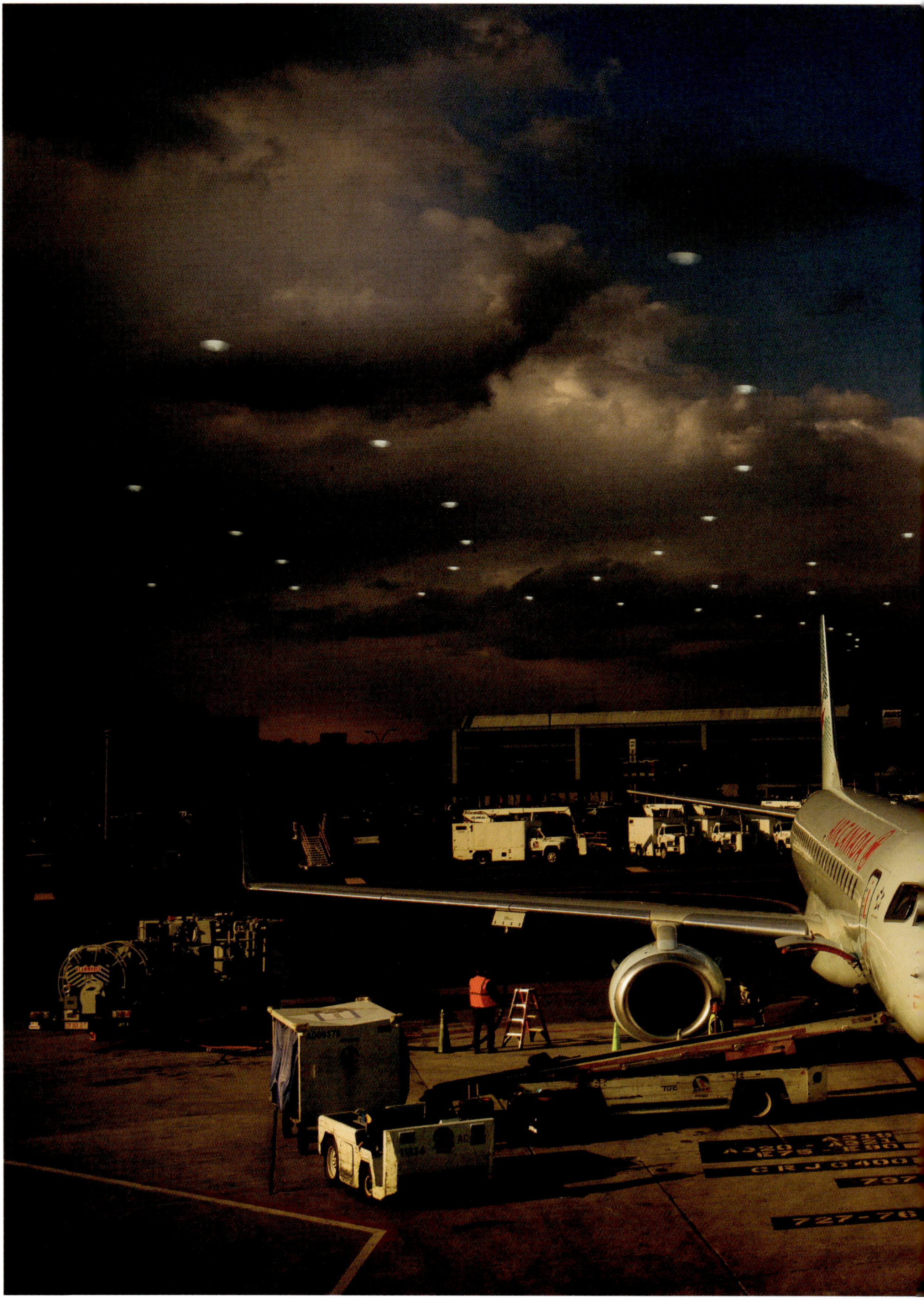
AIR CANADA

I.
BOLTS AND STEEL IN CALGARY

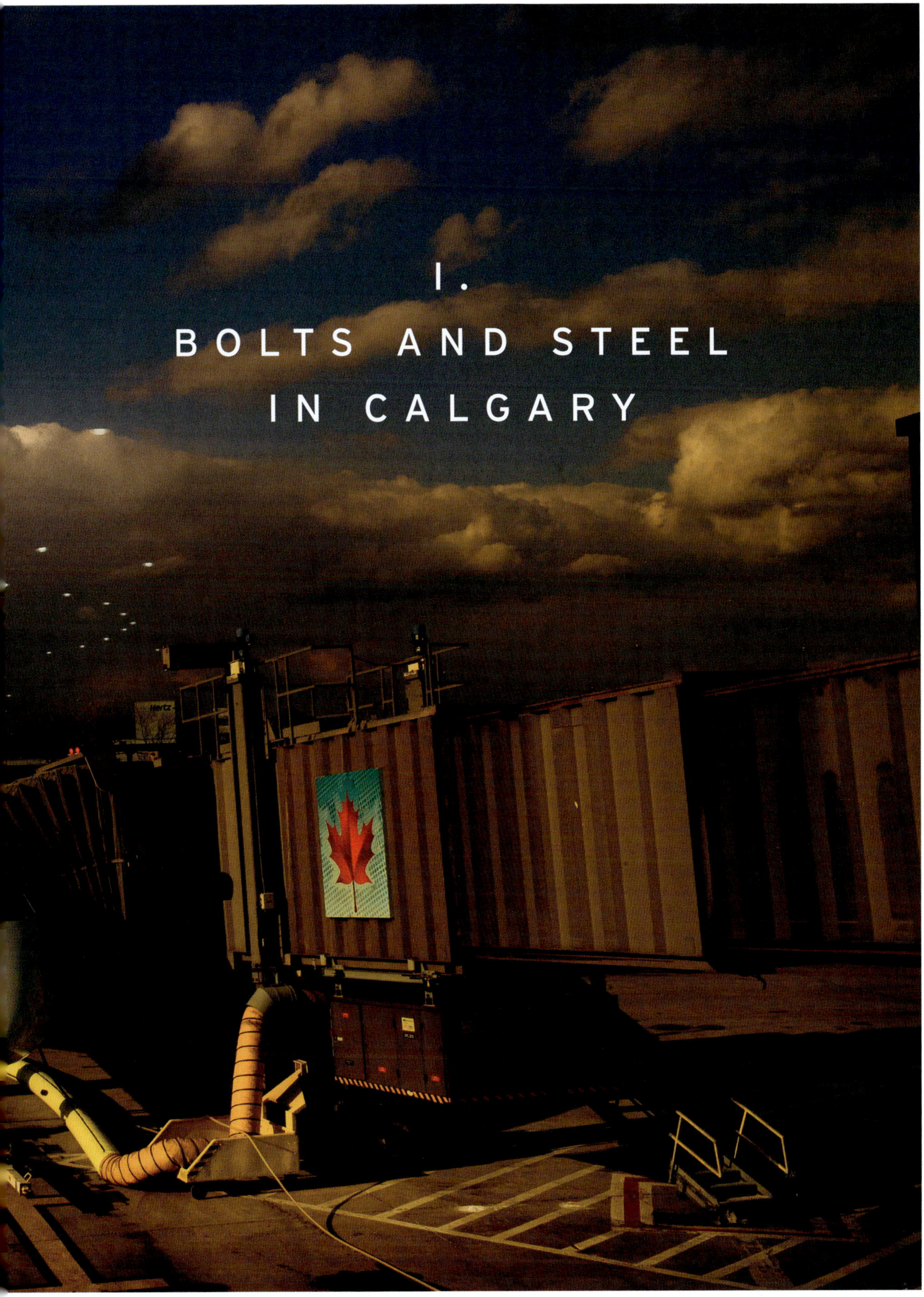

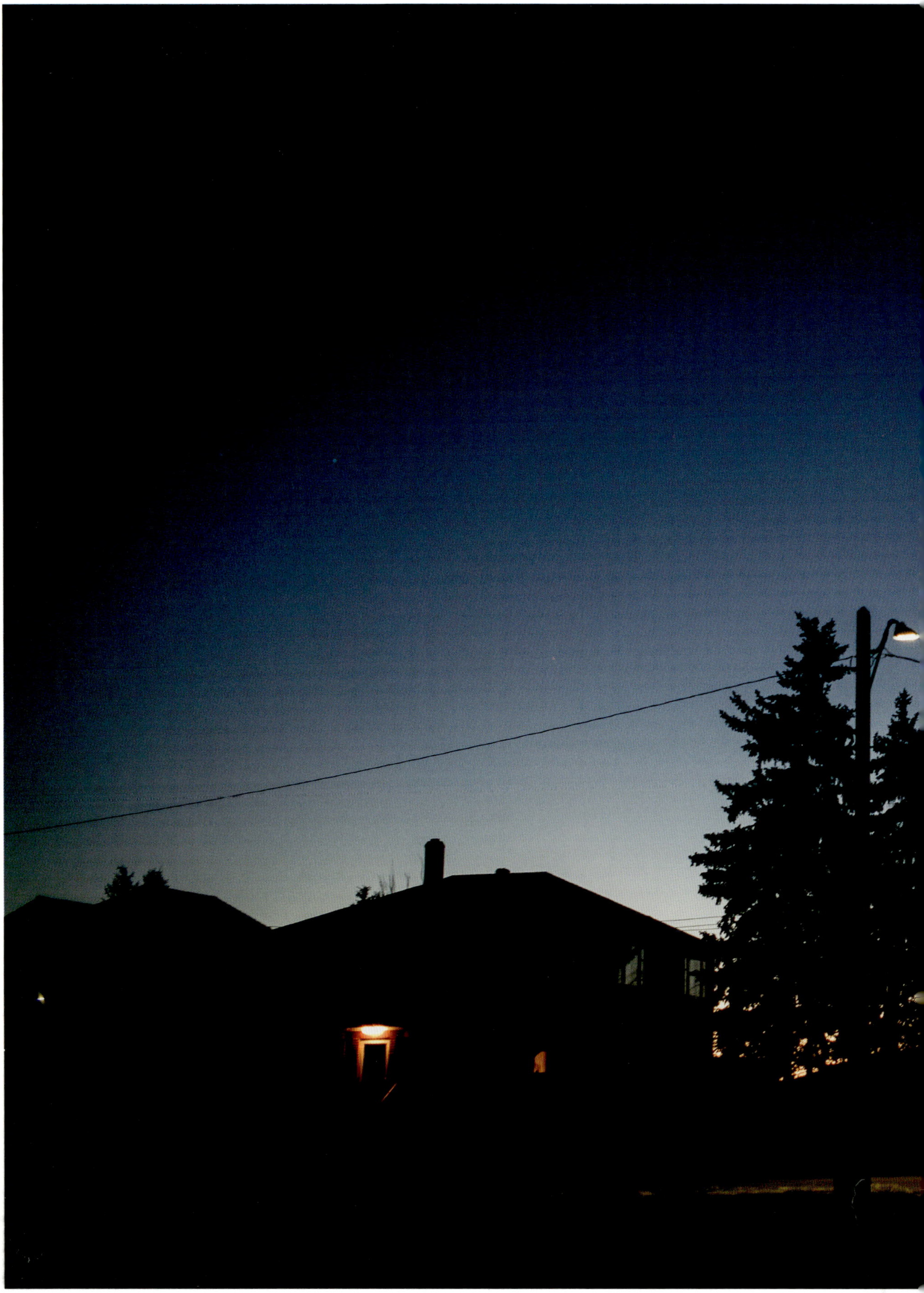

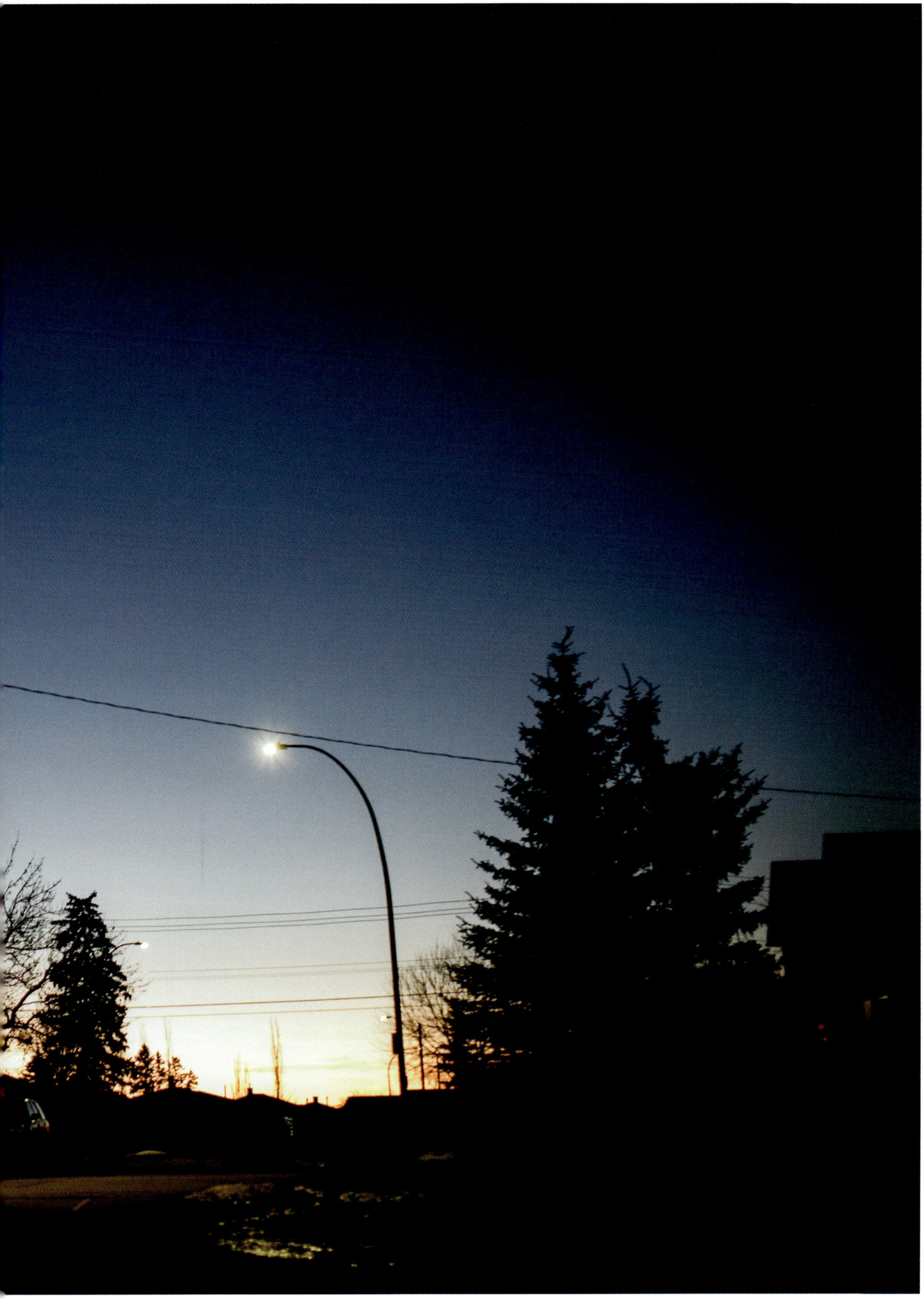

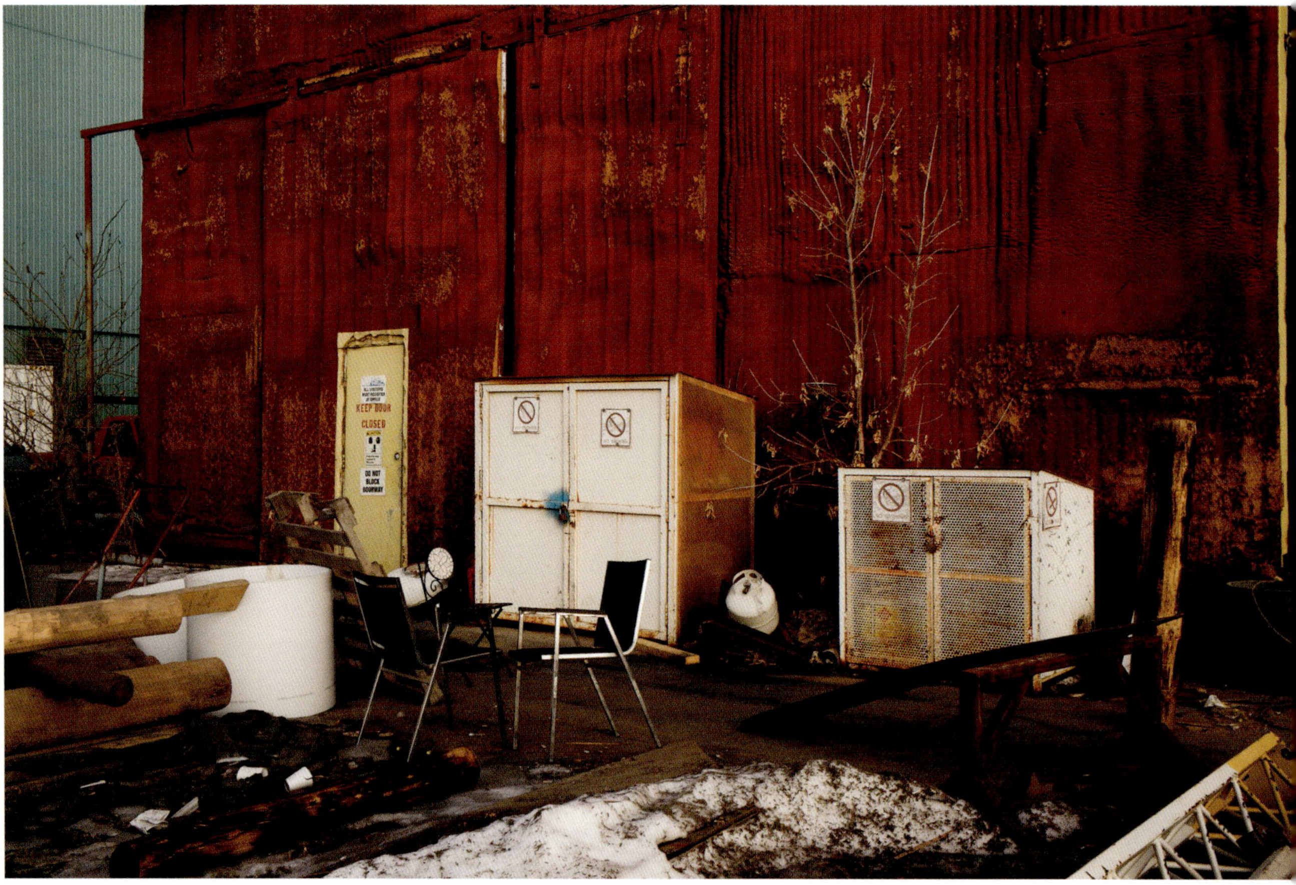
KEEP DOOR
CLOSED
DO NOT
BLOCK
DOORWAY

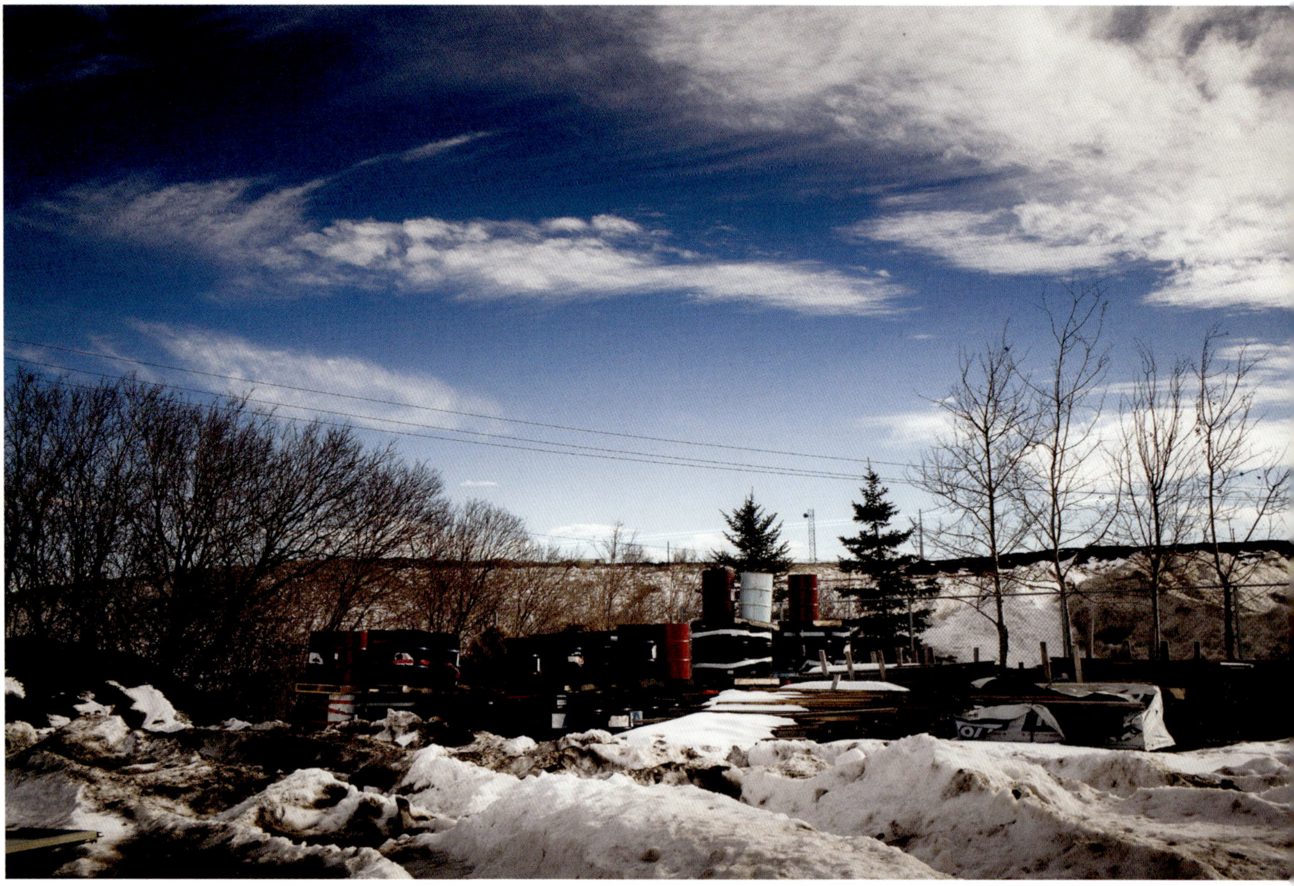

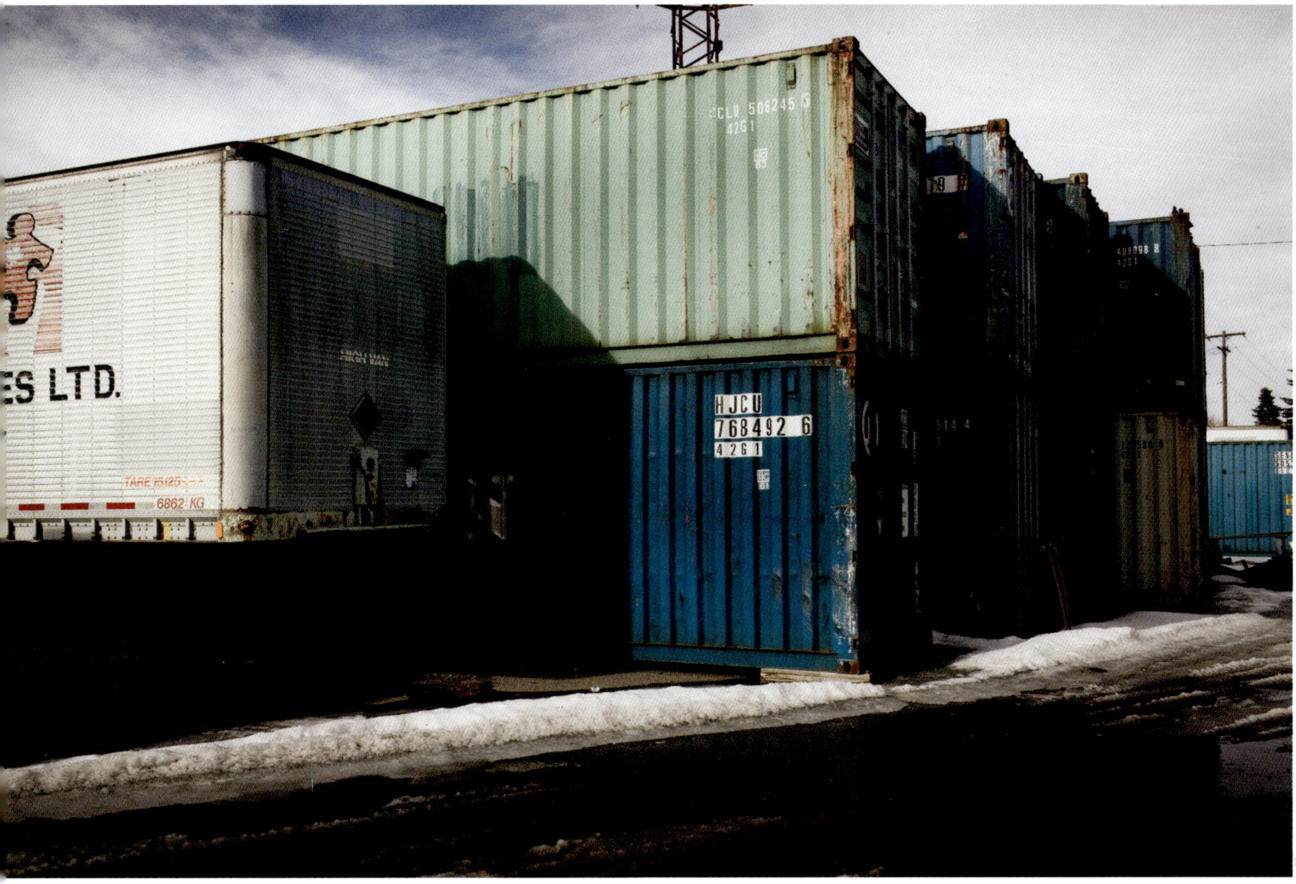
ES LTD.
HJCU
768492 6
42G1
6862 KG

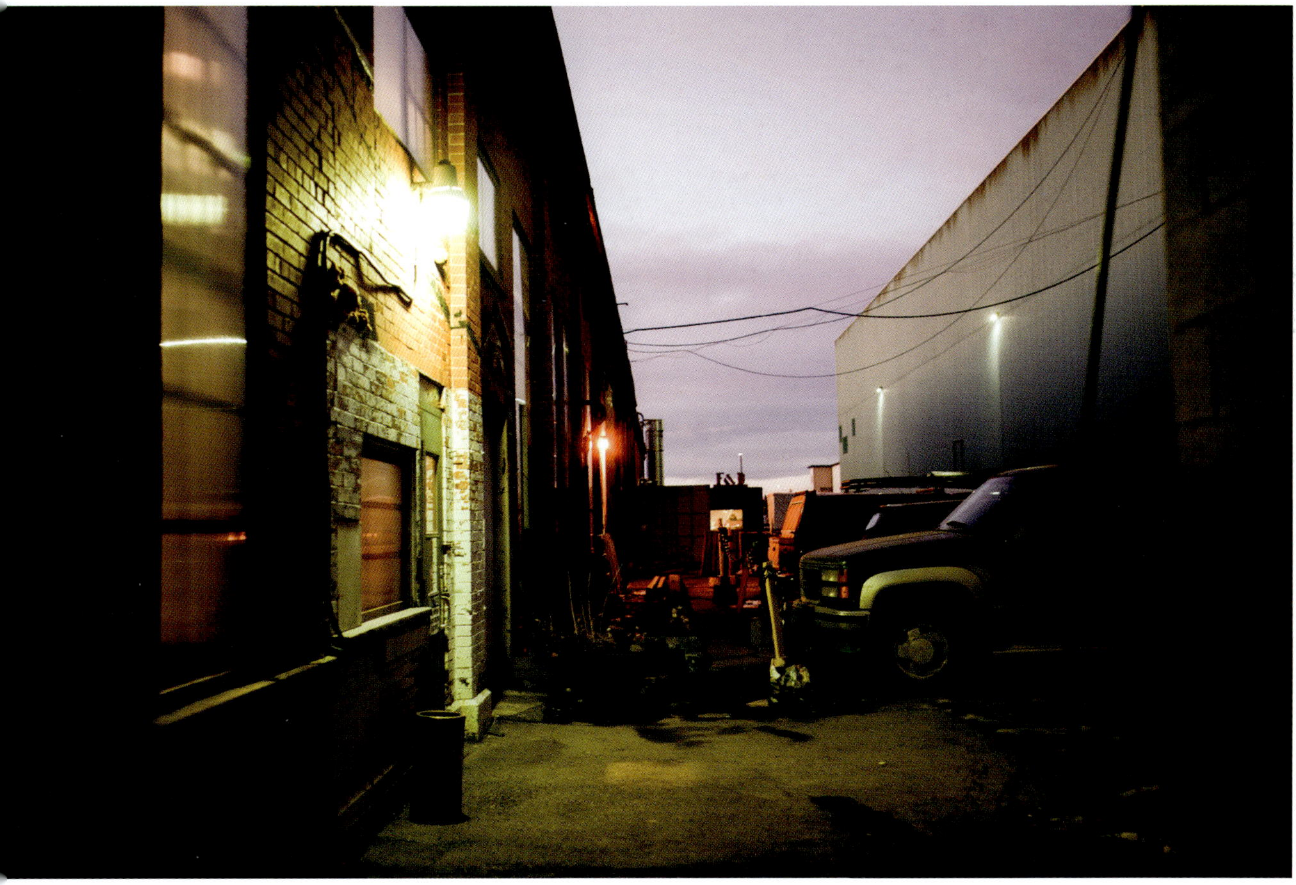

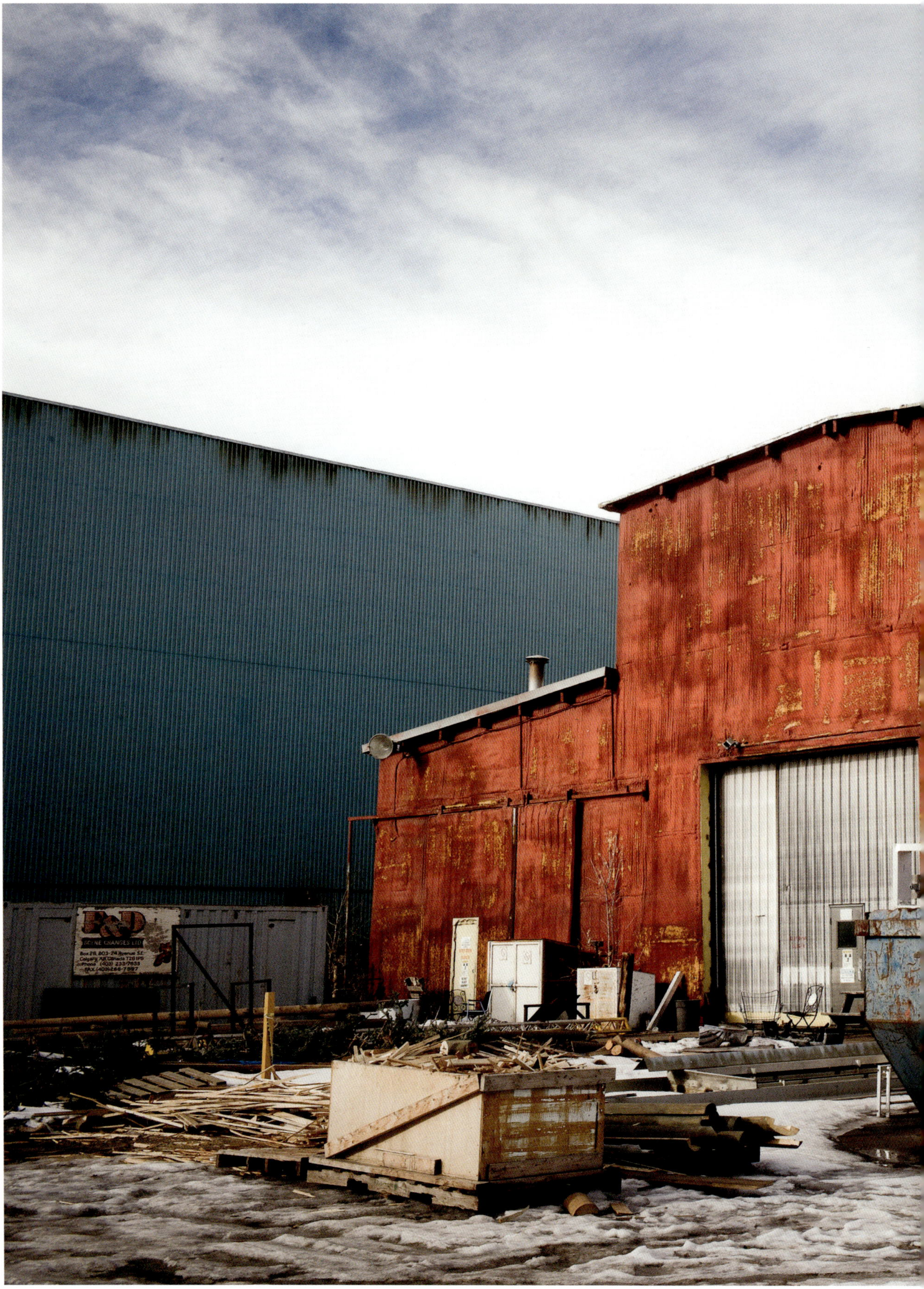
F&D

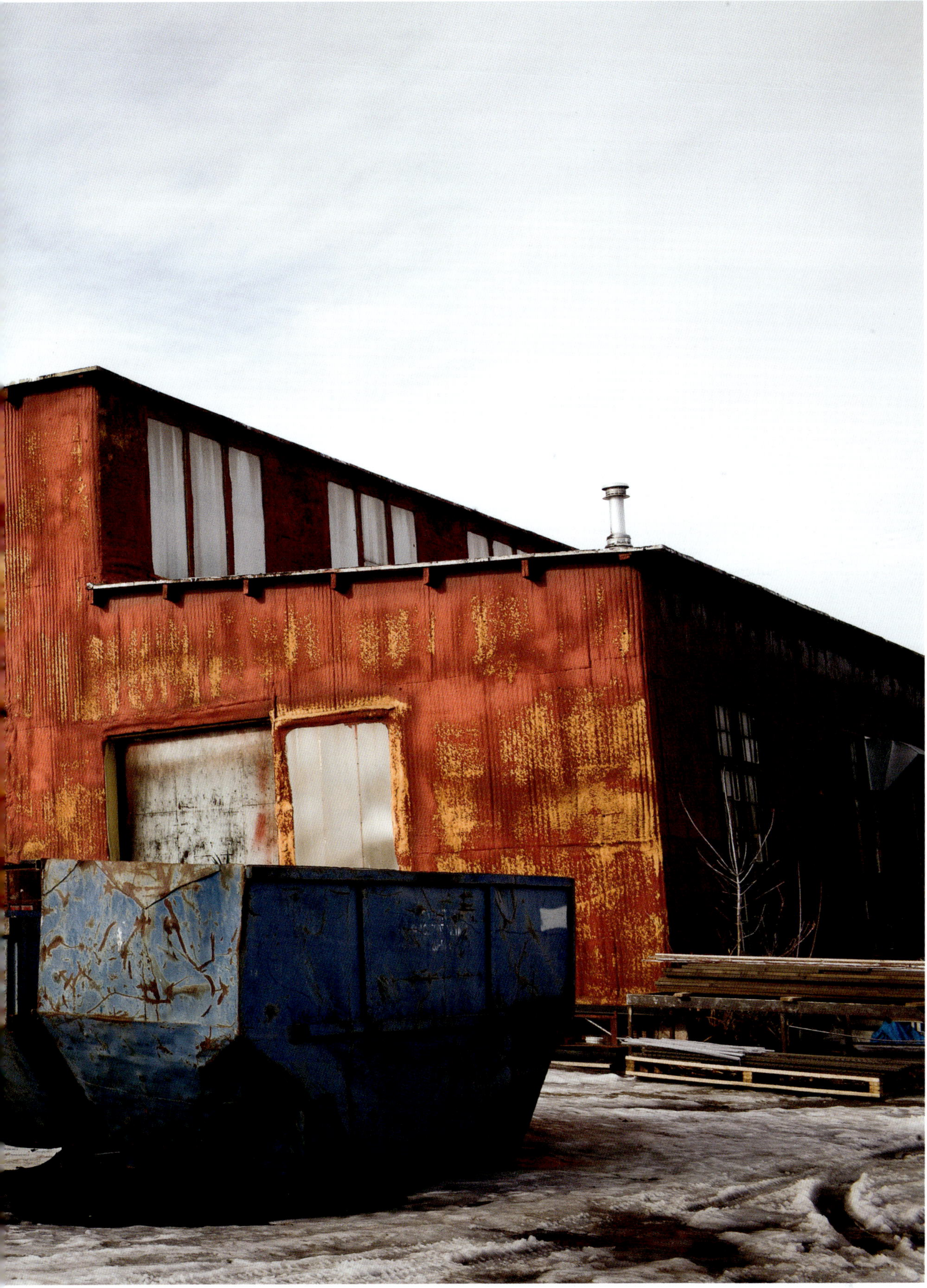

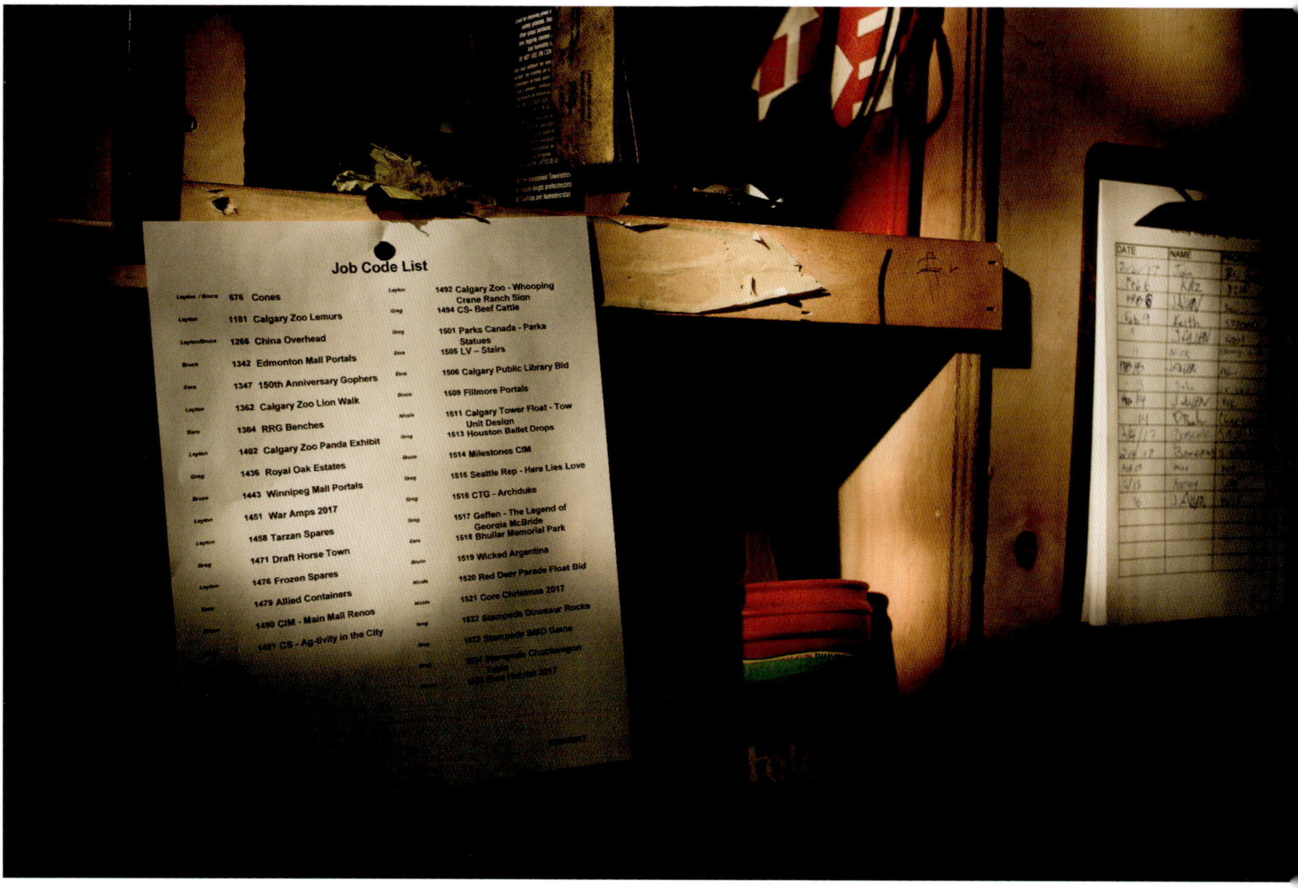
Job Code List
676 Cones
1181 Calgary Zoo Lemurs
1266 China Overhead
1342 Edmonton Mall Portals
1347 150th Anniversary Gophers
1362 Calgary Zoo Lion Walk
1384 RRG Benches
1402 Calgary Zoo Panda Exhibit
1436 Royal Oak Estates
1443 Winnipeg Mall Portals
1451 War Amps 2017
1458 Tarzan Spares
1471 Draft Horse Town
1476 Frozen Spares
1479 Allied Containers
1490 CIM - Main Mall Renos
CS - Ag-tivity in the City
1492 Calgary Zoo - Whooping Crane Ranch Sign
1494 CS- Beef Cattle
1501 Parks Canada - Parka Statues
1505 LV – Stairs
1506 Calgary Public Library Bid
1509 Fillmore Portals
1511 Calgary Tower Float - Tow Unit Design
1513 Houston Ballet Drops
1514 Milestones CIM
1515 Seattle Rep - Here Lies Love
1516 CTG - Archduke
1517 Geffen - The Legend of Georgia McBride
1518 Bhullar Memorial Park
1519 Wicked Argentina
1520 Red Deer Parade Float Bid
1521 Core Christmas 2017
1522 Stampede Dinosaur Rocks
DATE
NAME

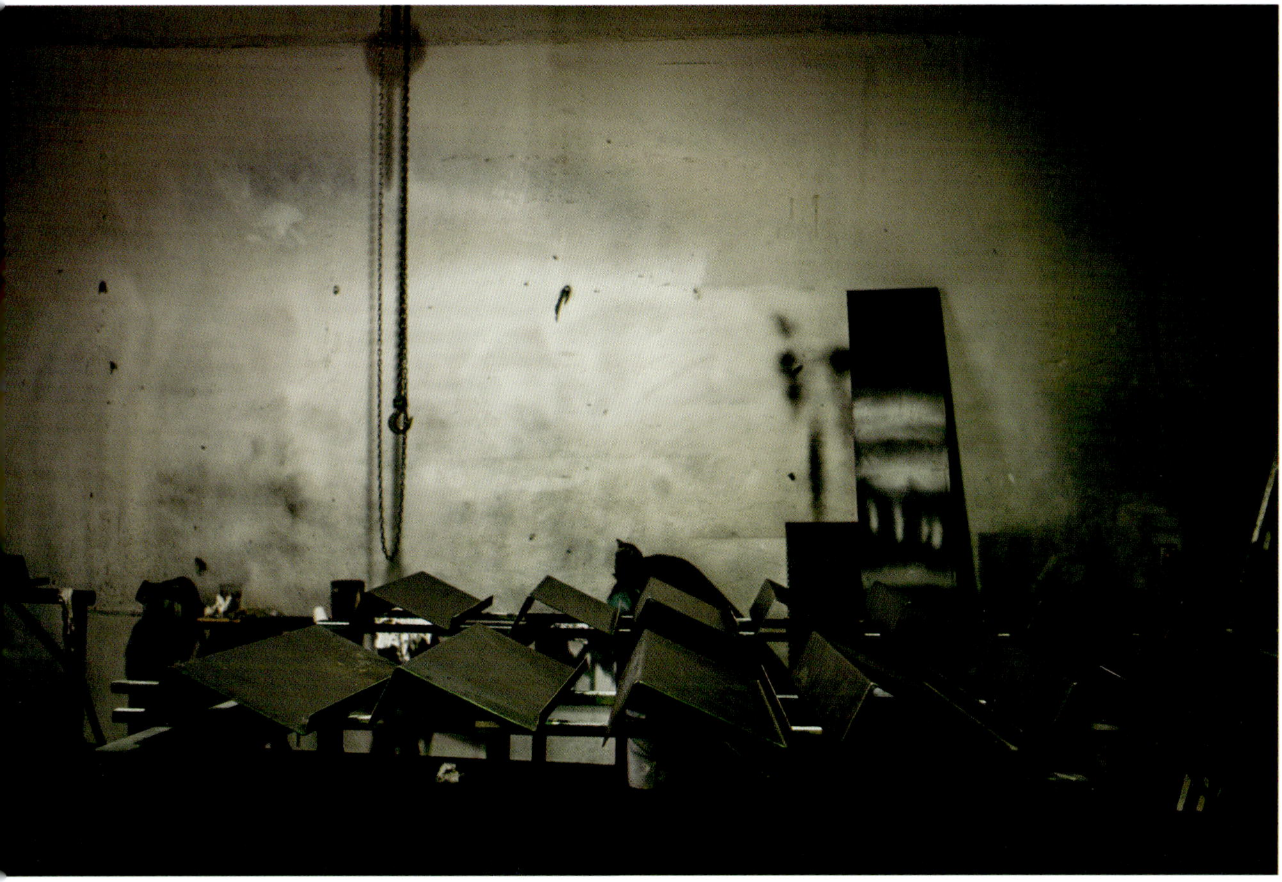

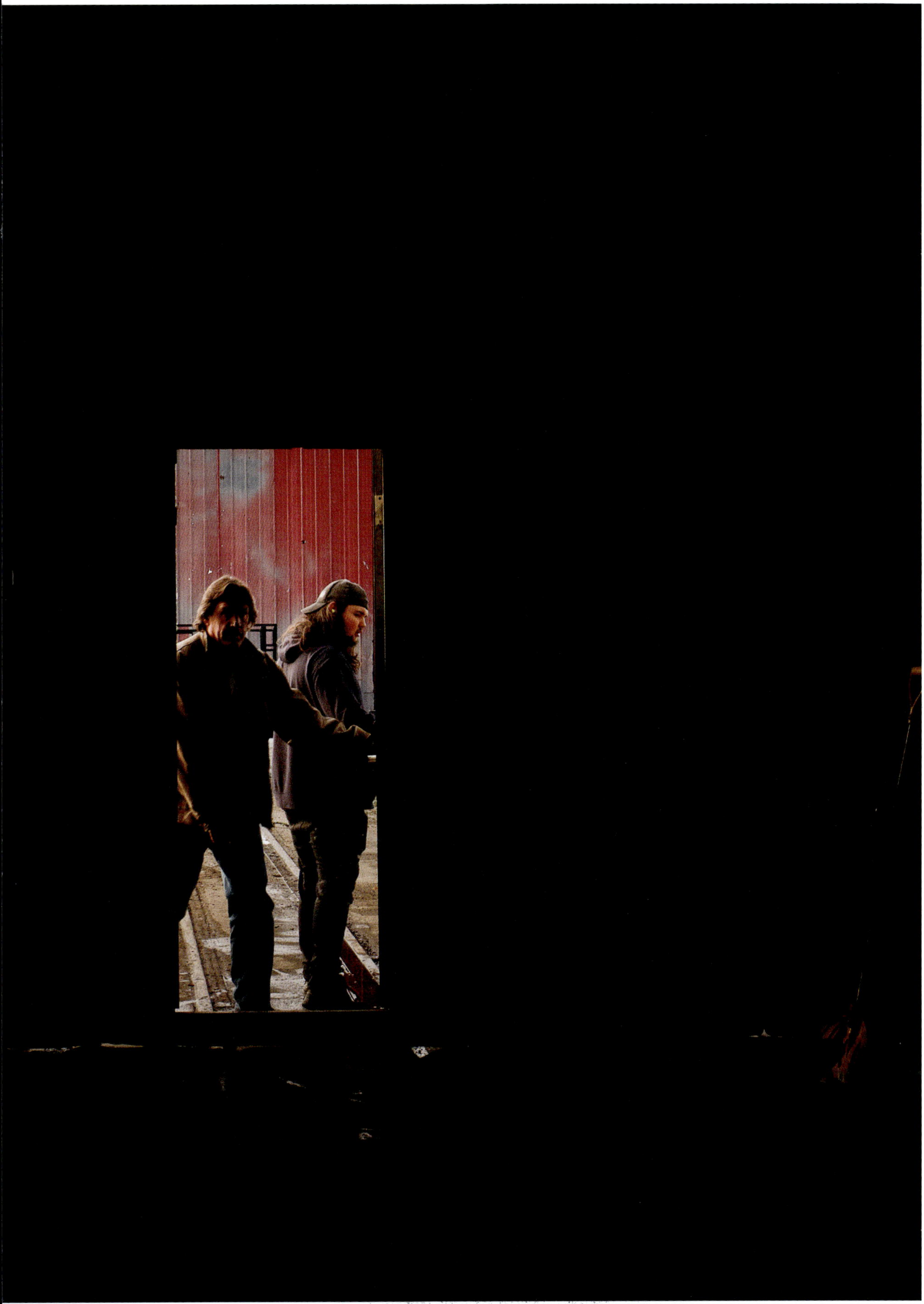

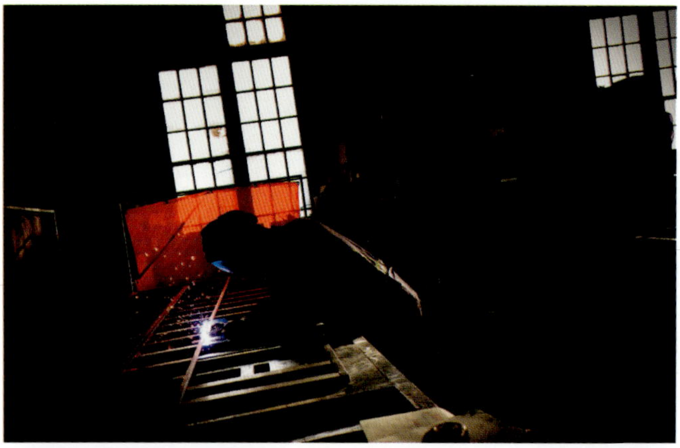
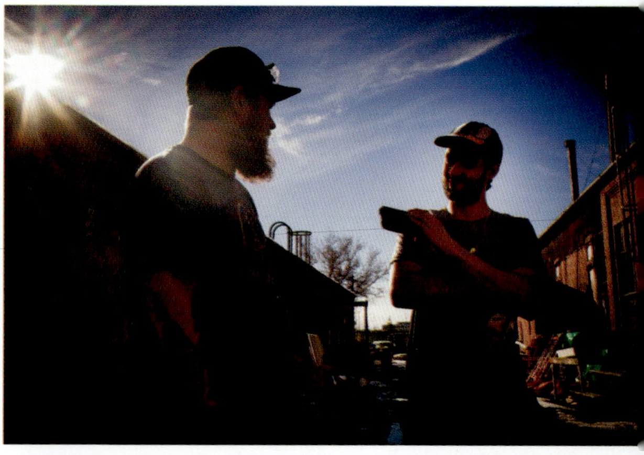
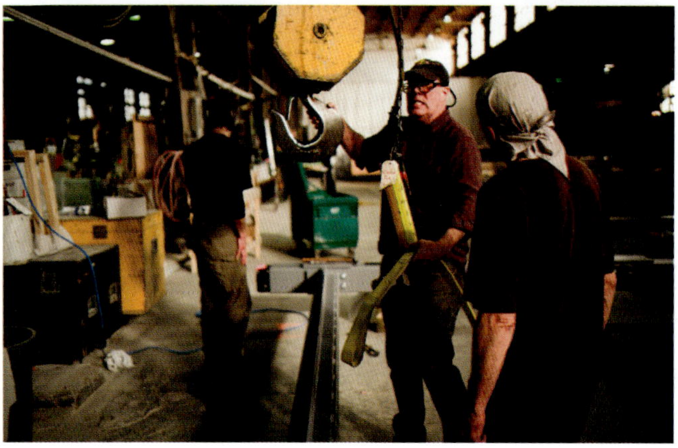
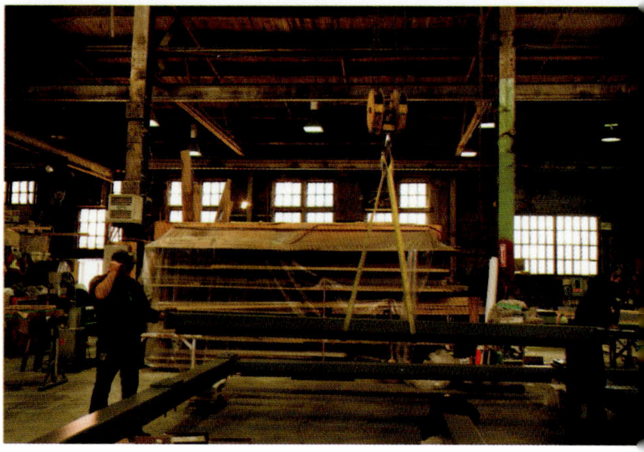

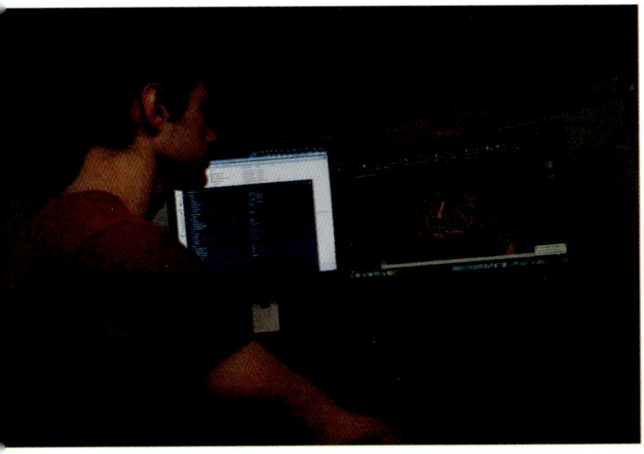

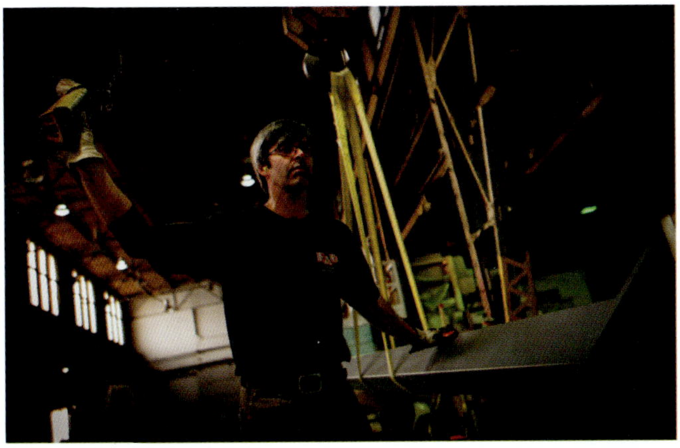

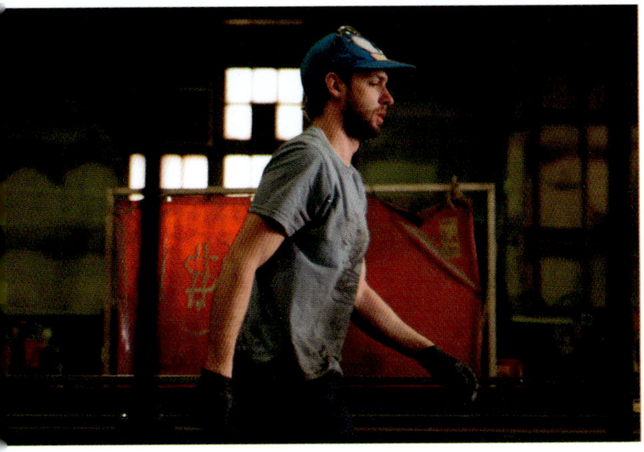

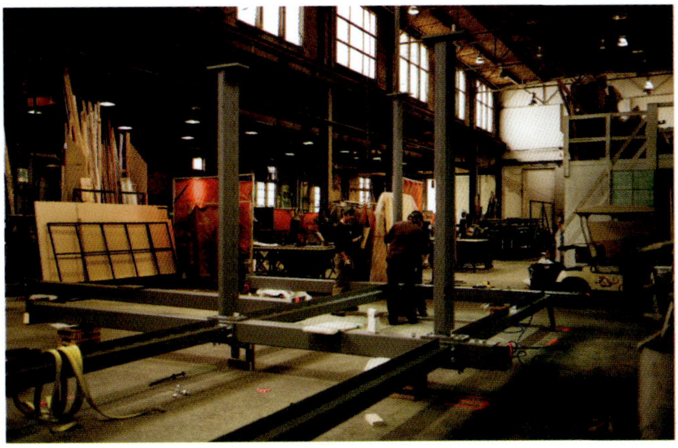

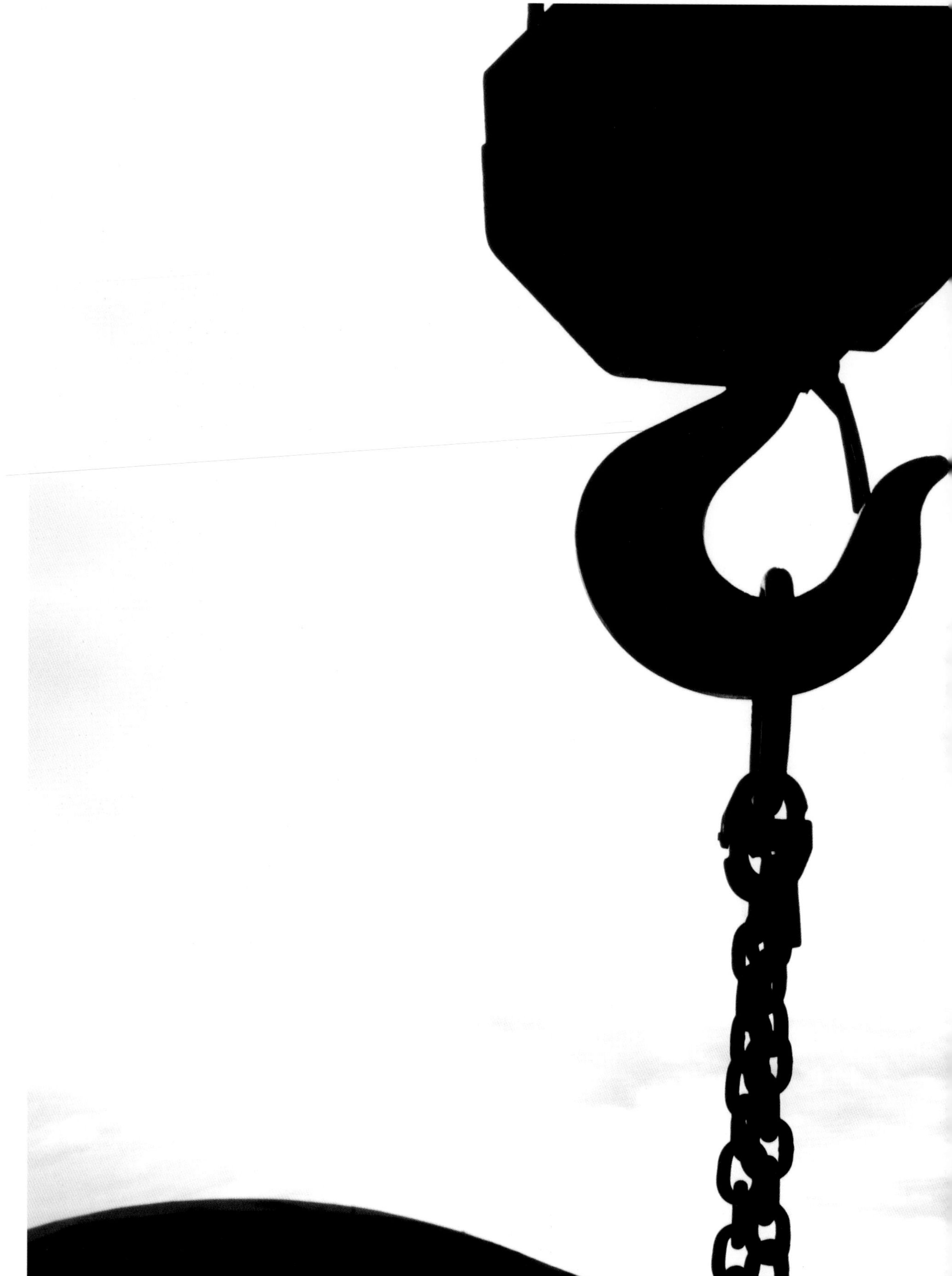

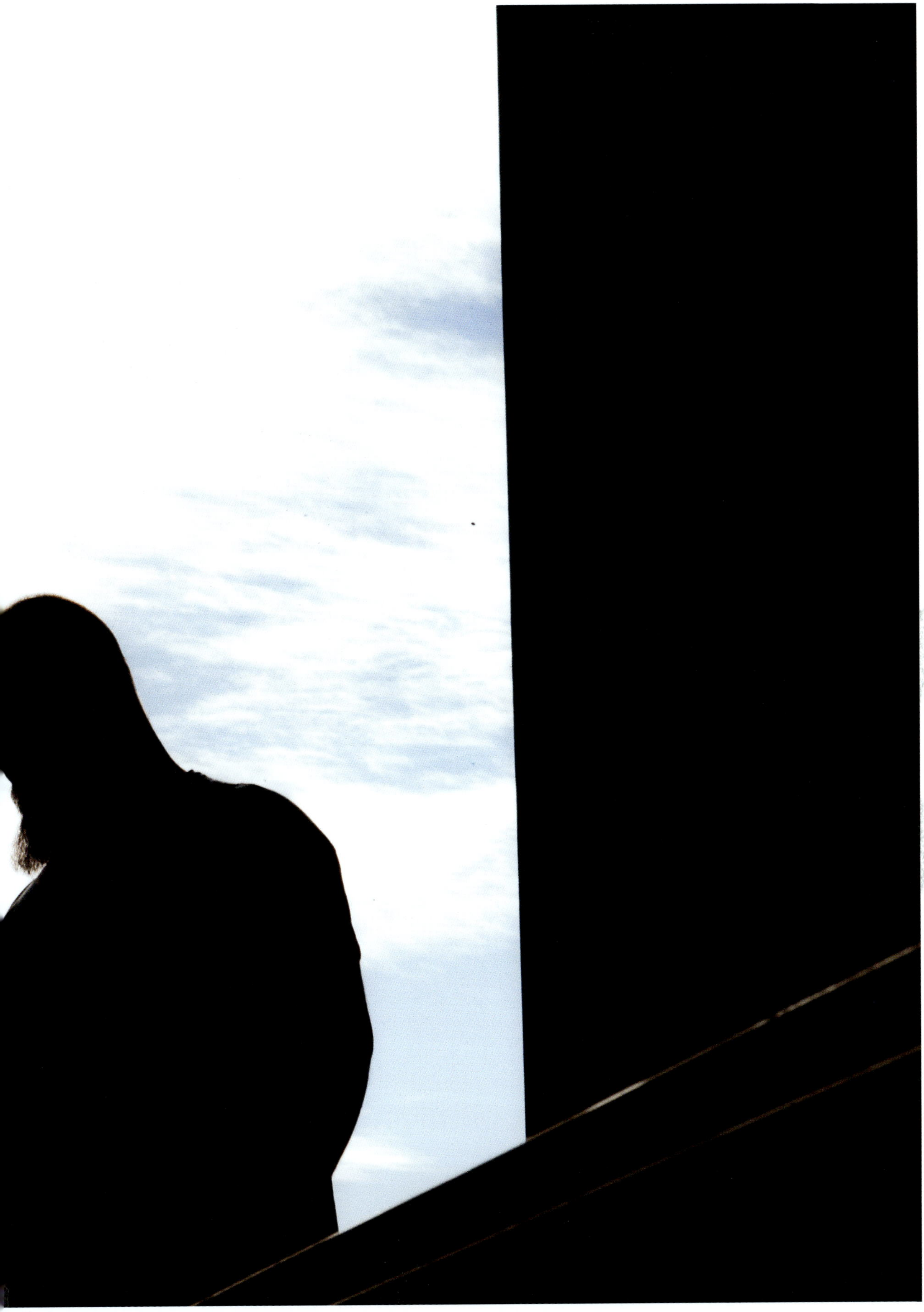

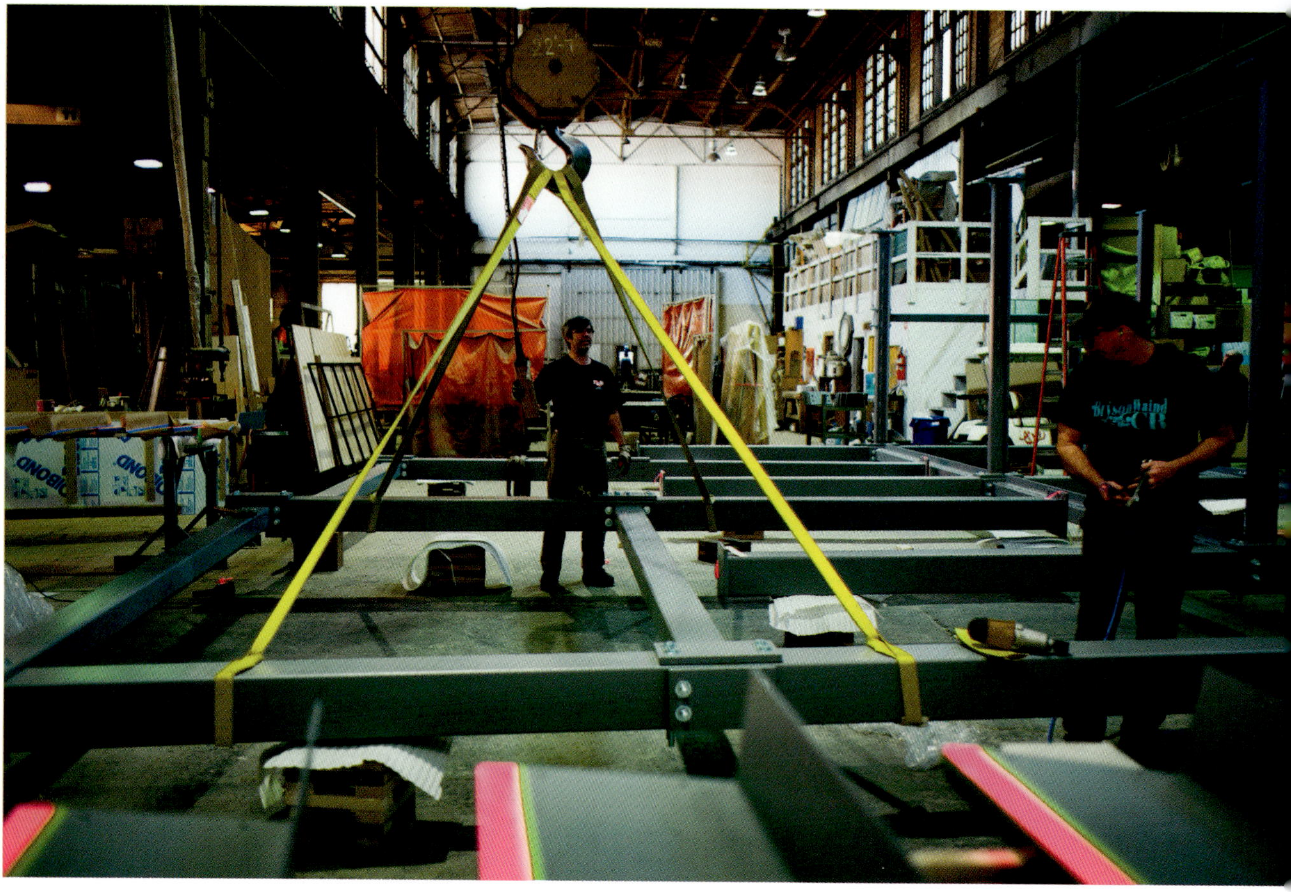

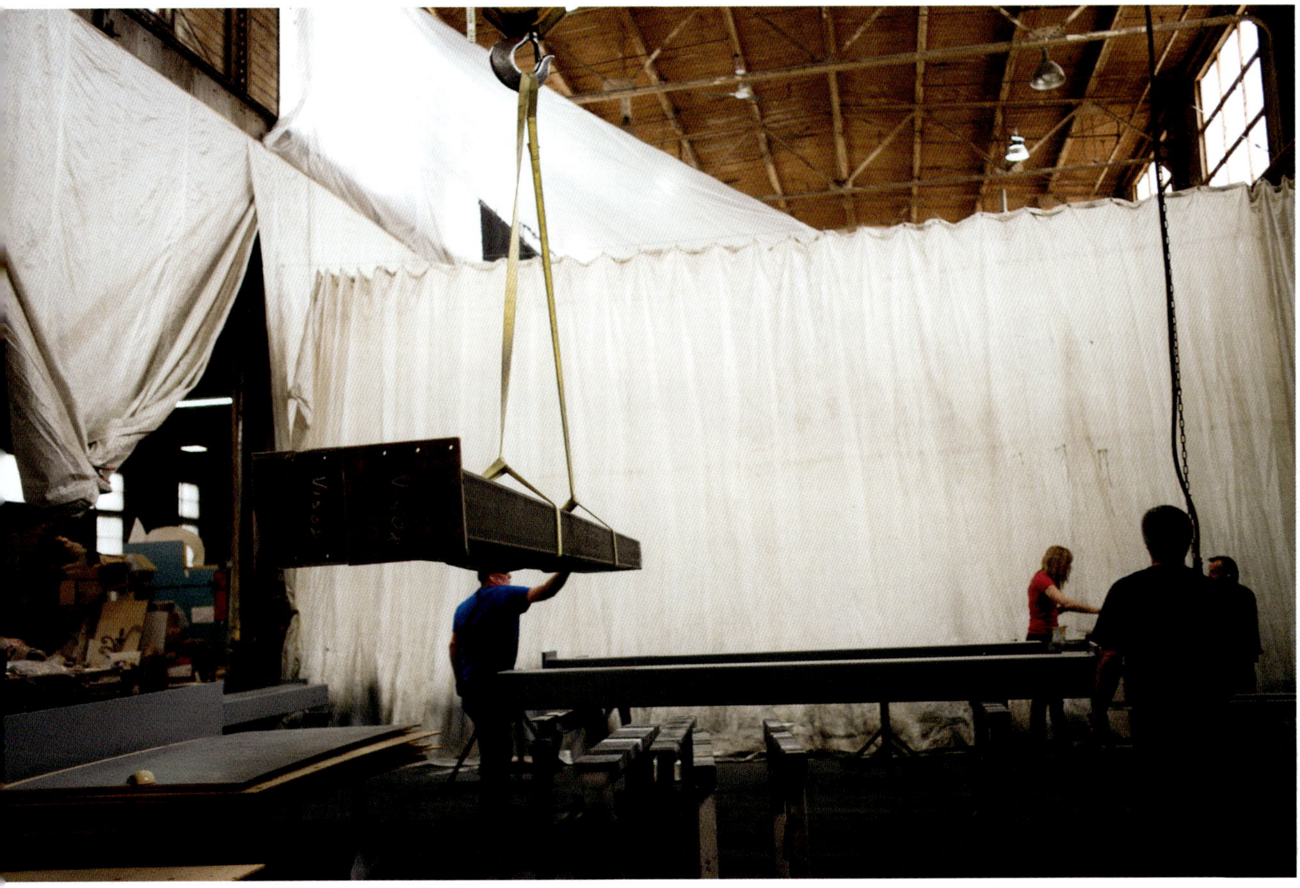

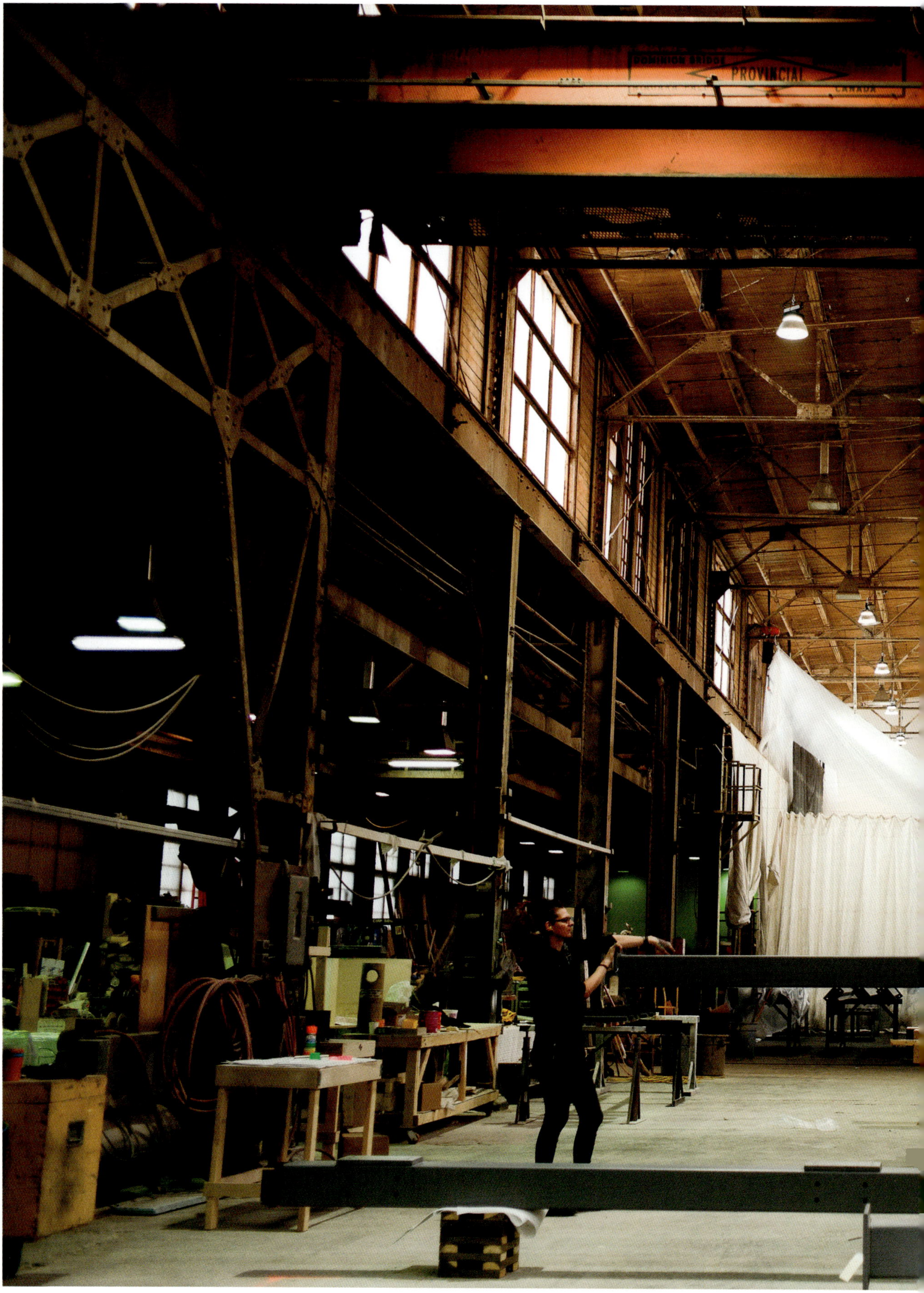
DOMINION BRIDGE
PROVINCIAL
CANADA

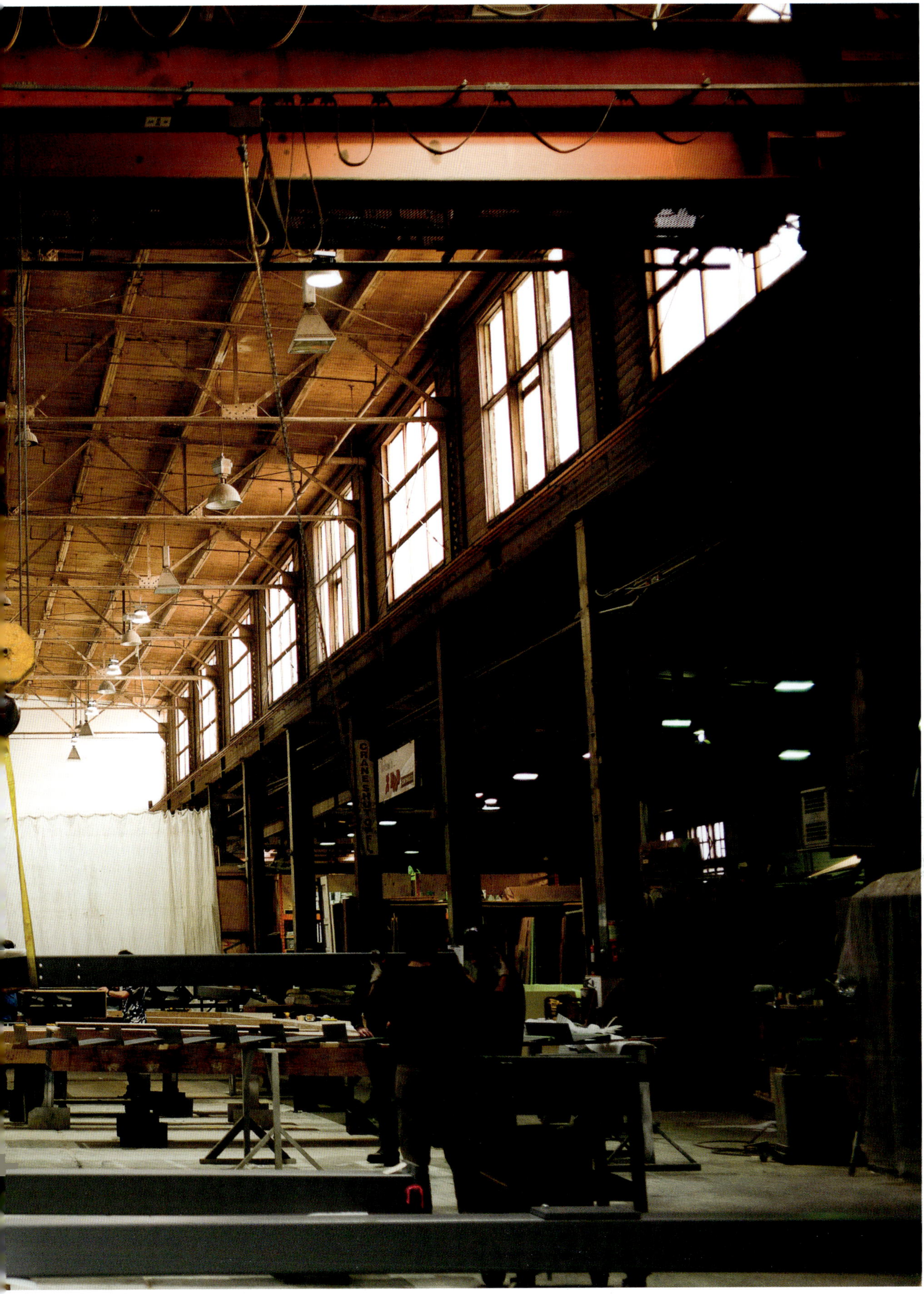
CRANE SHUT OFF

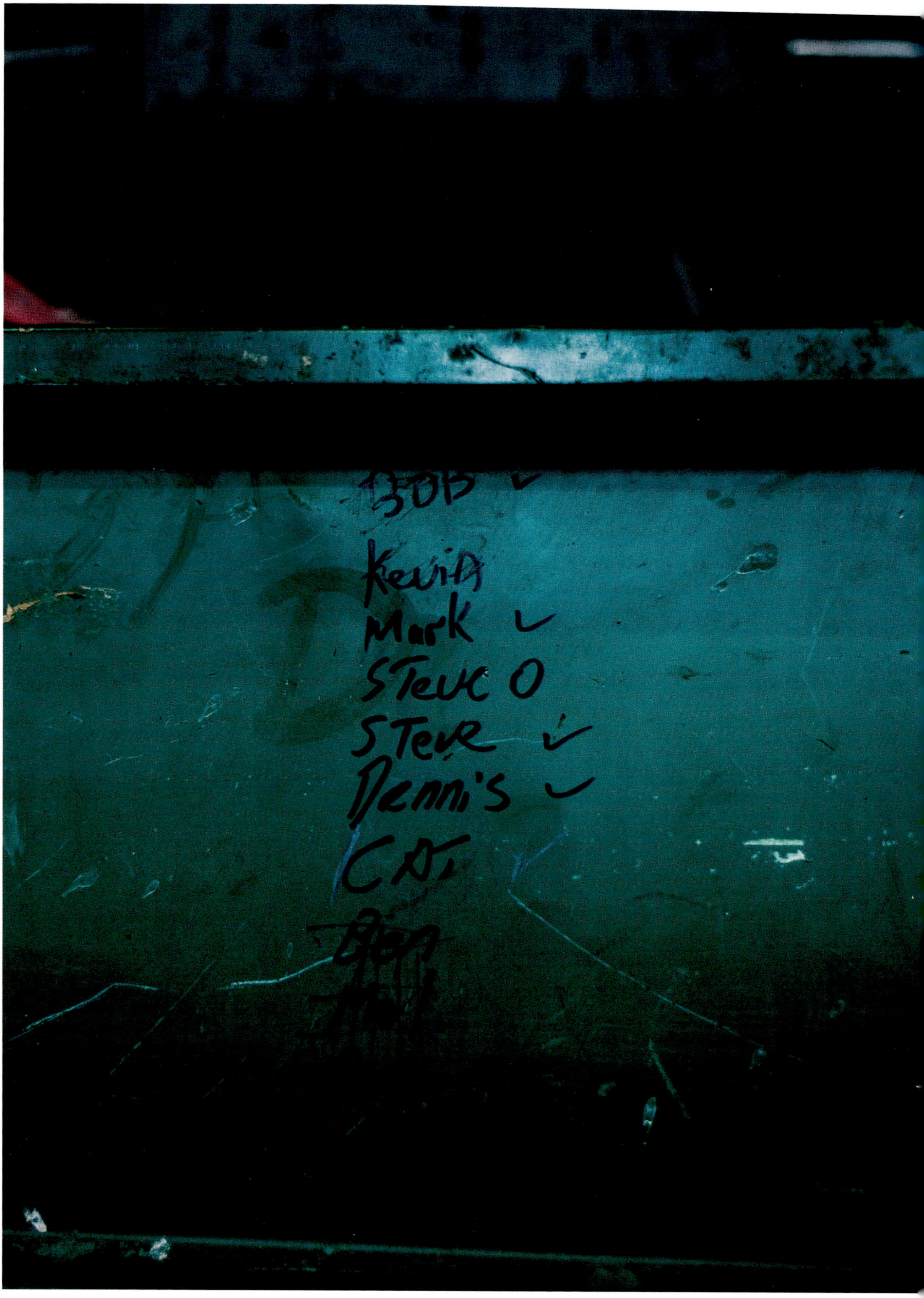
BOB
Kevin
Mark
Steve O
Steve
Dennis
C.A.

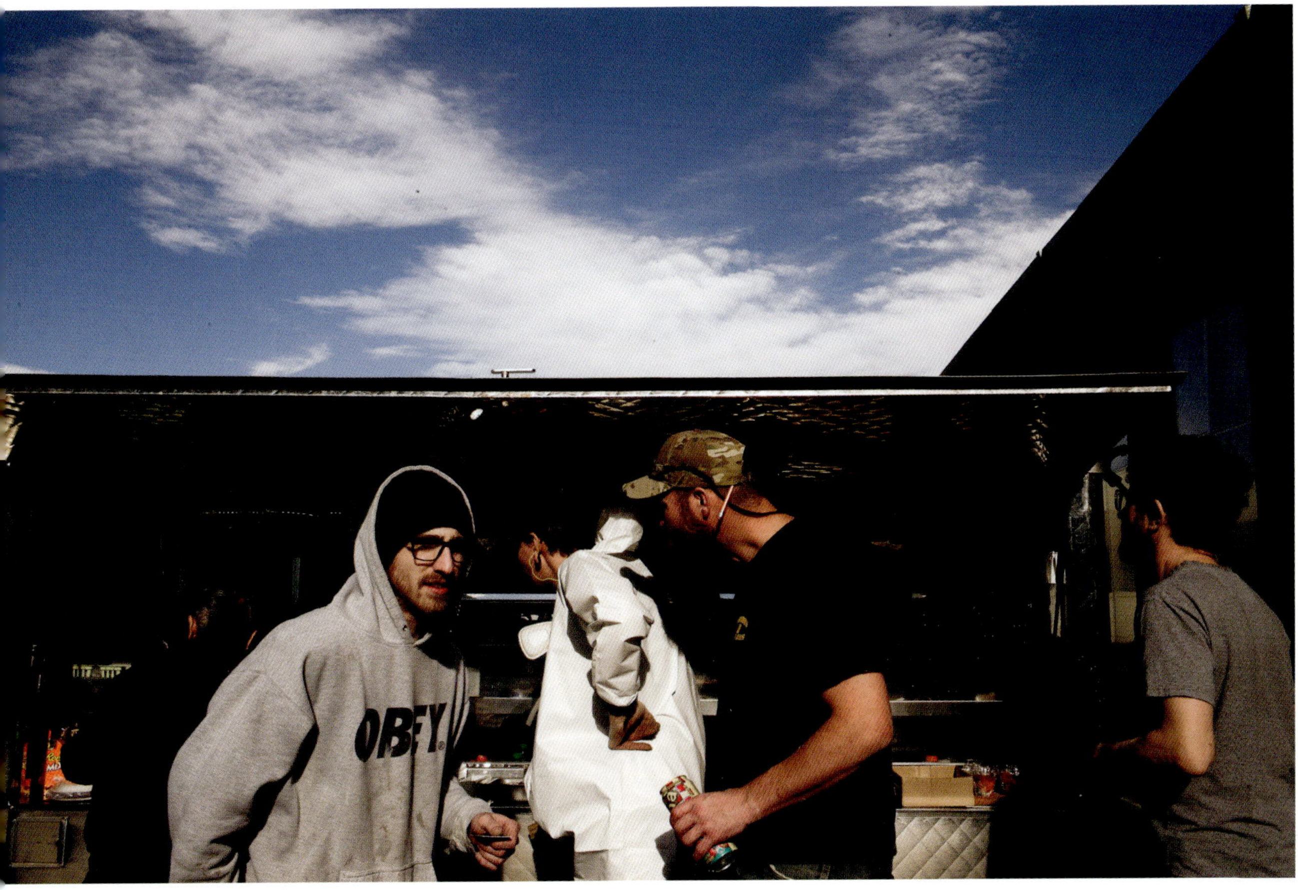
OBEY

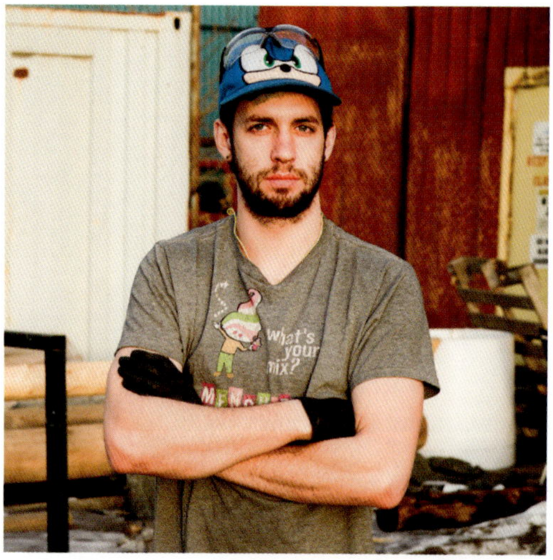
what's
your
mix?
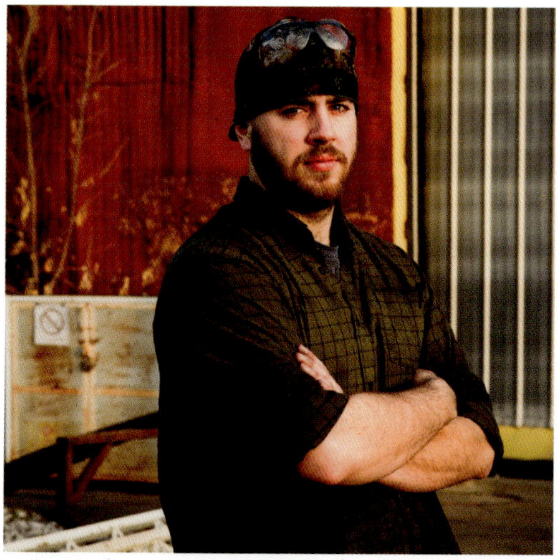
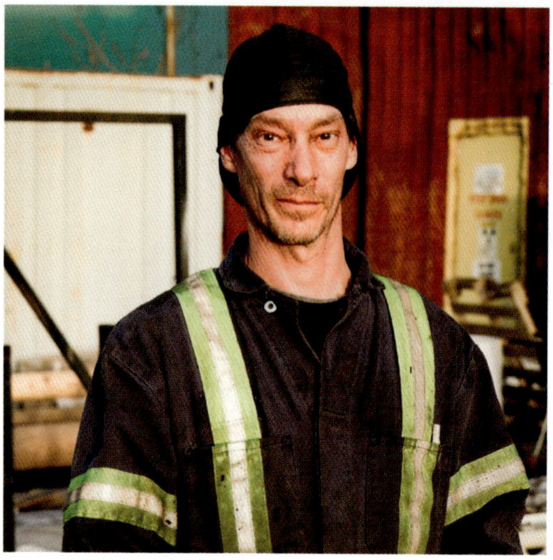
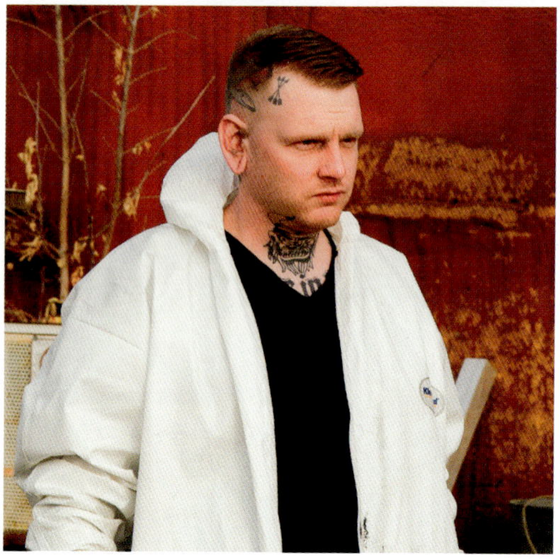

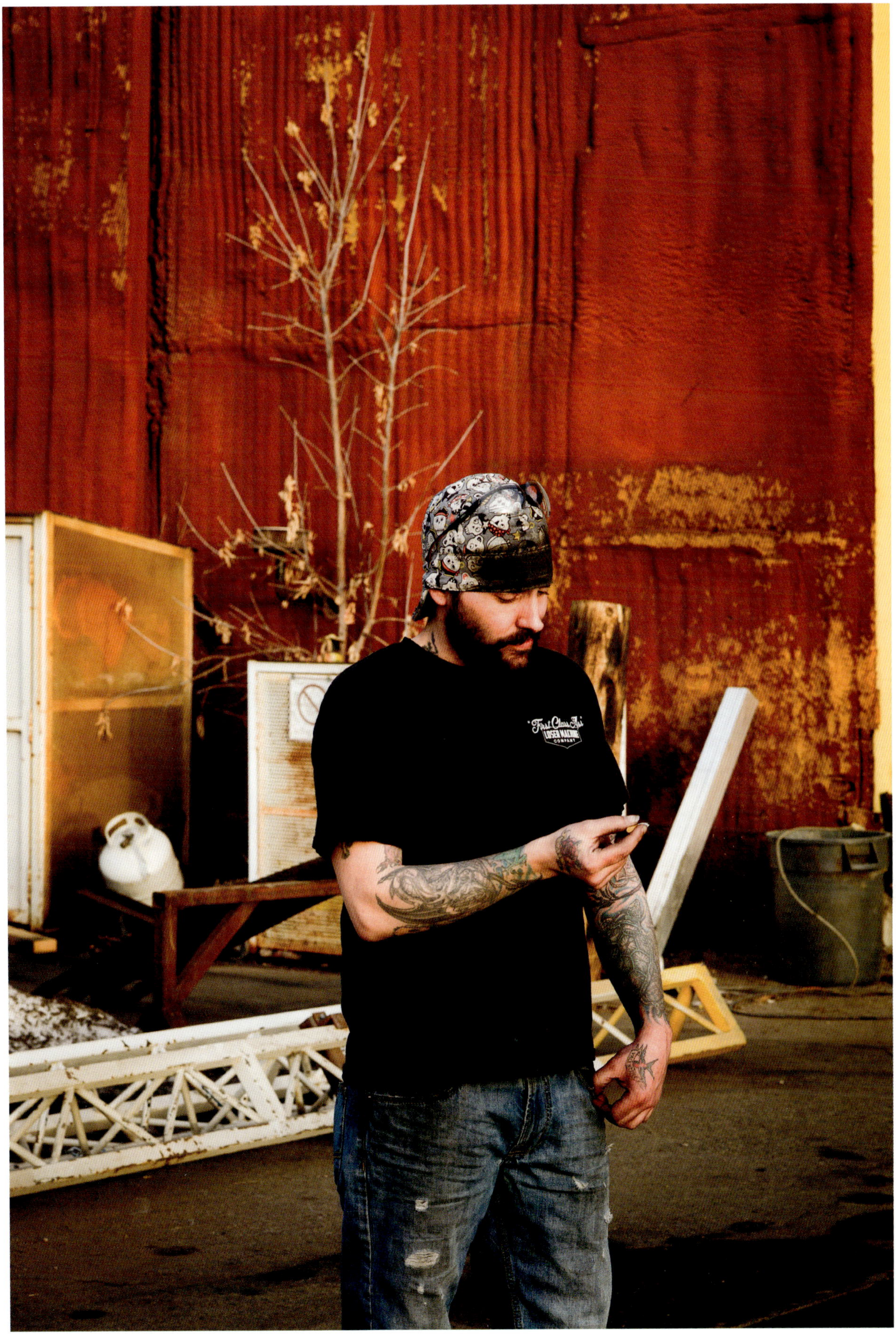
LOSER MACHINE
COMPANY

HE GAVE ME TWO ROSES
ONE IS OPEN
ONE IS CLOSED

ONE IS THE FUTURE

AND ONE IS MY LOVE

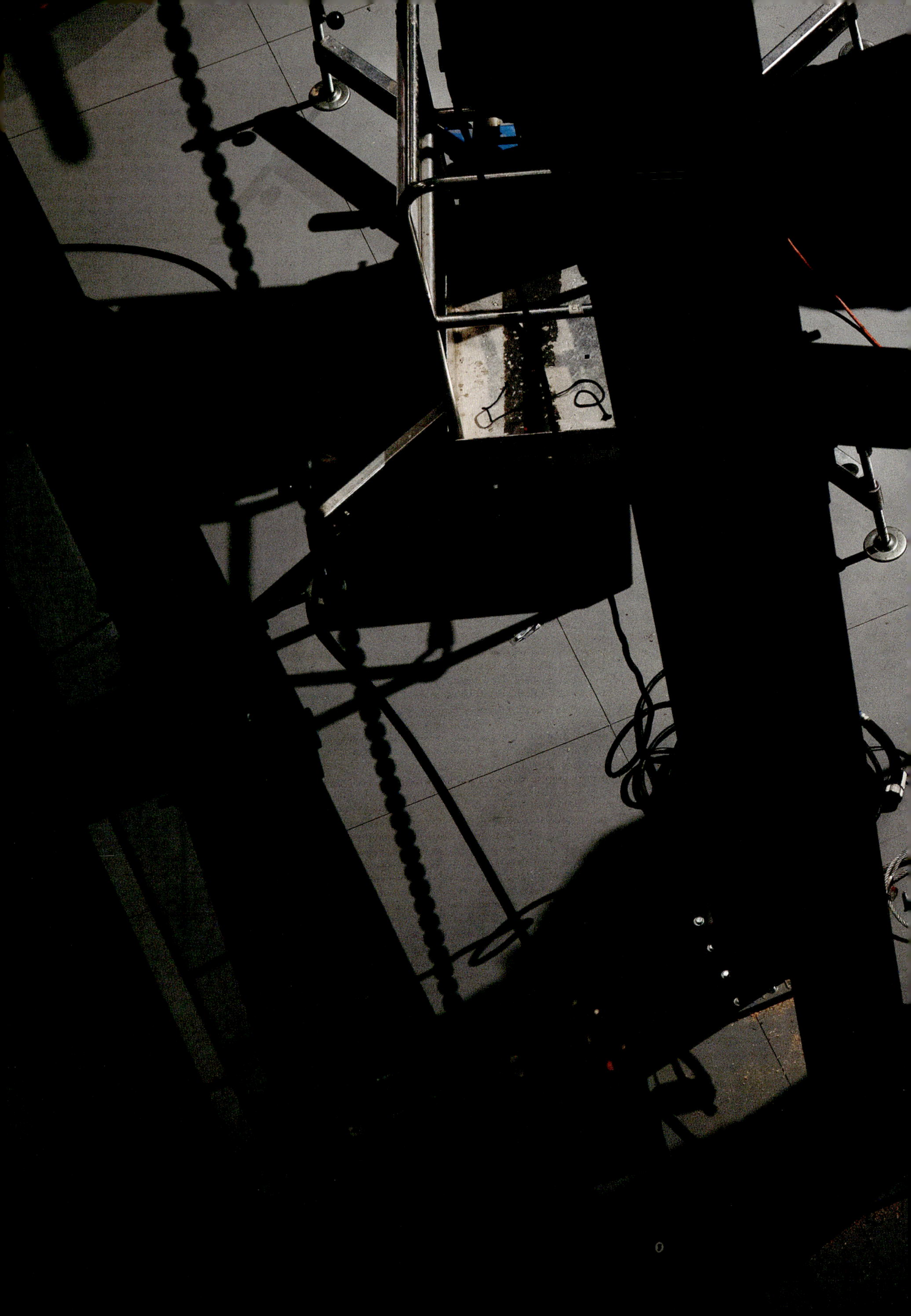

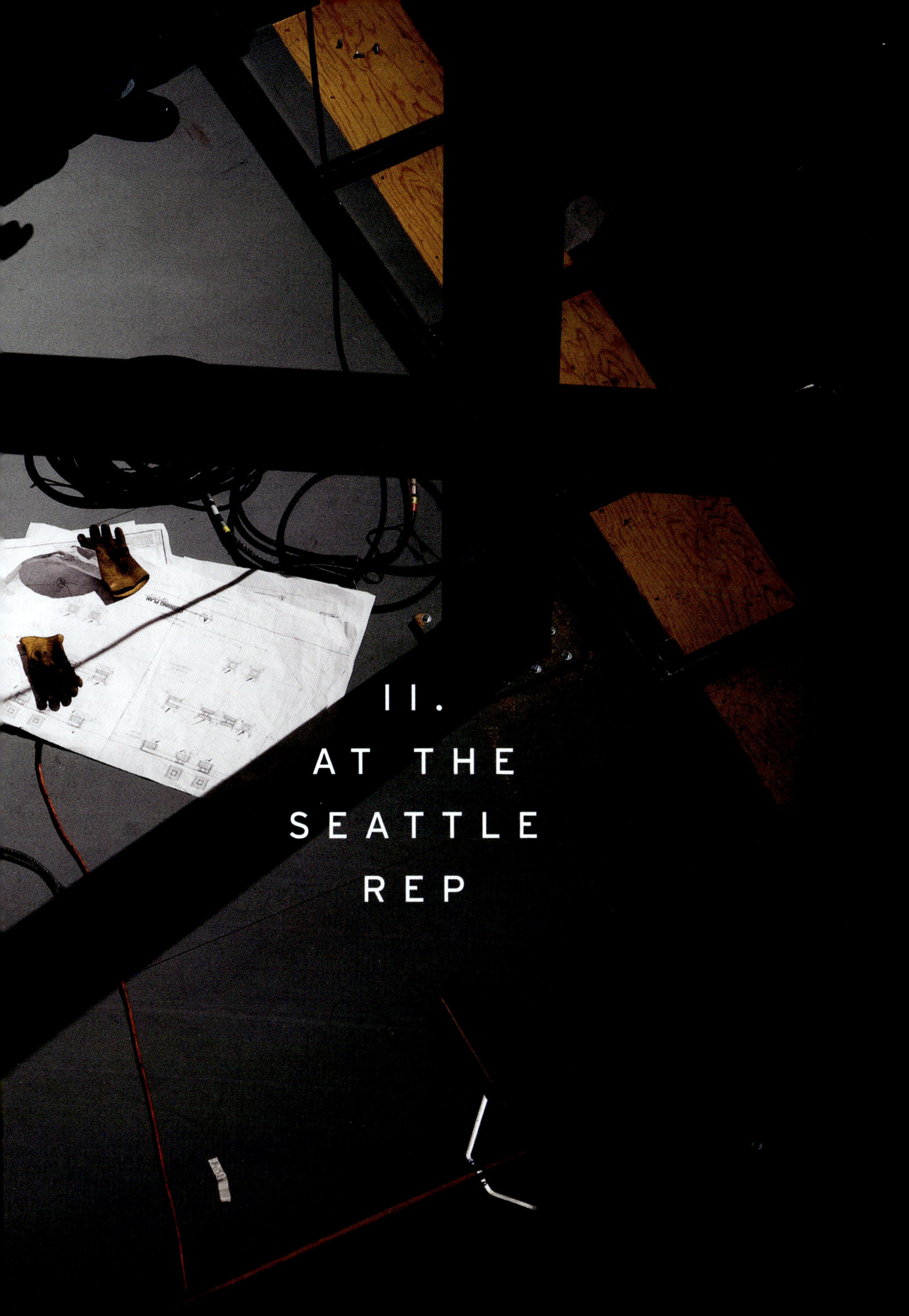

II. AT THE SEATTLE REP

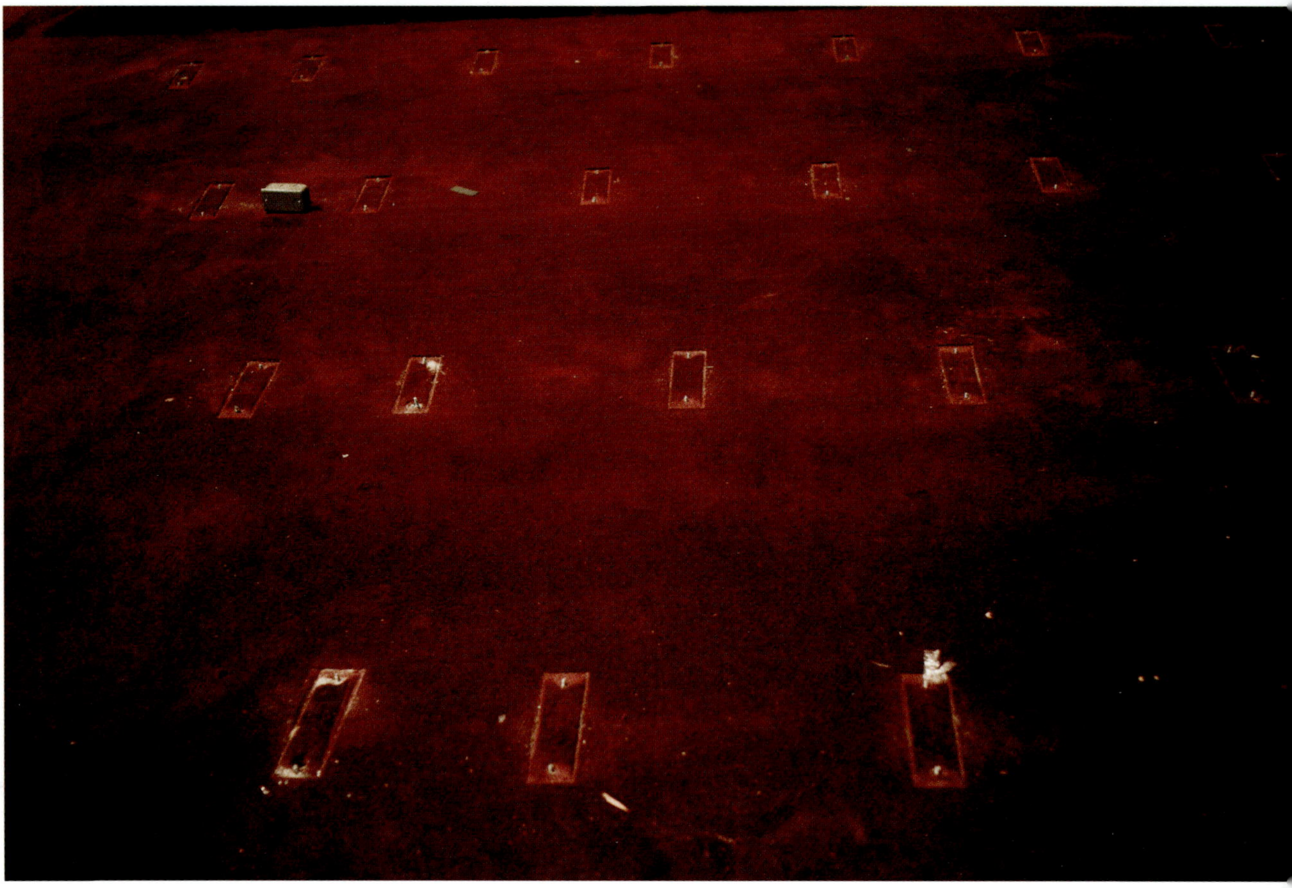

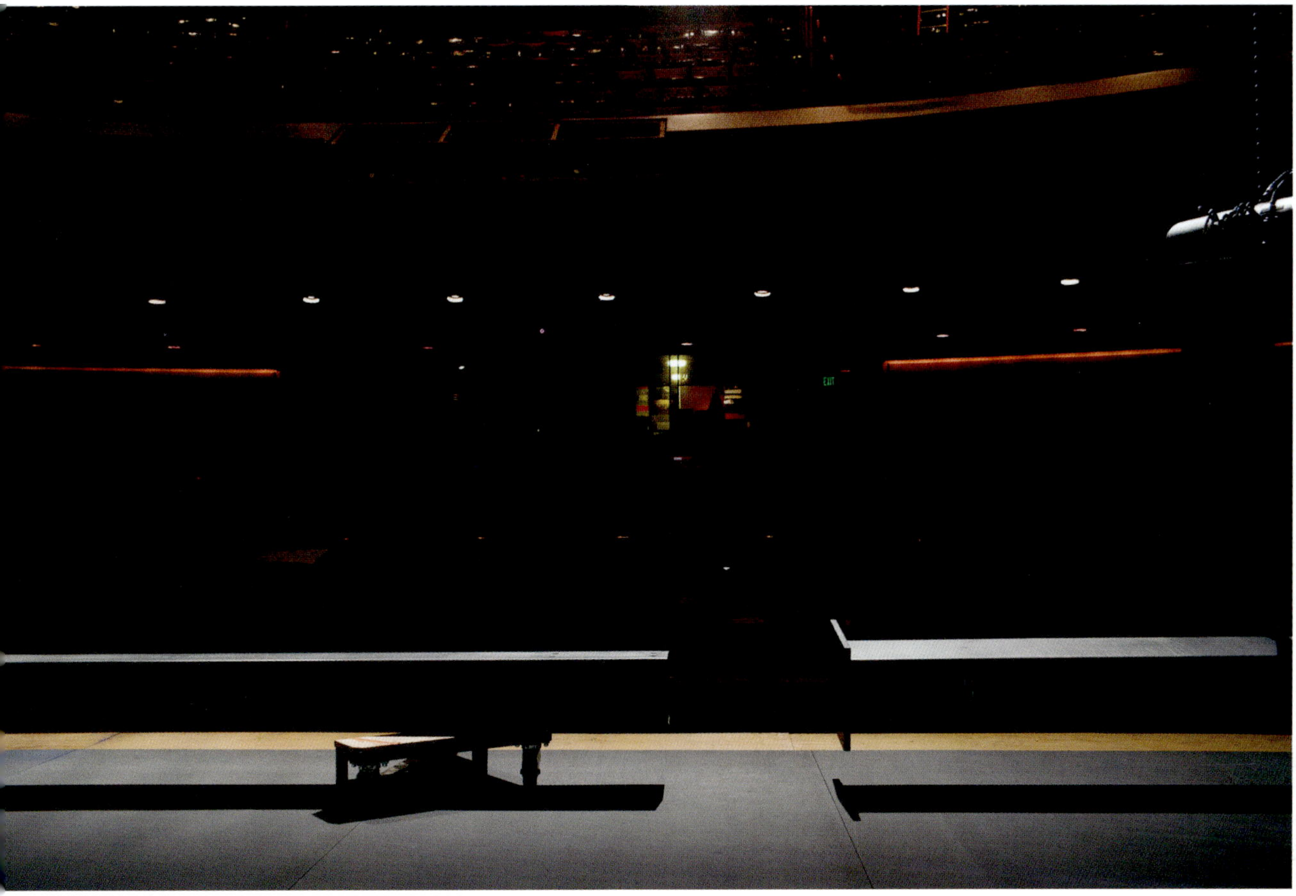

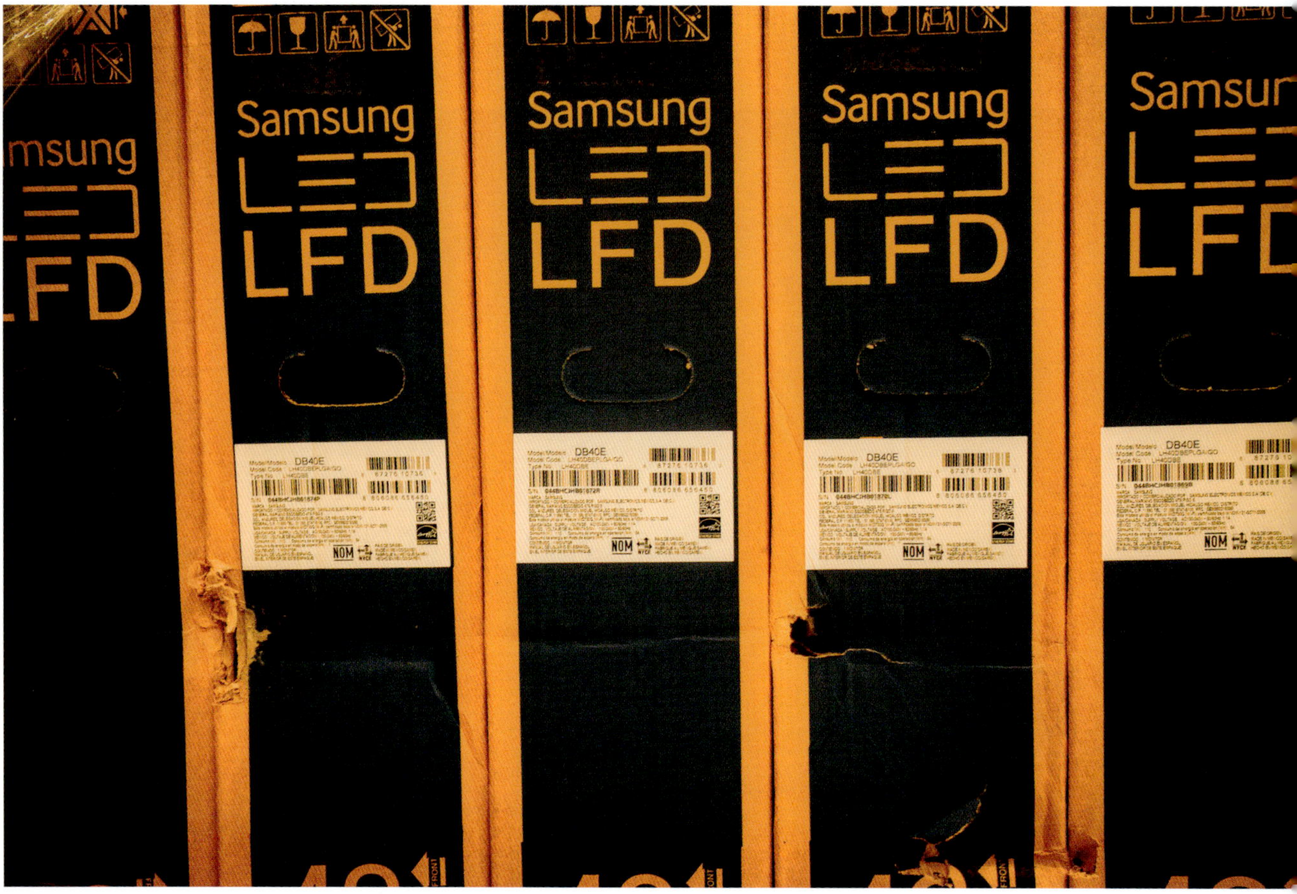
Samsung
LFD
DB40E
Samsung
LFD
DB40E
Samsung
LFD
DB40E

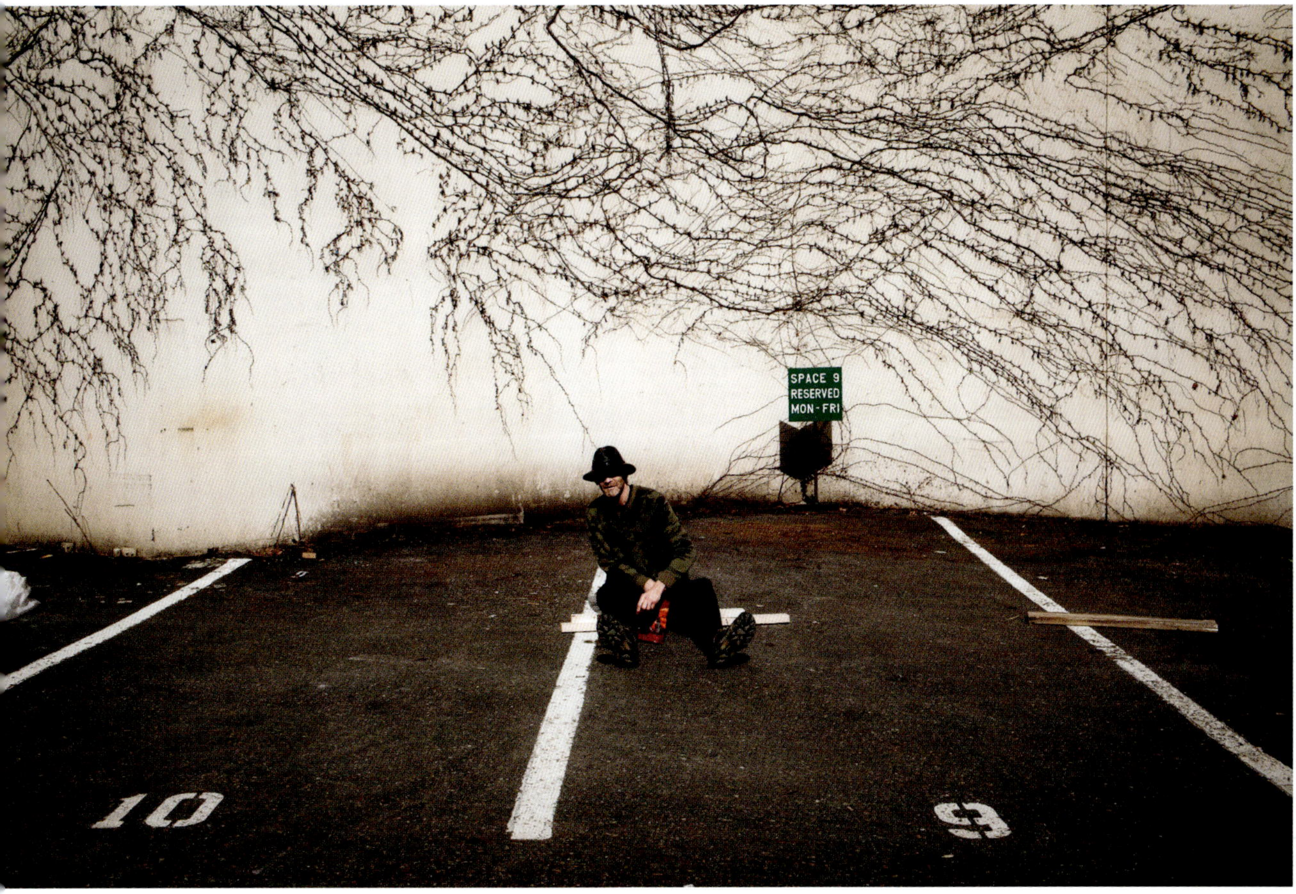
SPACE 9
RESERVED
MON-FRI
10
9

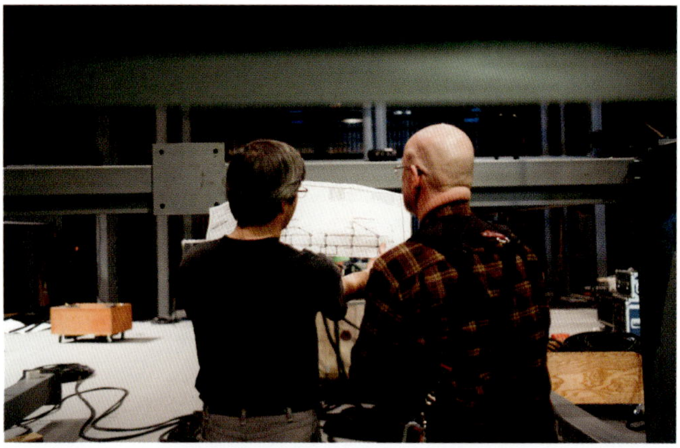

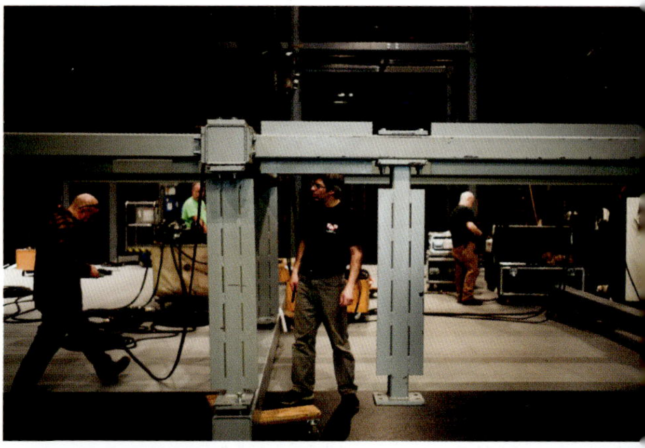

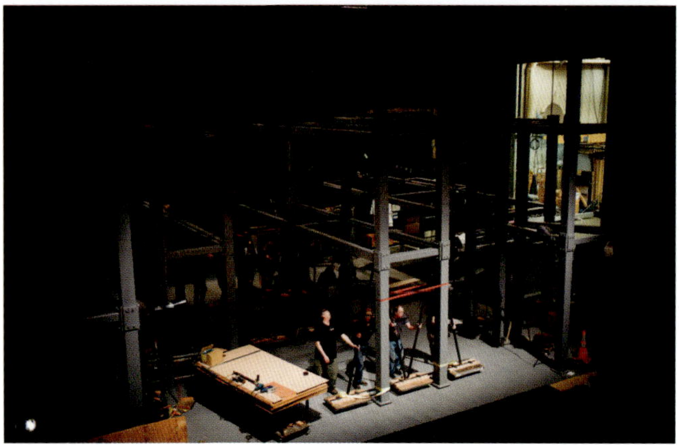

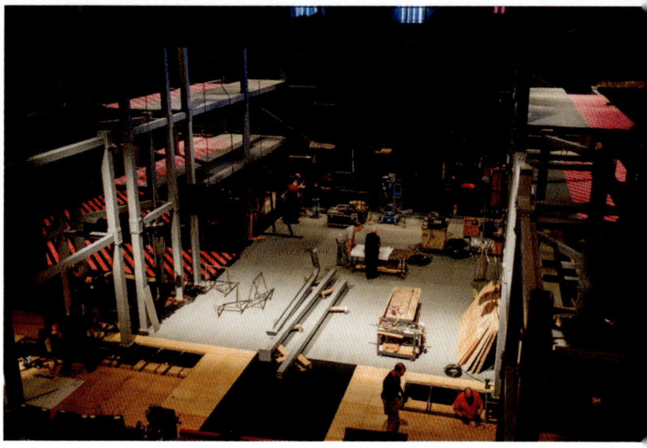

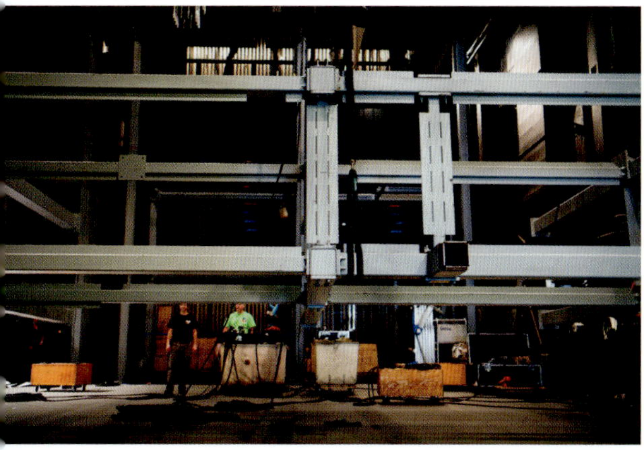

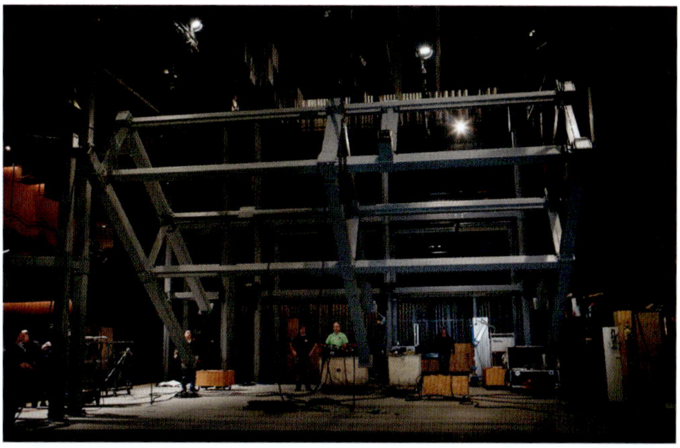

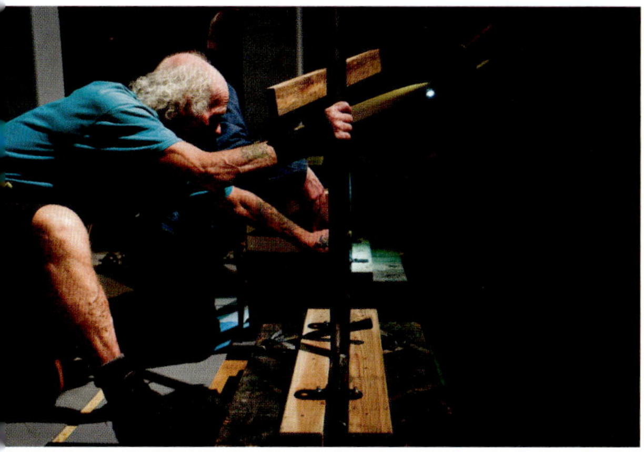

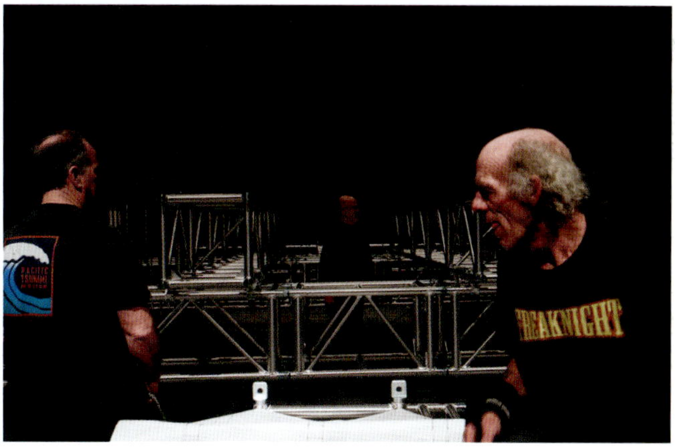
PACIFIC
TSUNAMI
REAKNIGHT

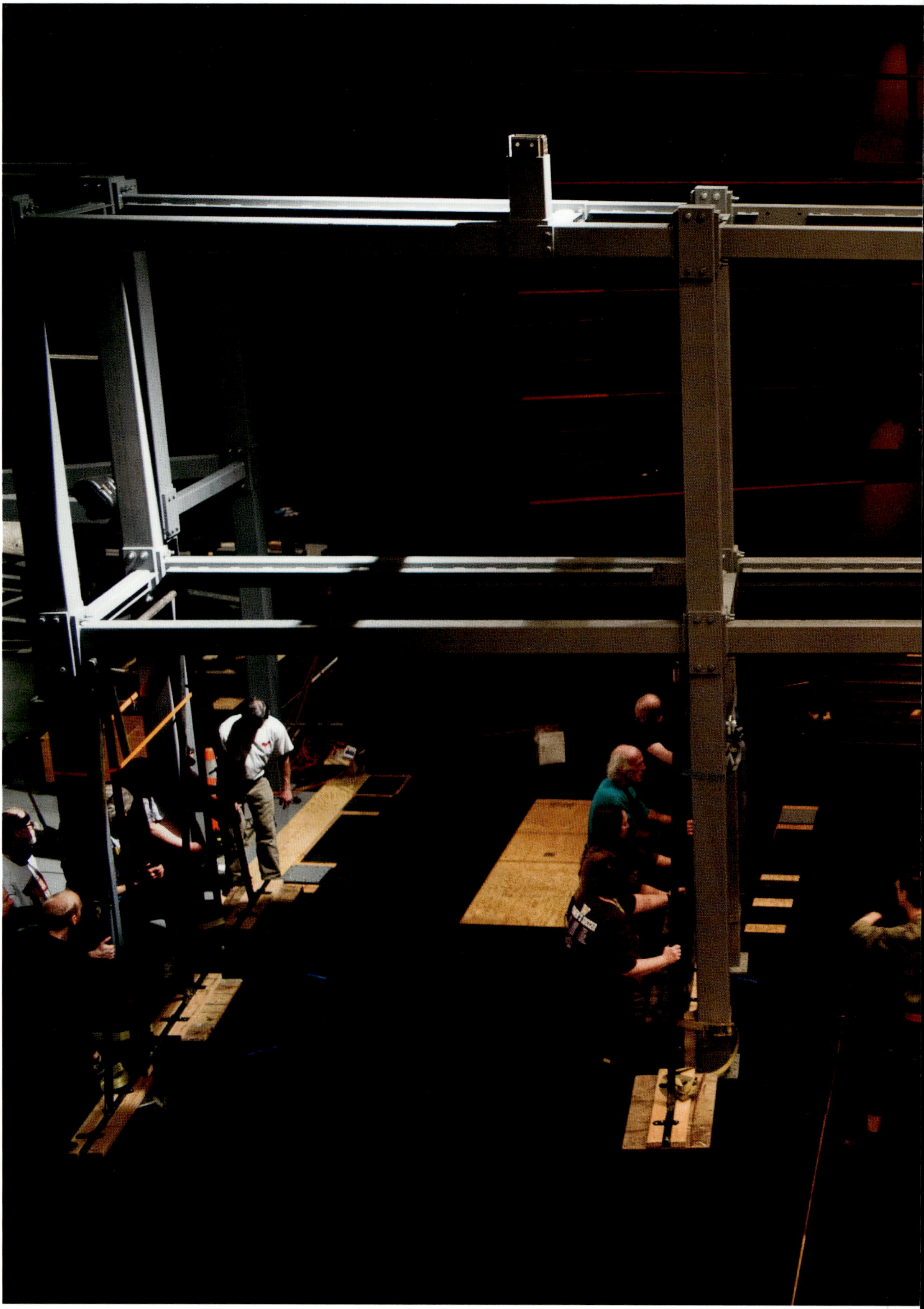

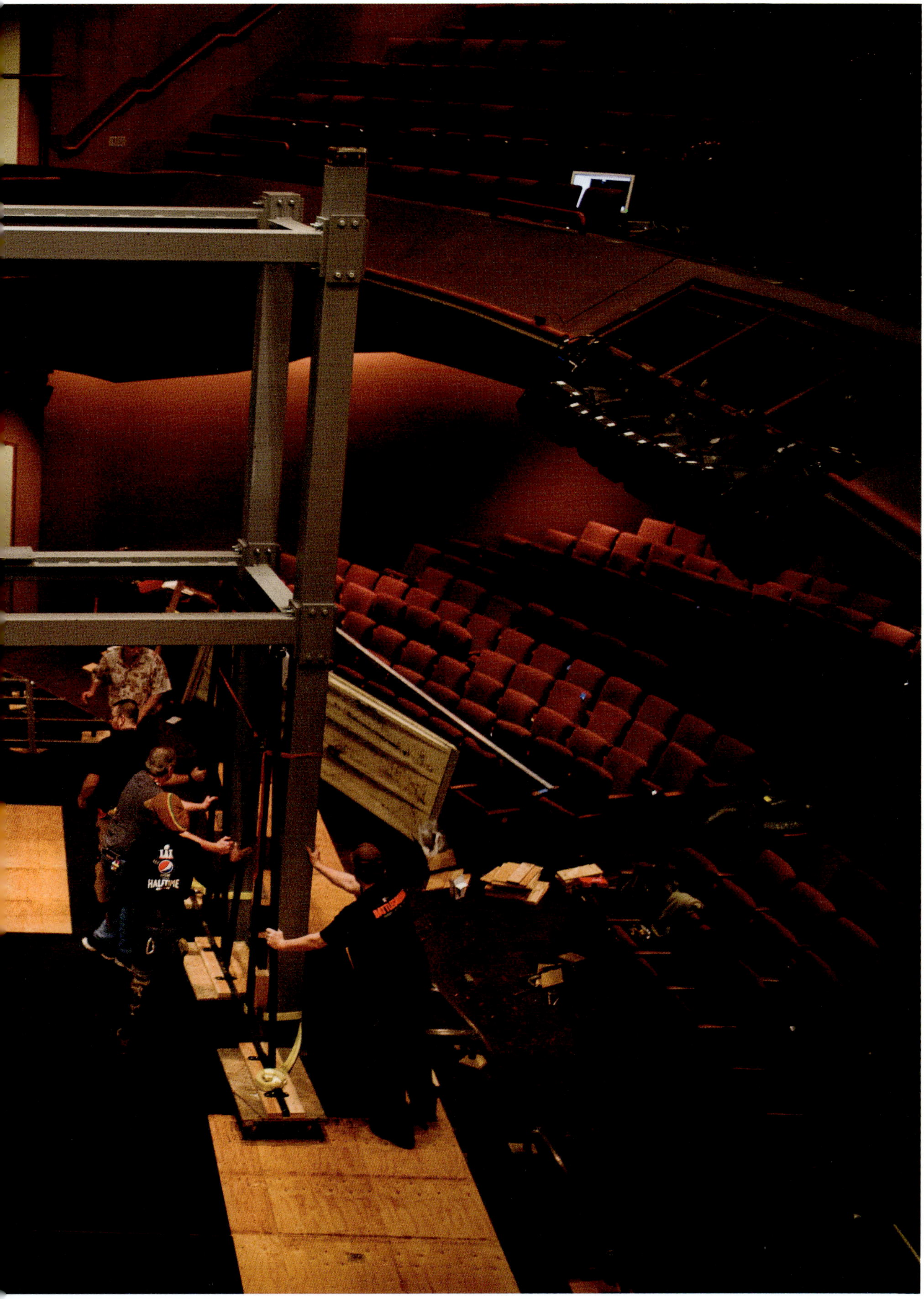

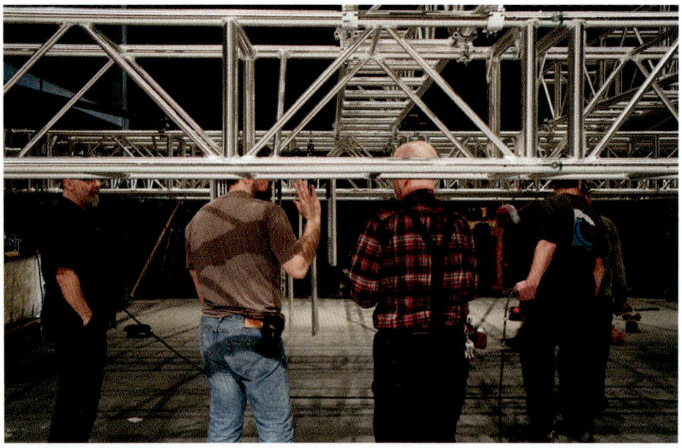
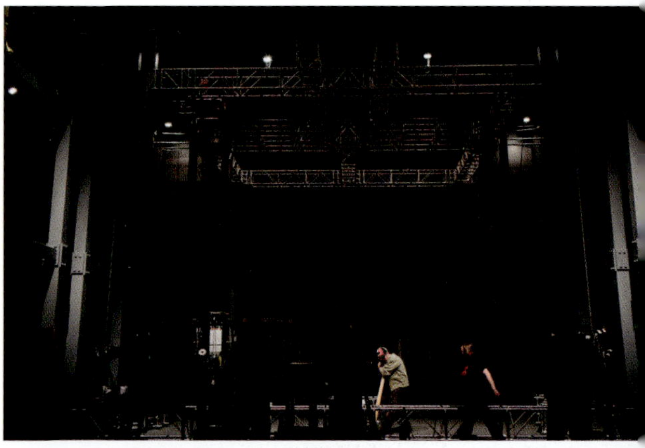
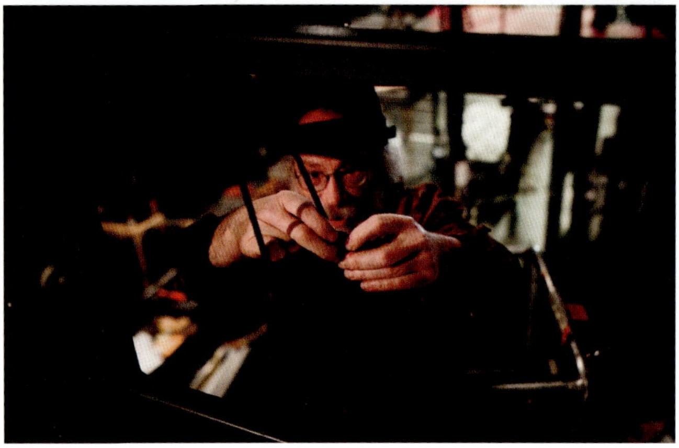
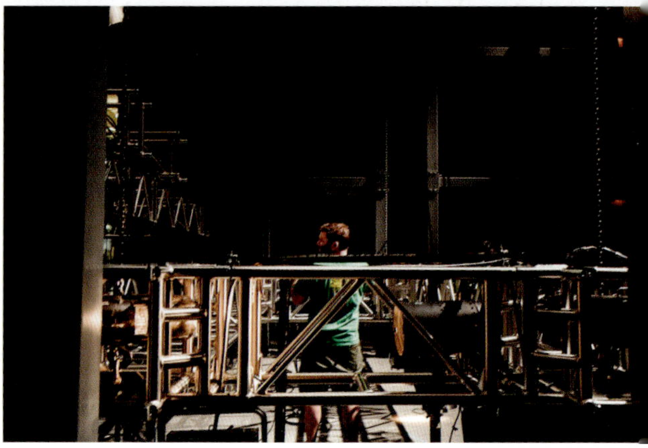

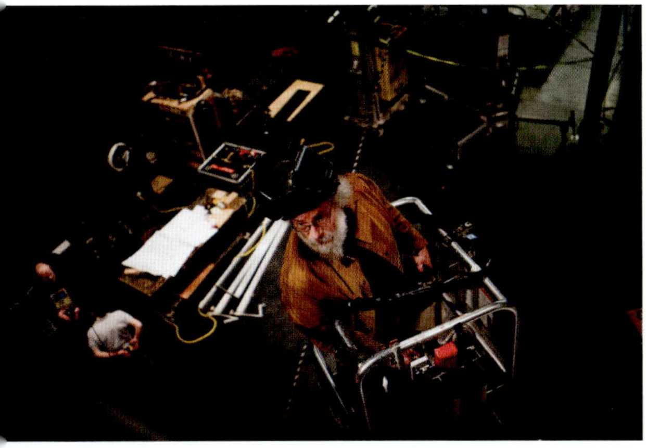

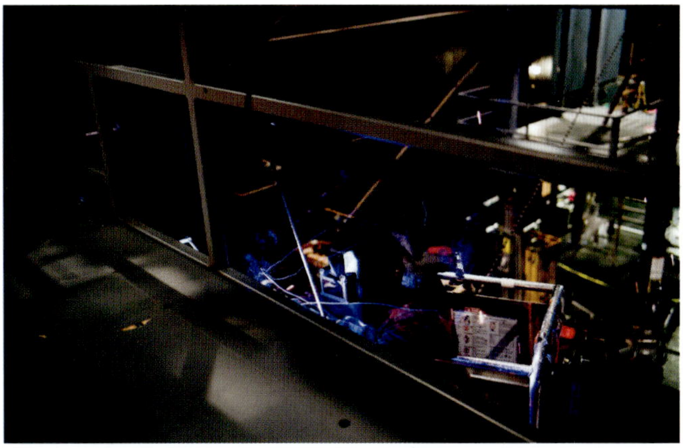

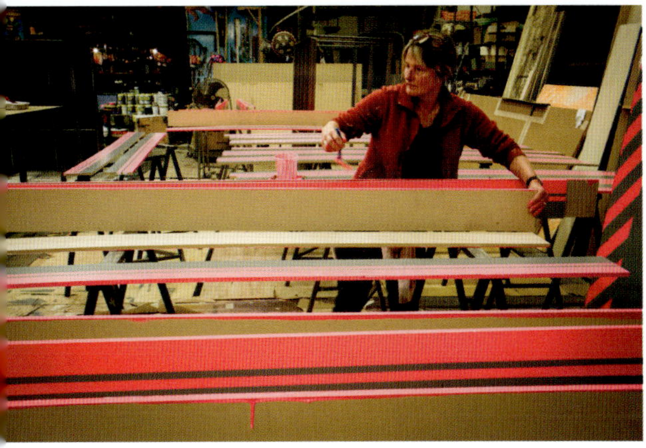

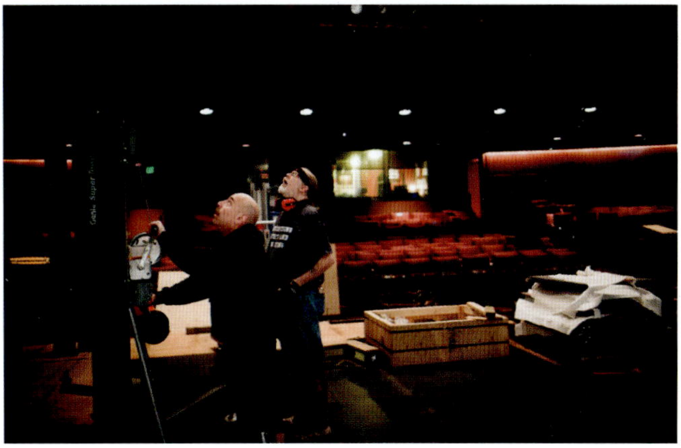

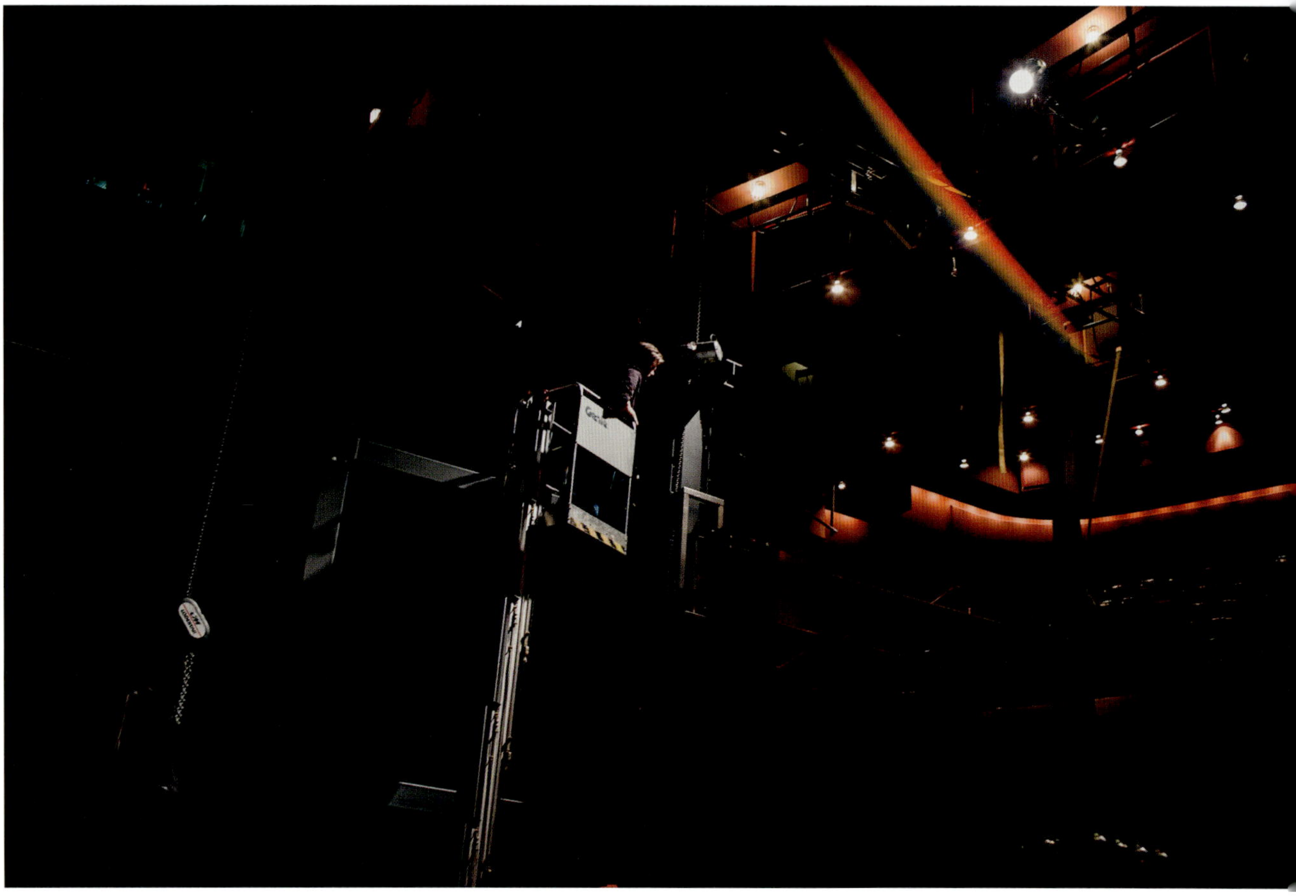

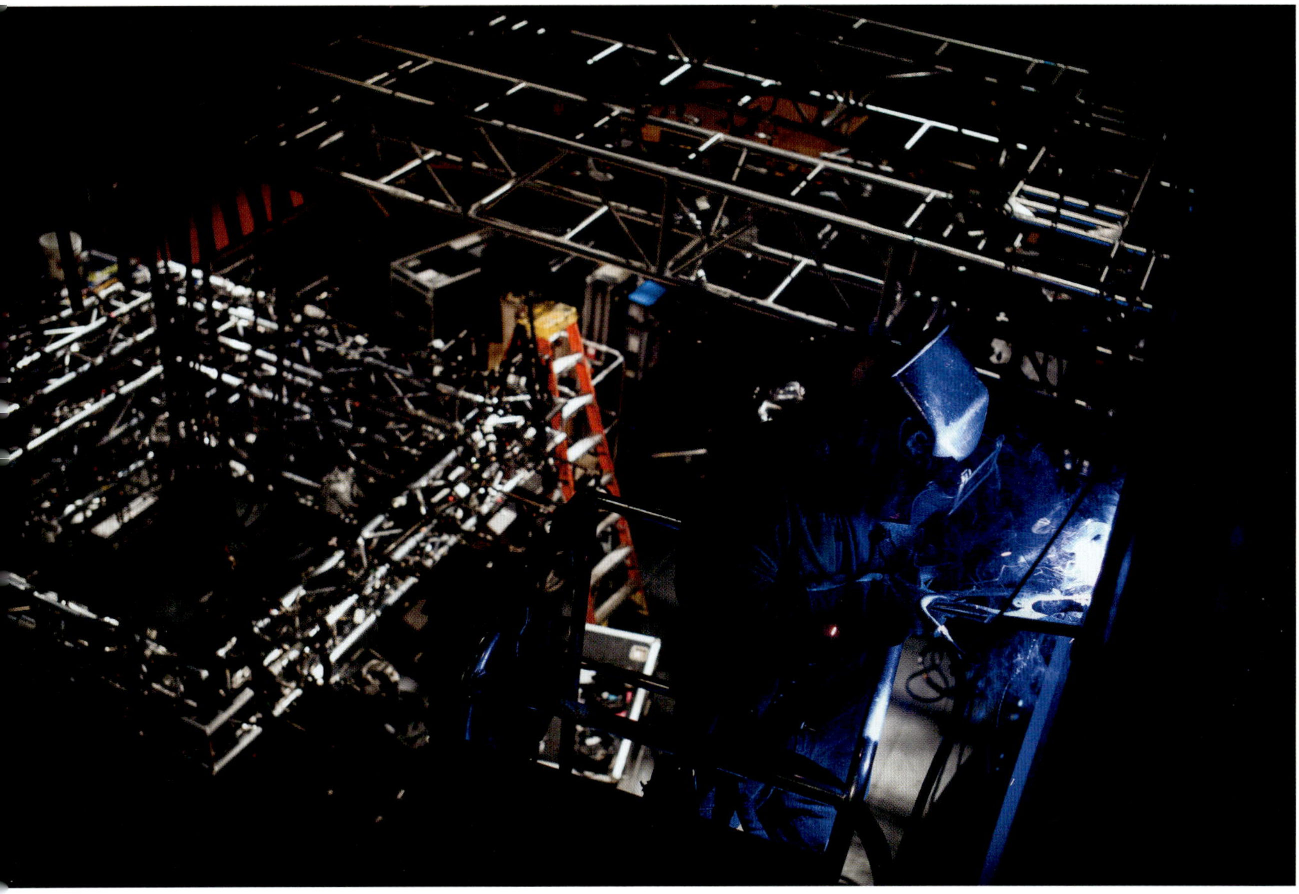

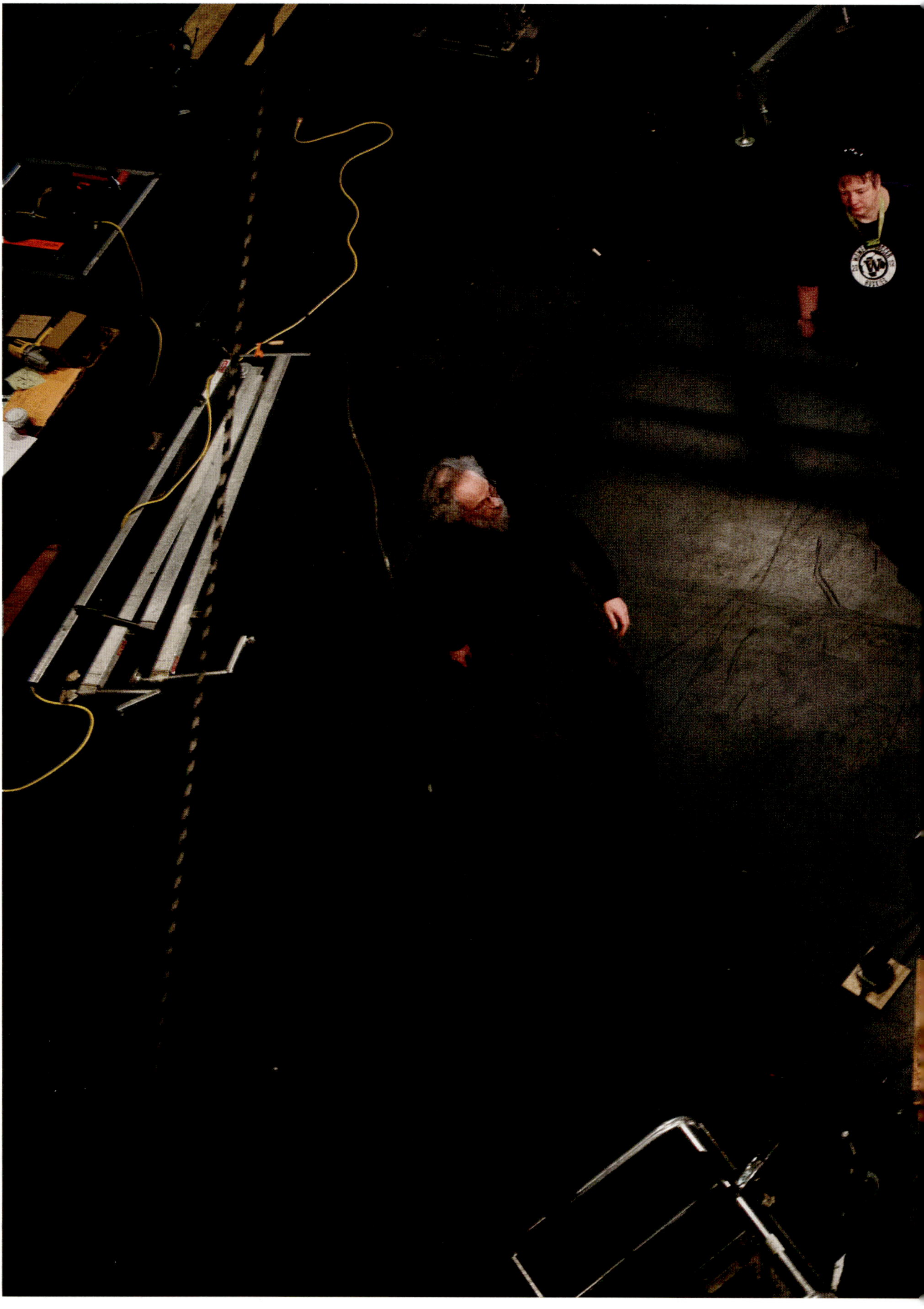

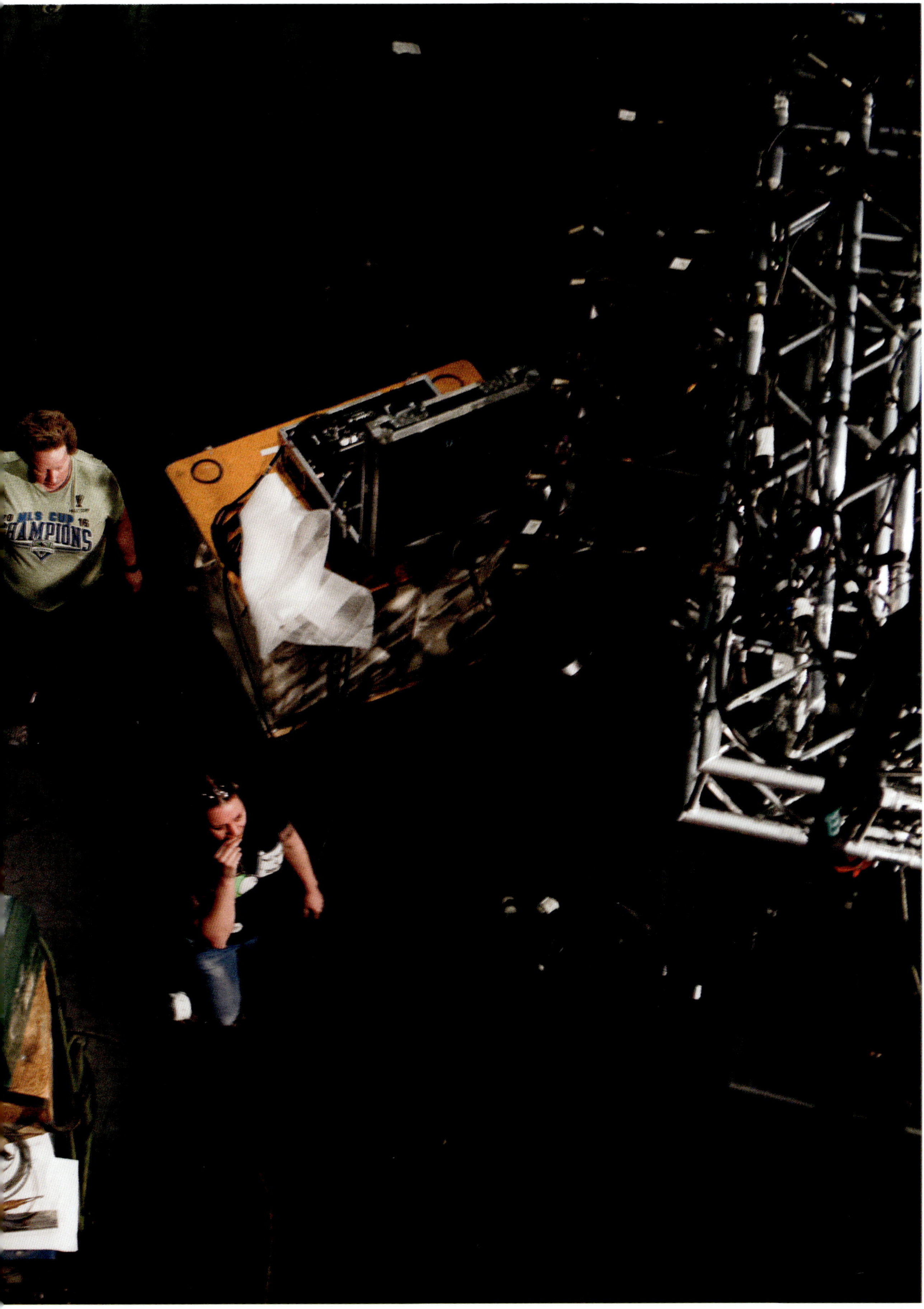
MLS CUP

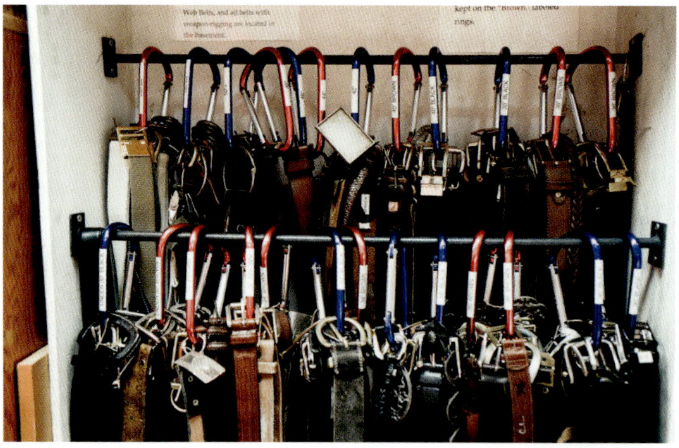
Web Belts, and all belts with
weapon-rigging are located in
the basement.
kept on the "Brown" labeled
rings.

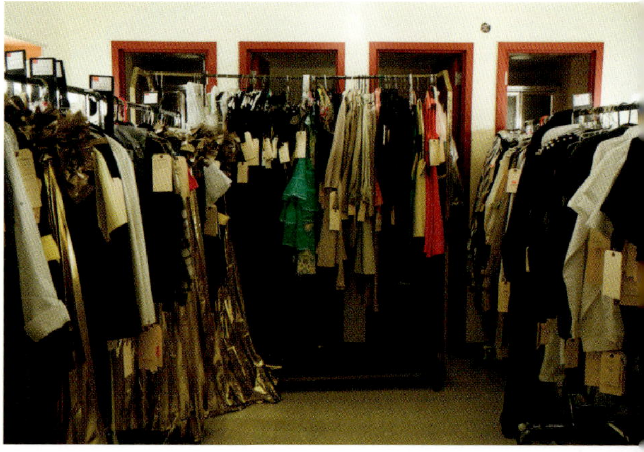

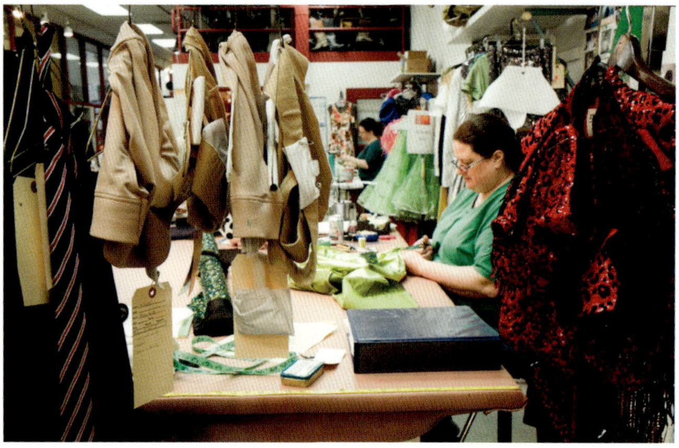

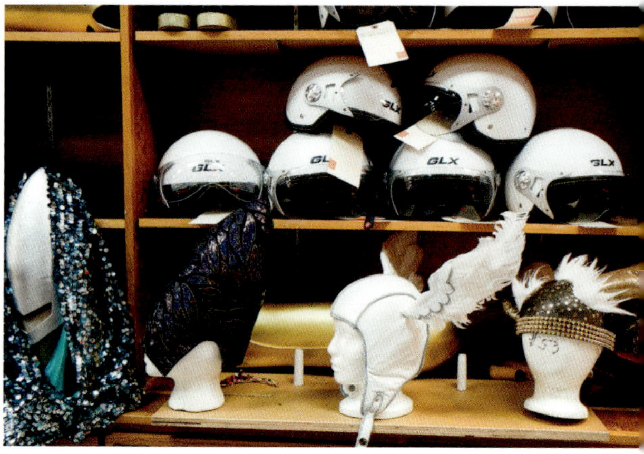
GLX

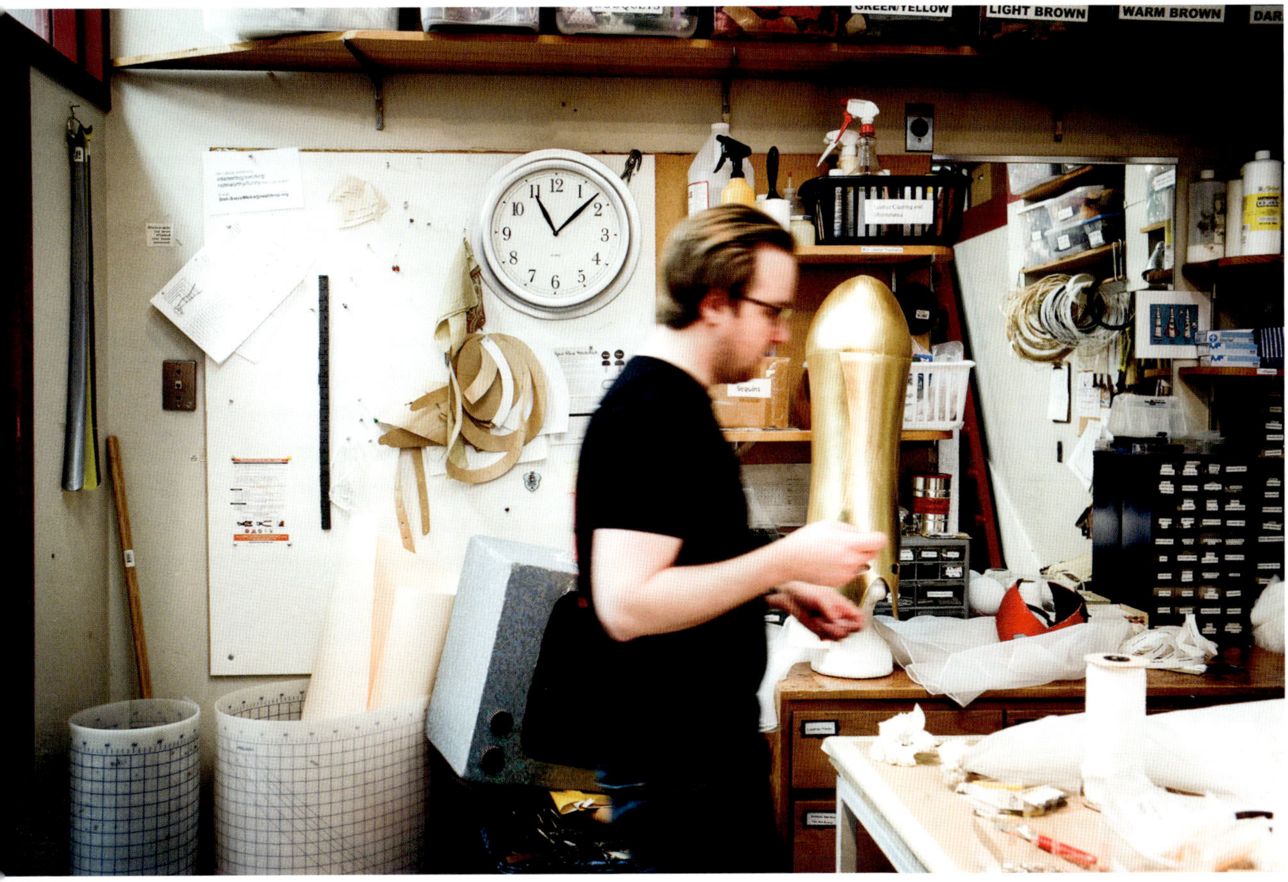
LIGHT BROWN
WARM BROWN

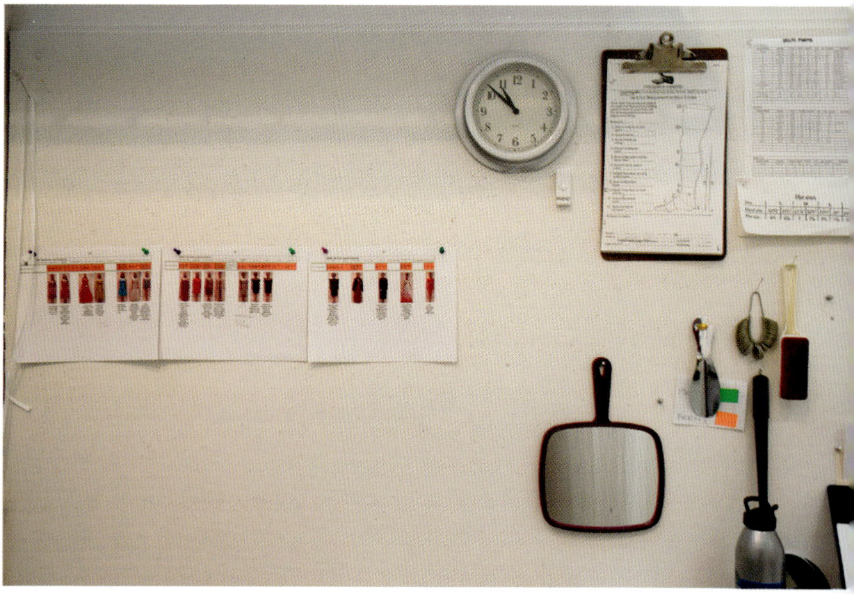

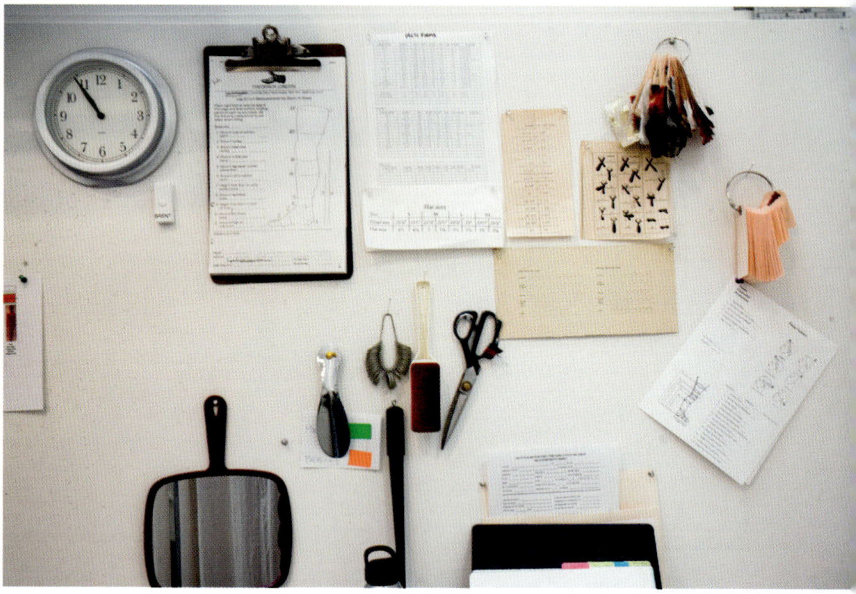

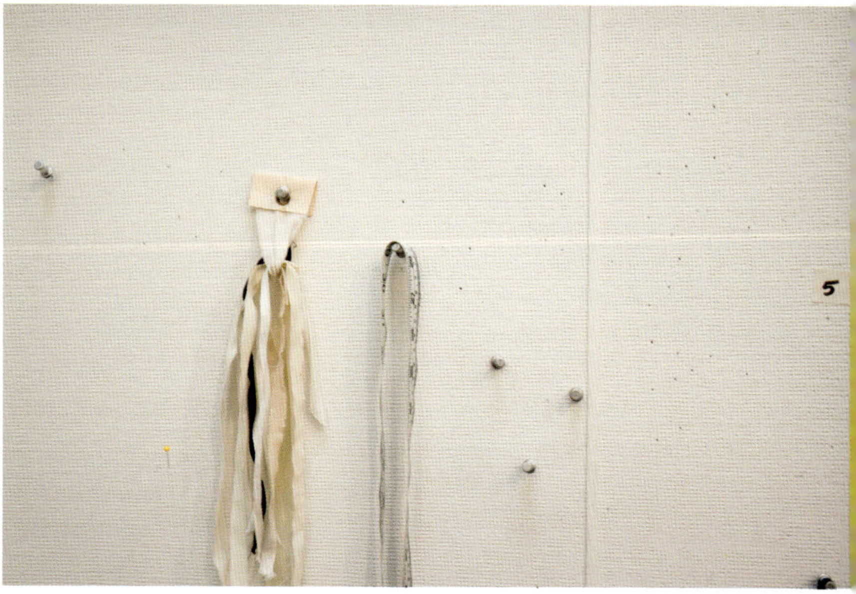

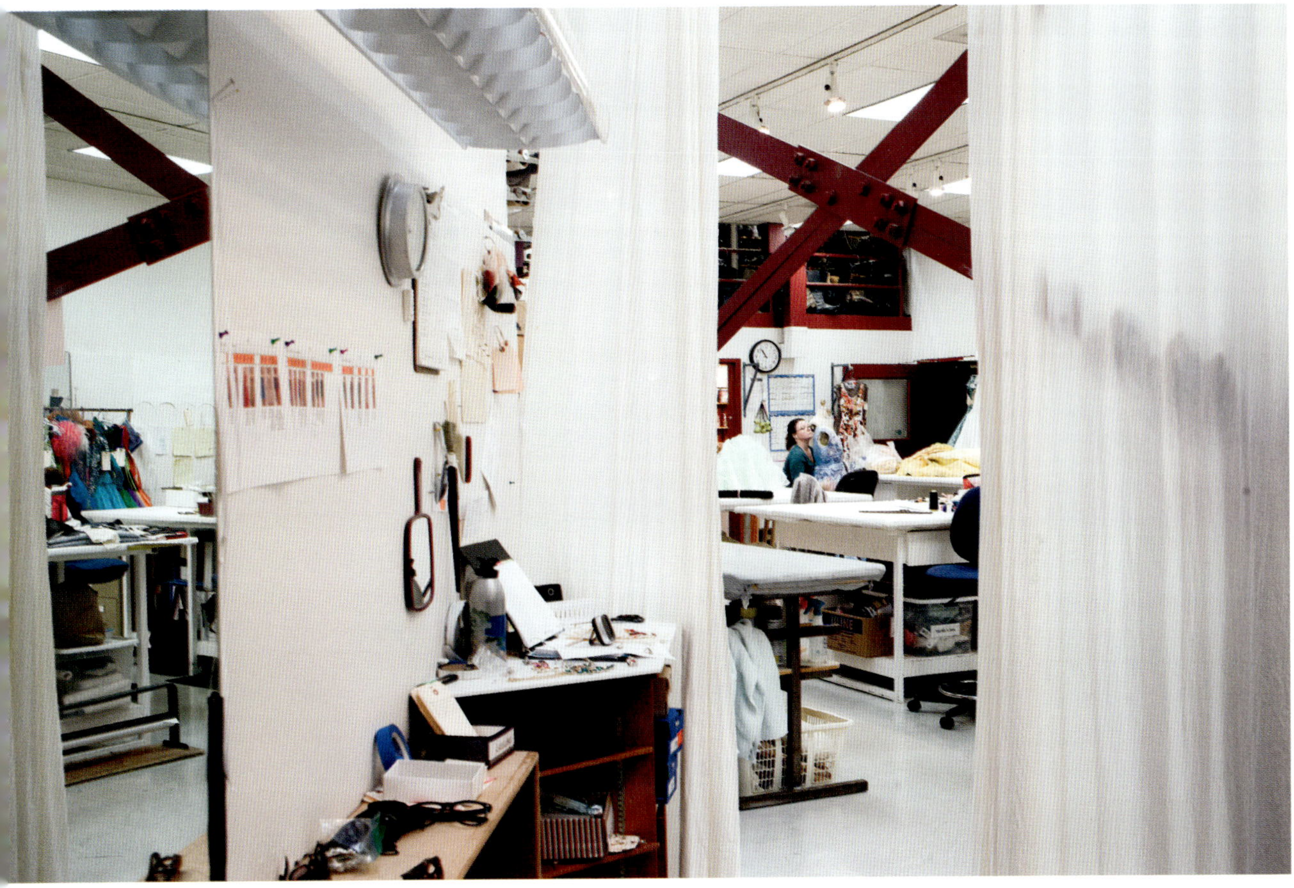

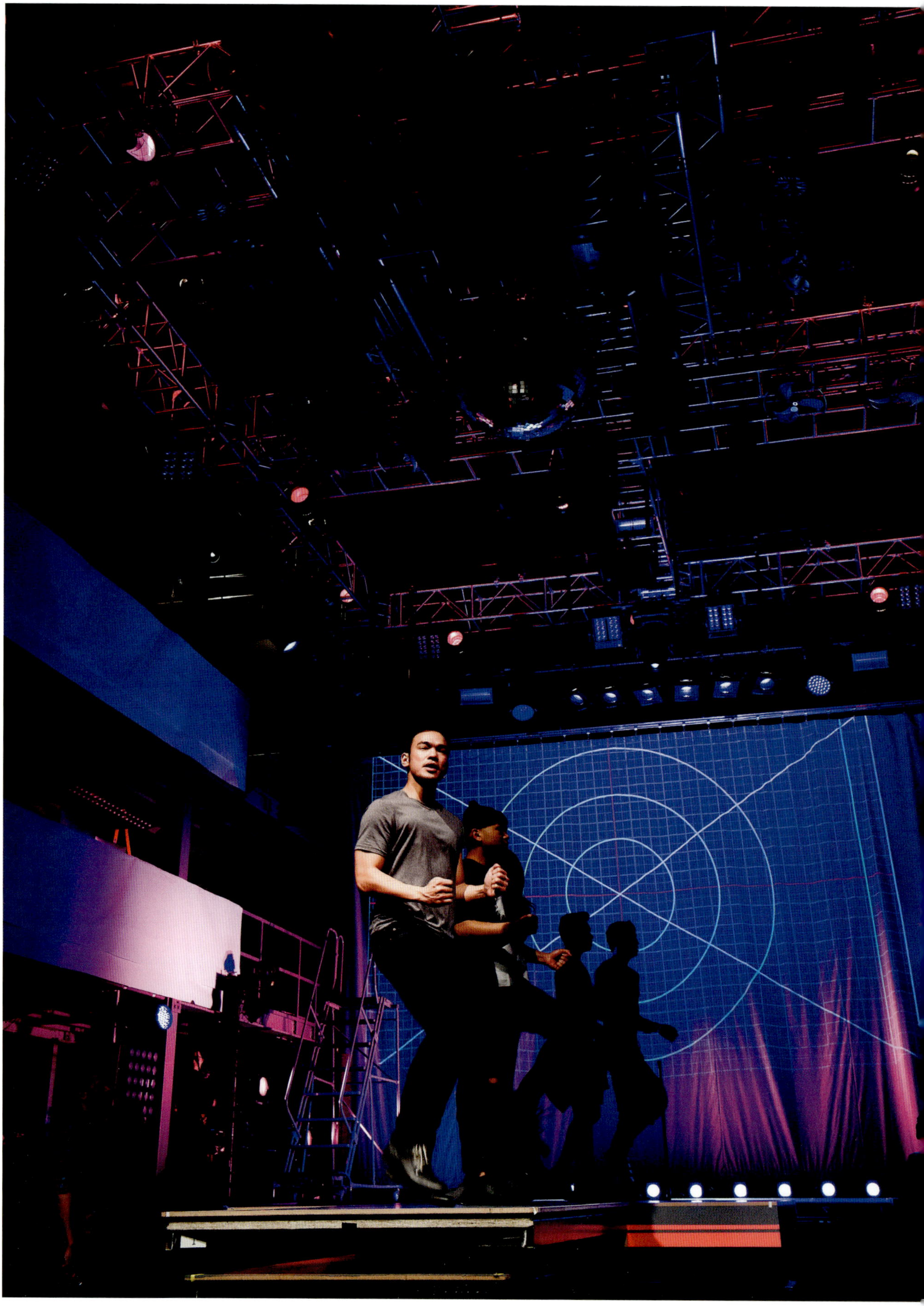

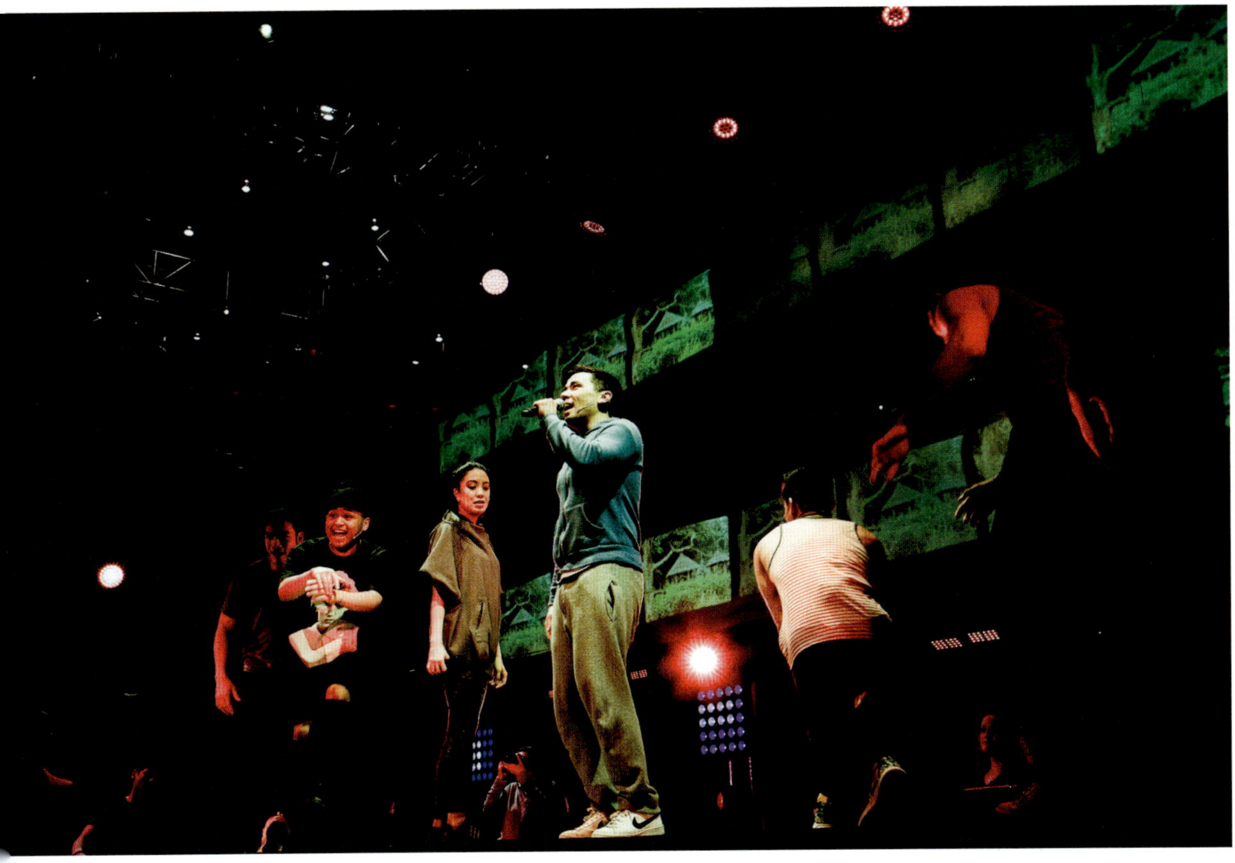

"On my first day, I was wearing a rubber mask on this platform, and they're like, "Do it full out," and I'm like, "Where am I?" And it turned into the experience of my life so far."

COMMENT FROM A CAST MEMBER

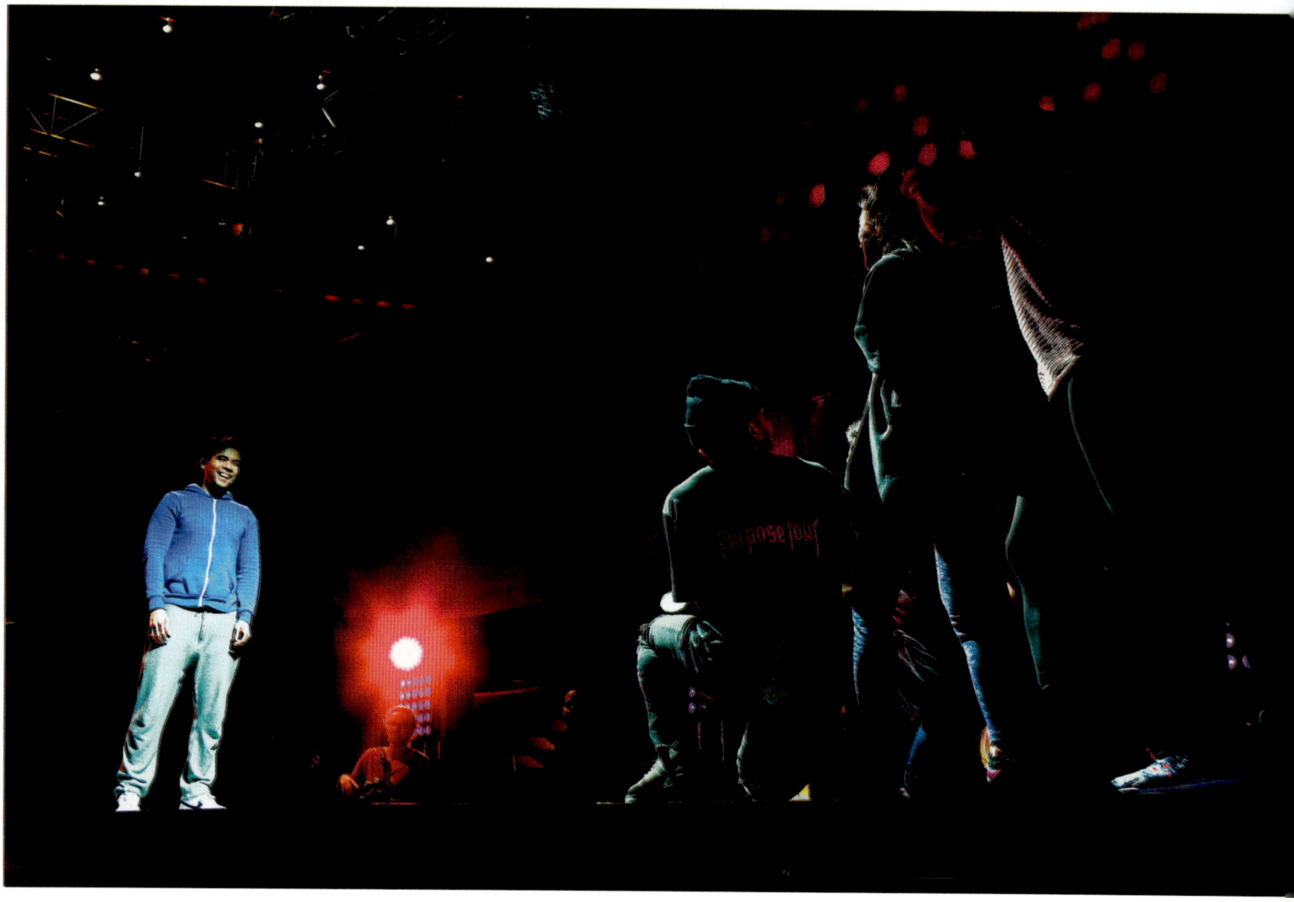

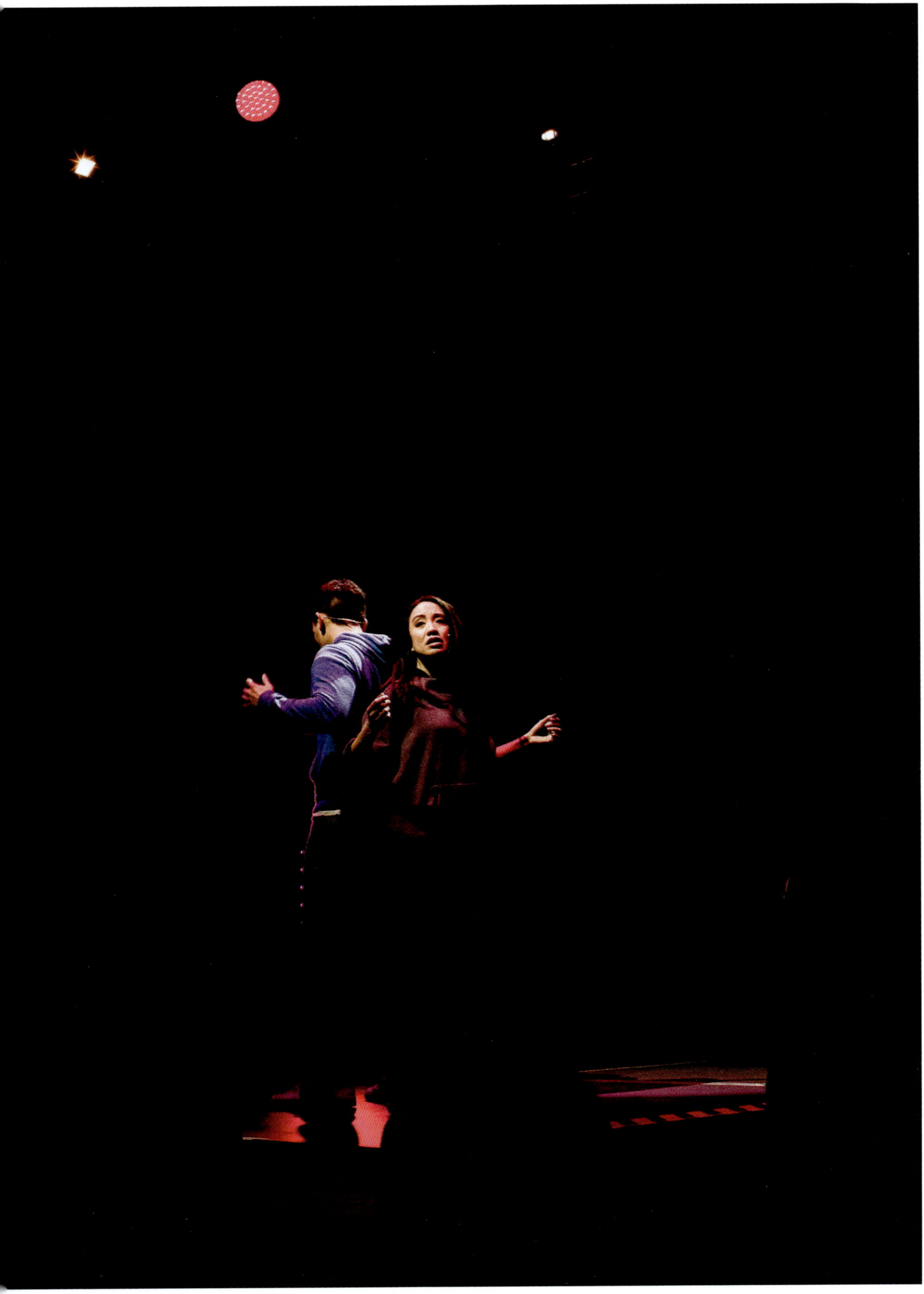

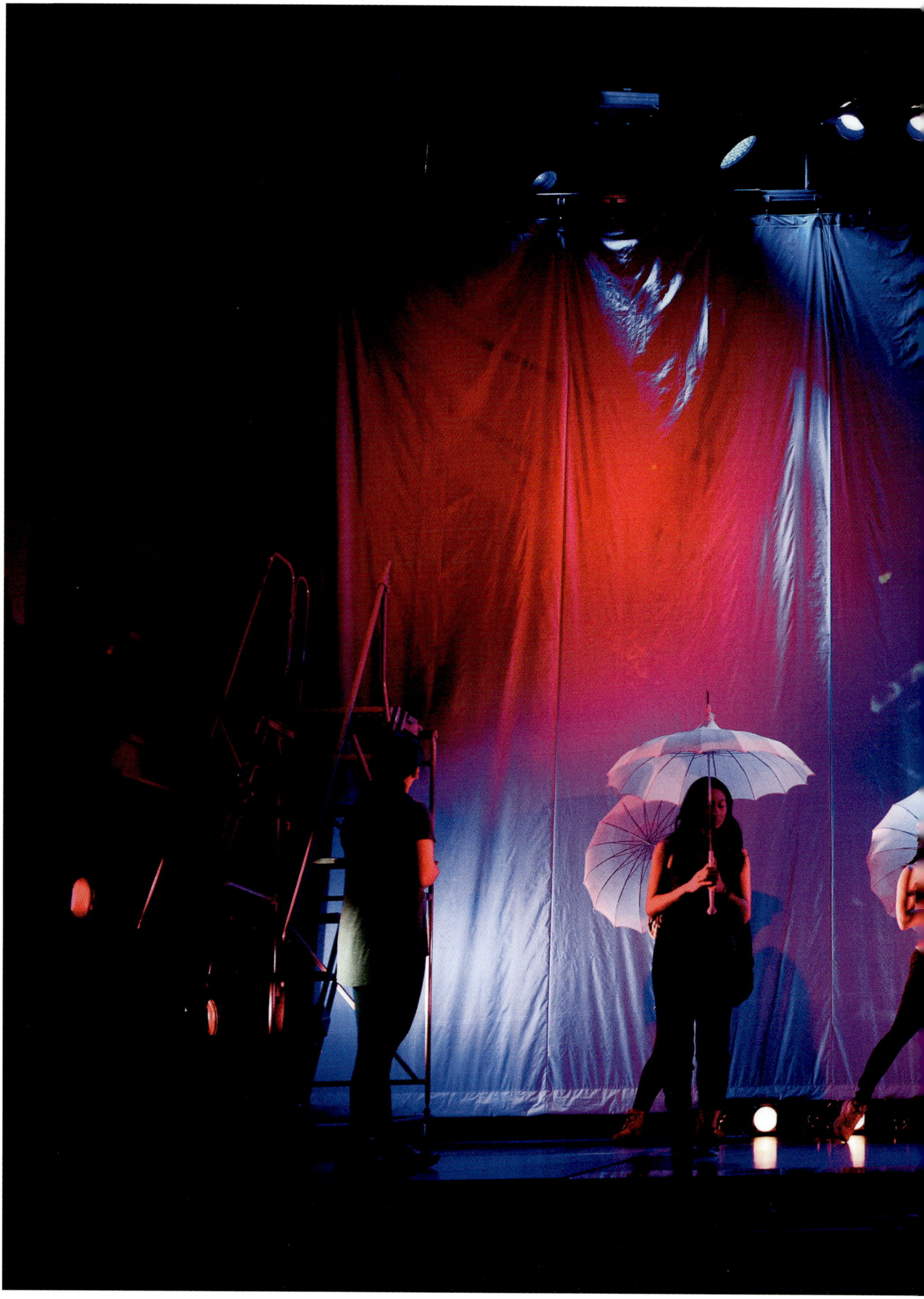

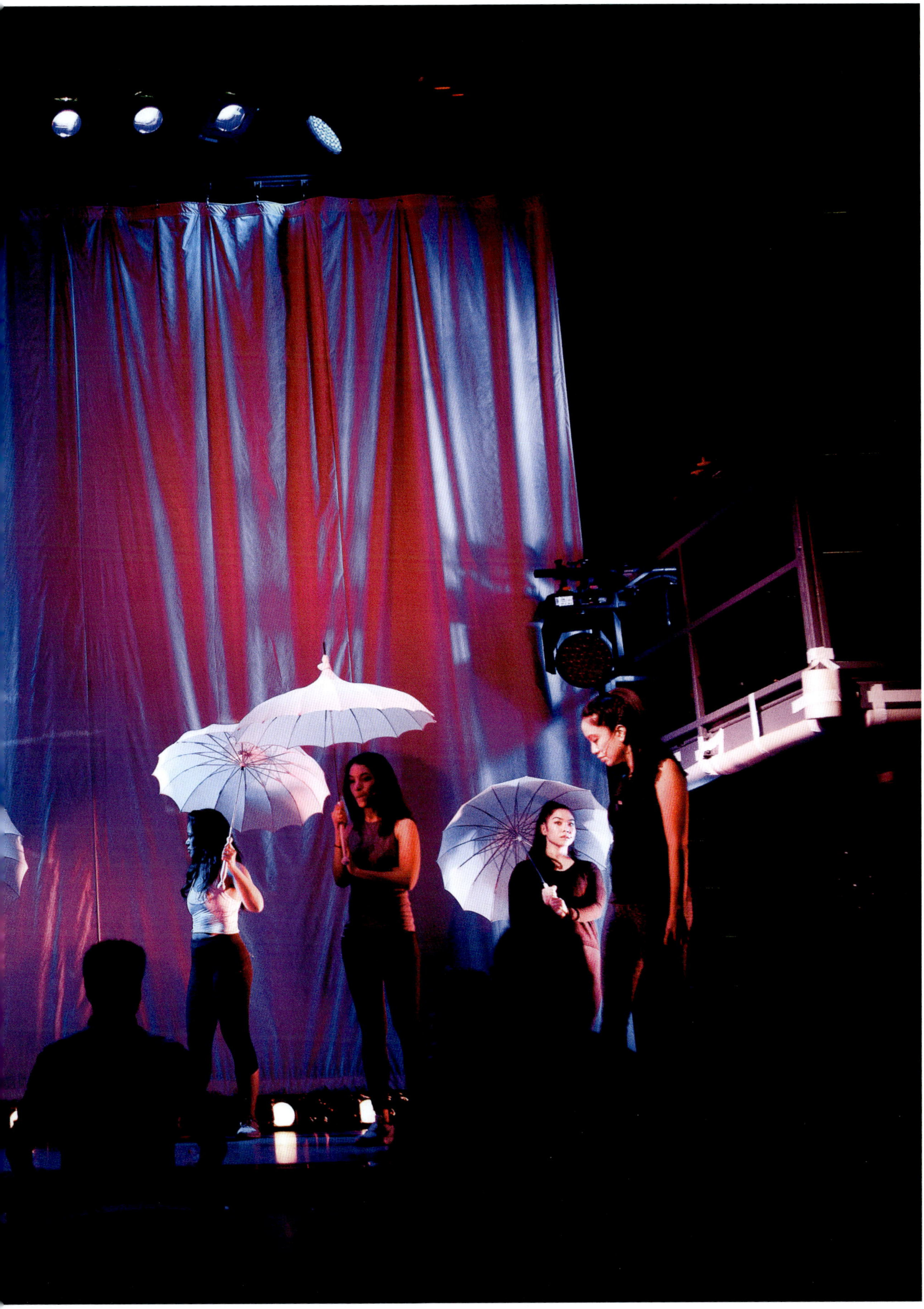

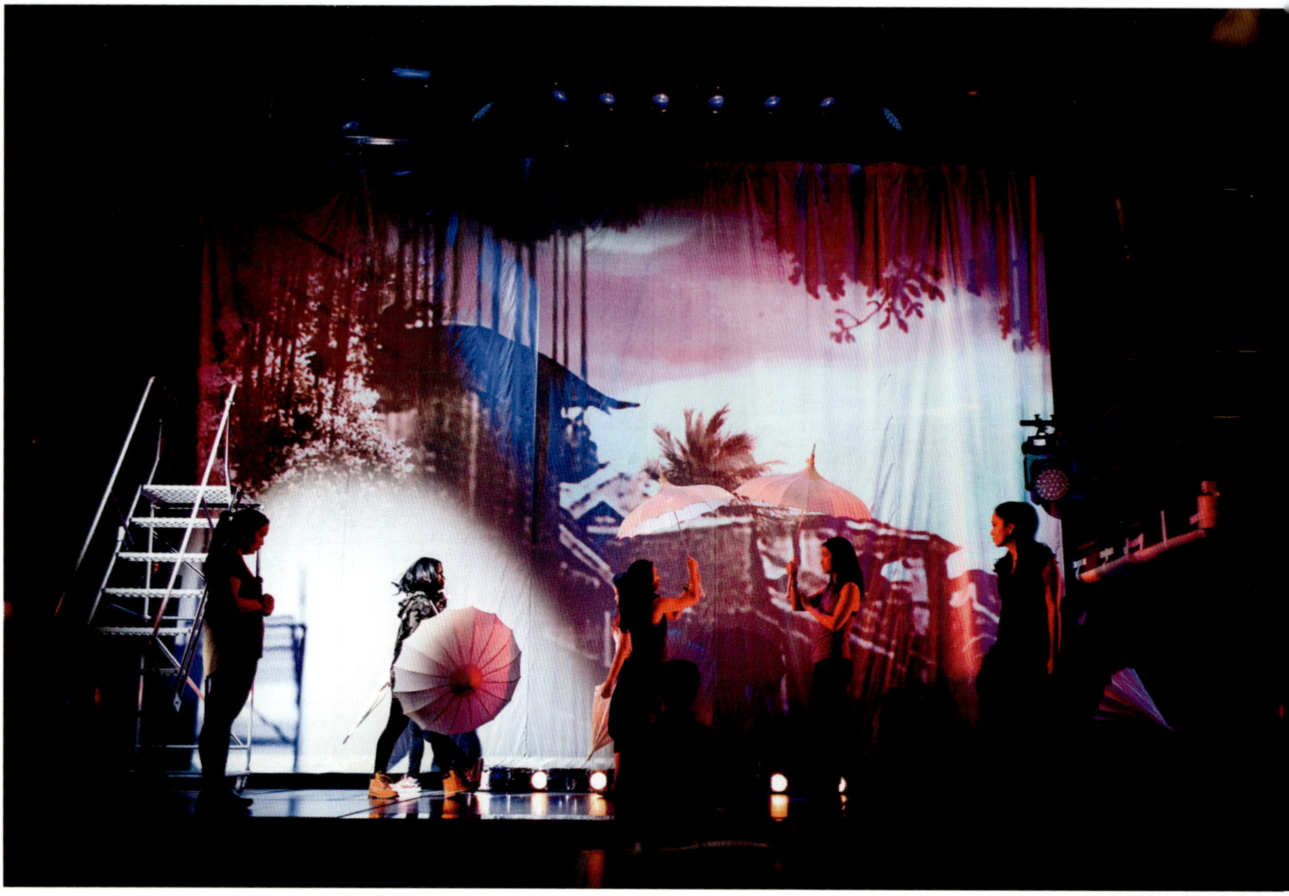

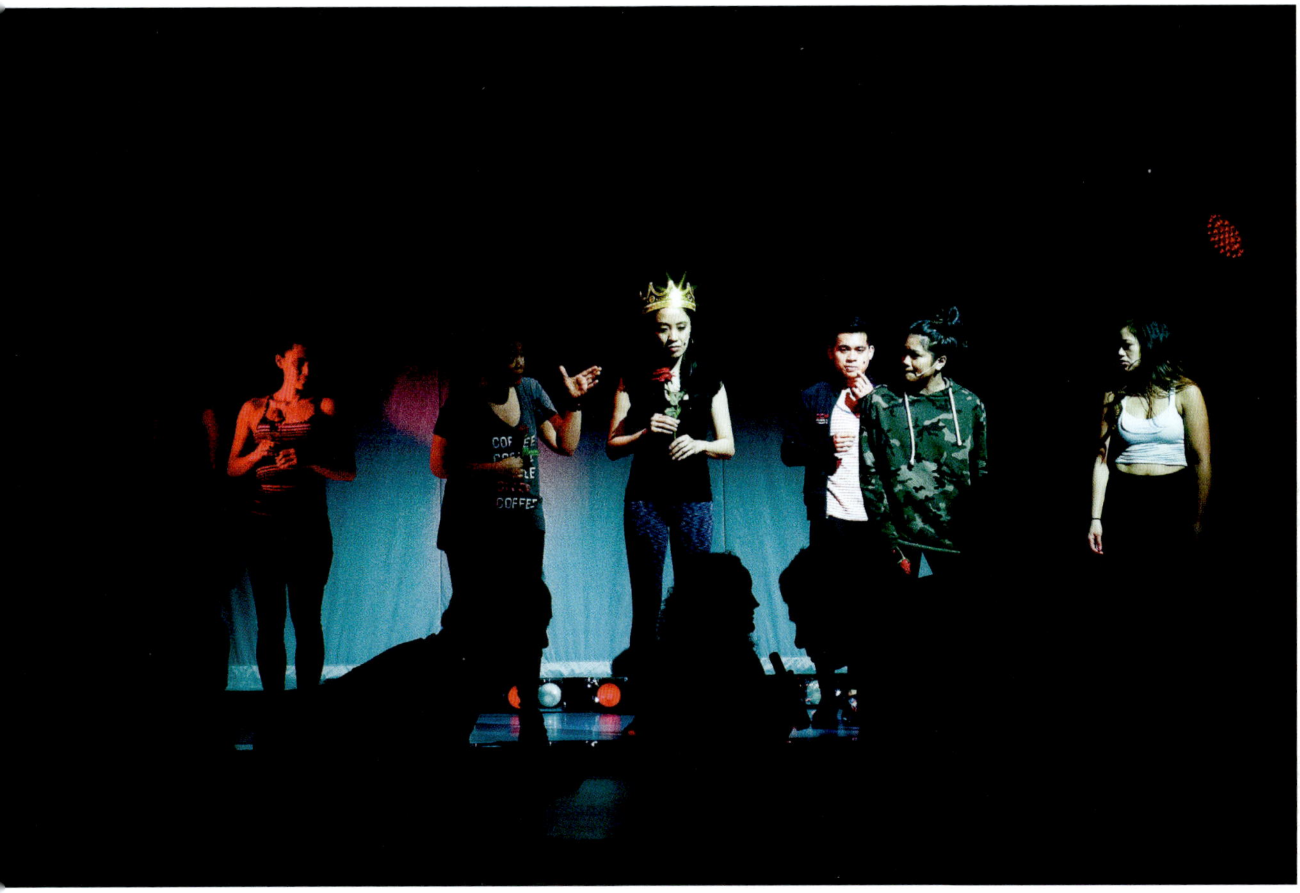
COFFEE

EVERY LITTLE TINY DROP
OF RAIN YOU FEEL

EVERY DROP OF RAIN

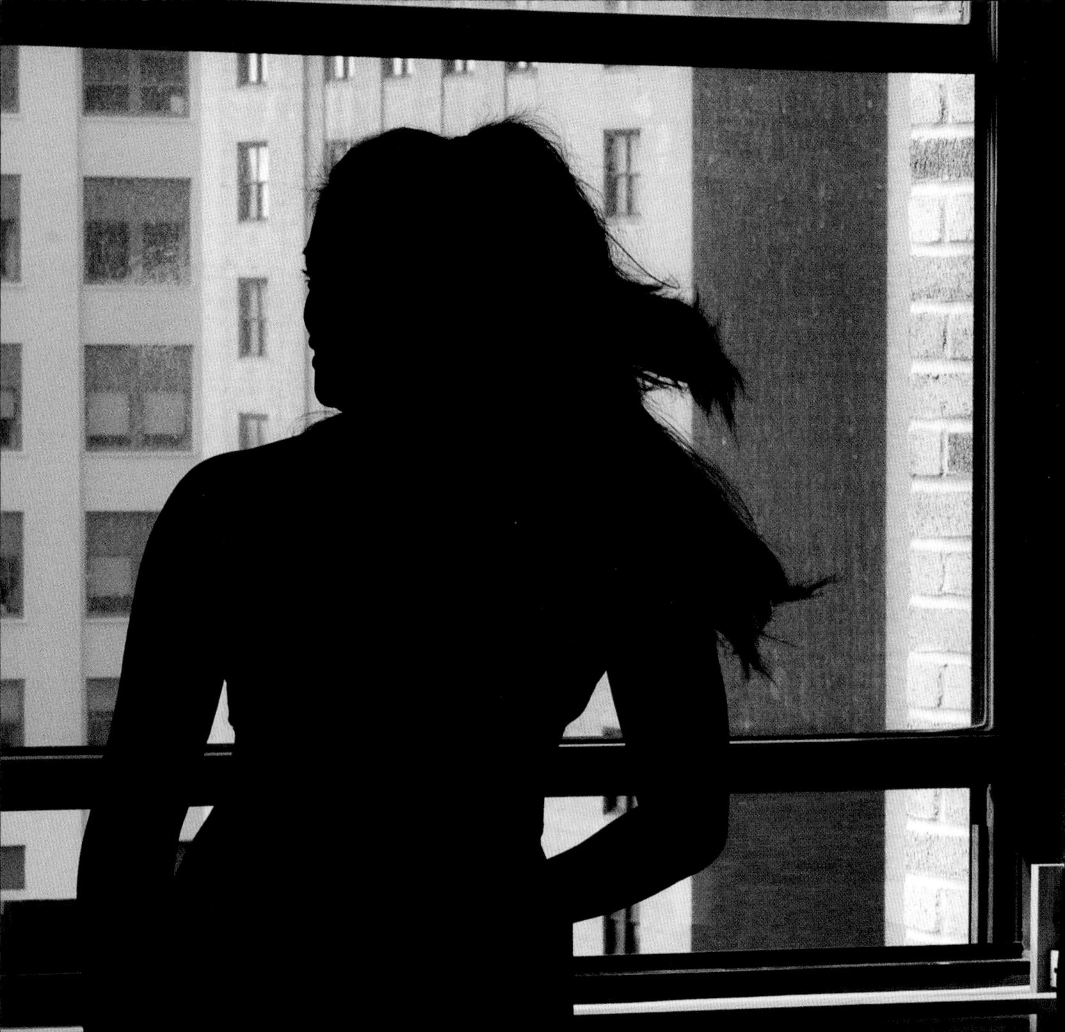

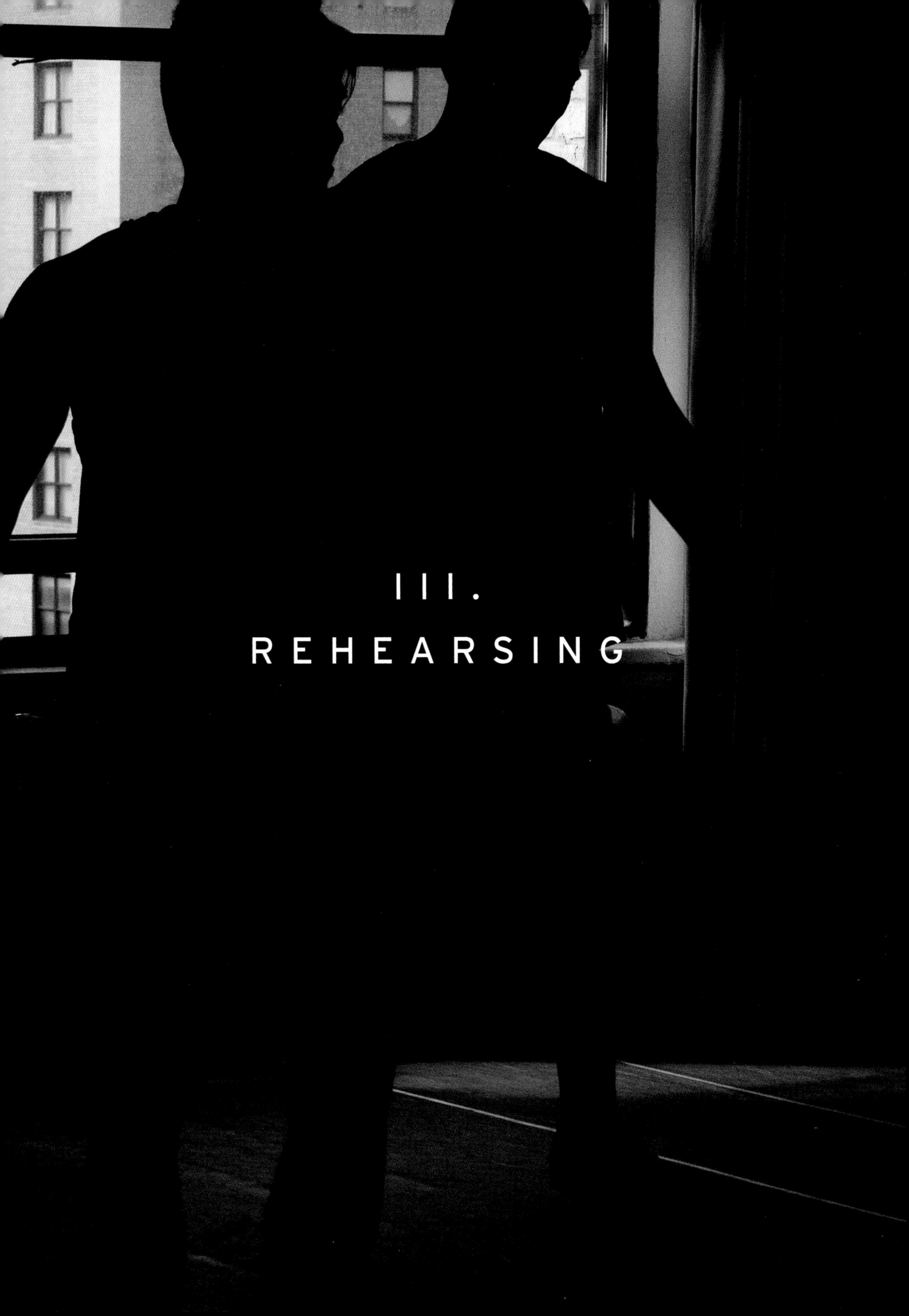

III.

REHEARSING

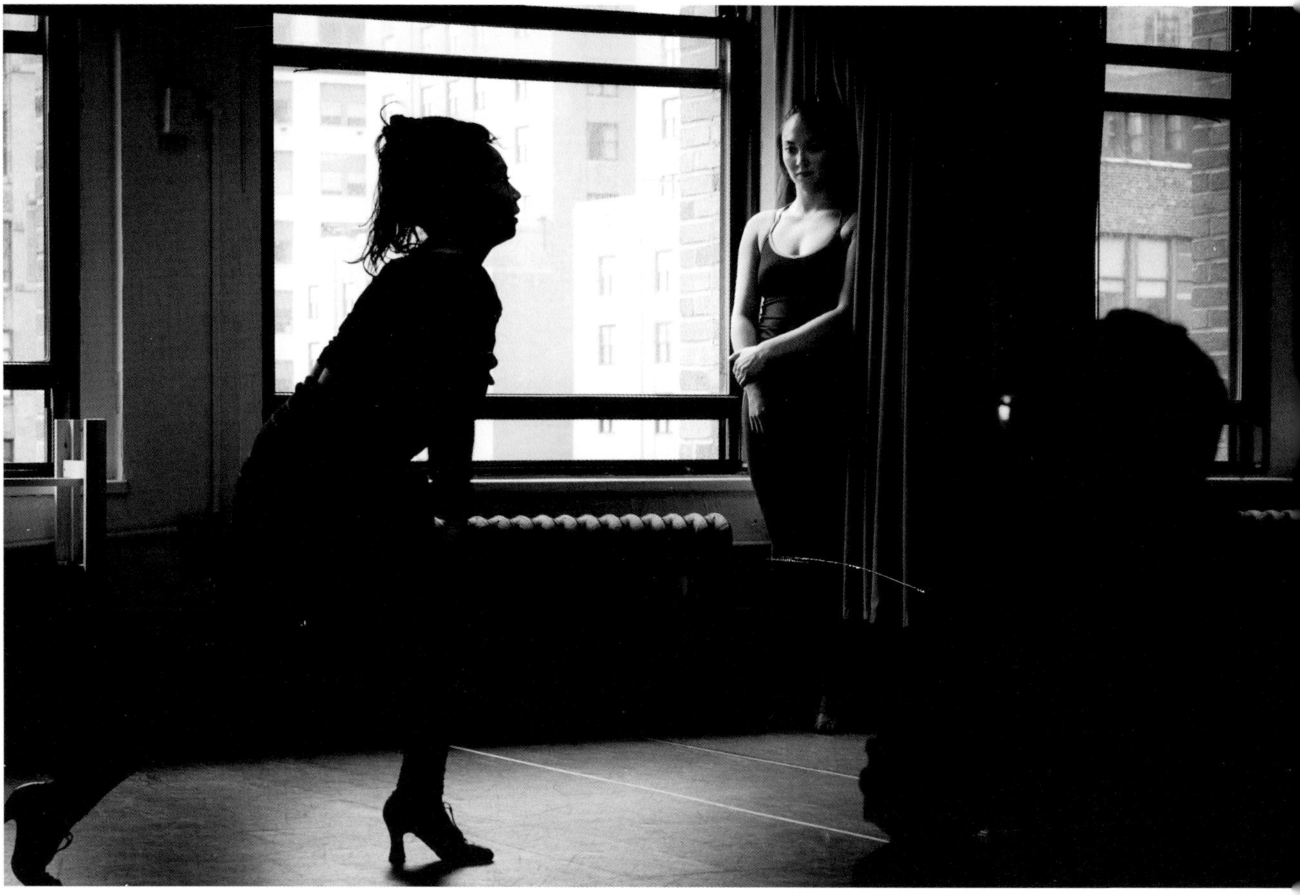

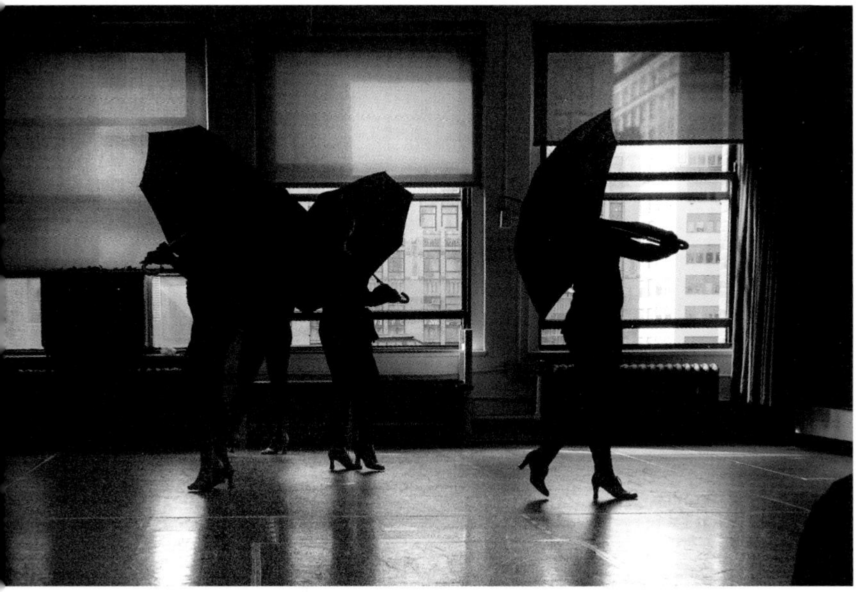
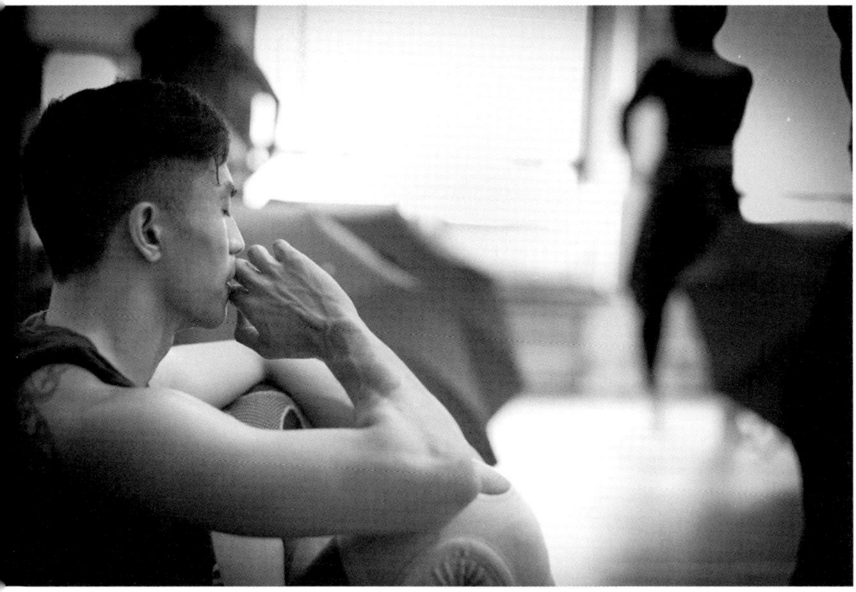
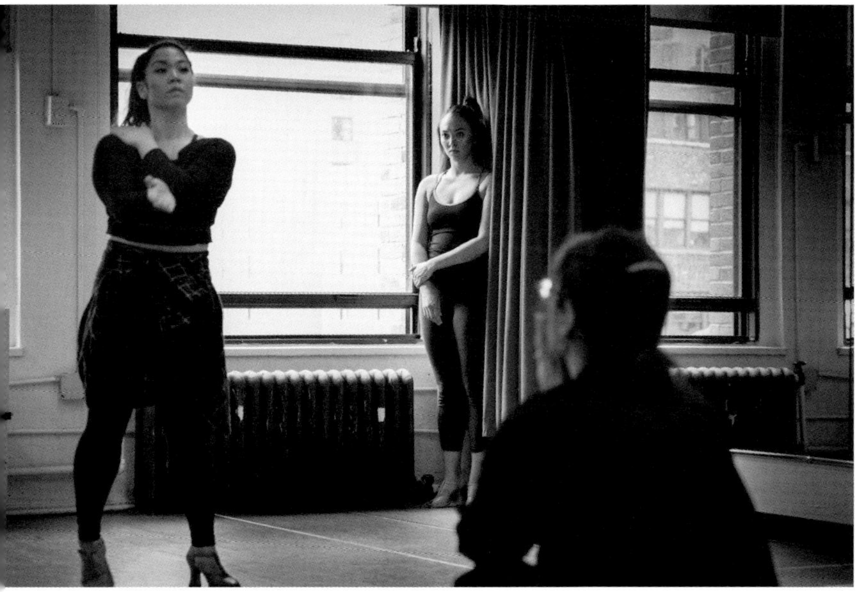

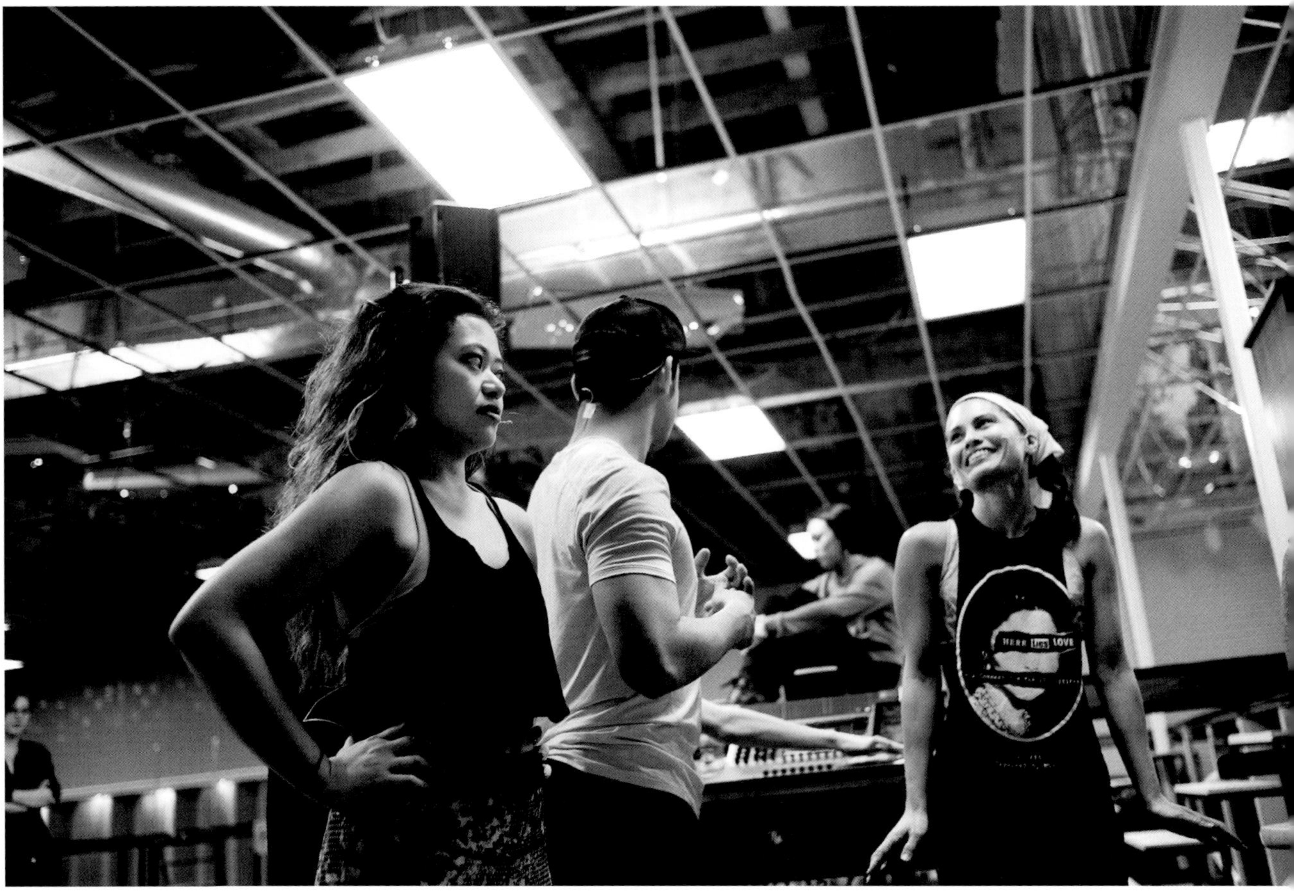

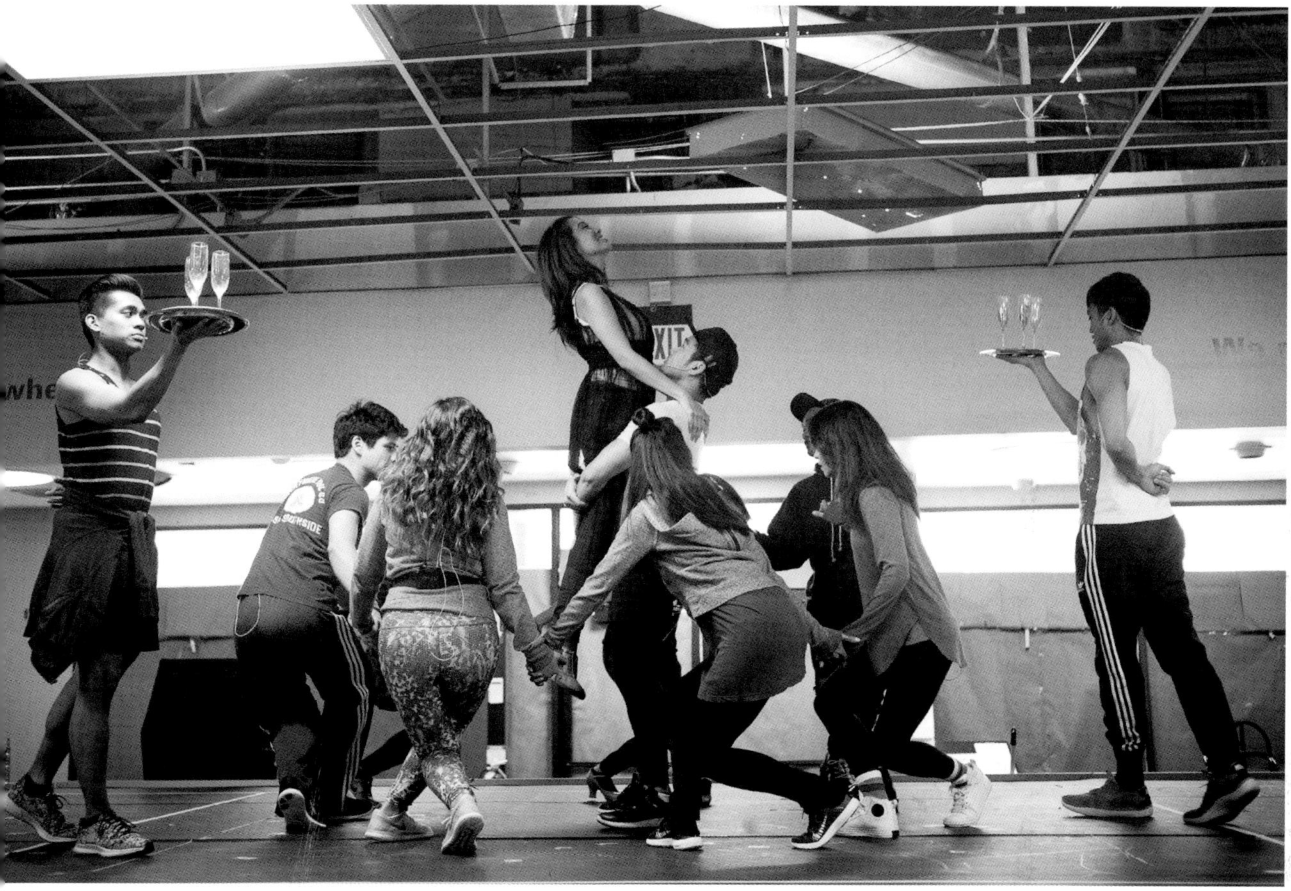

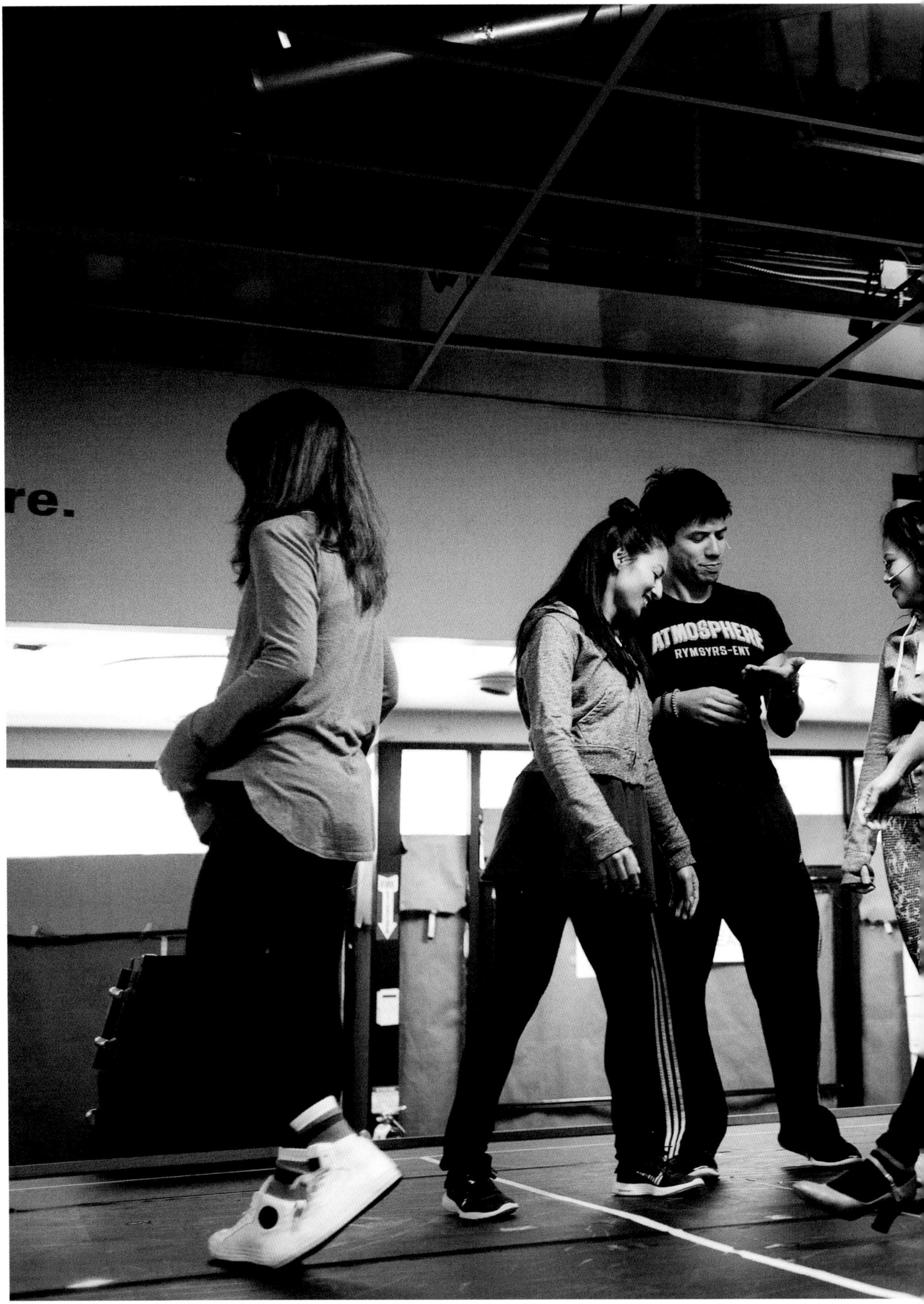
re.
ATMOSPHERE
RYMSYRS-ENT

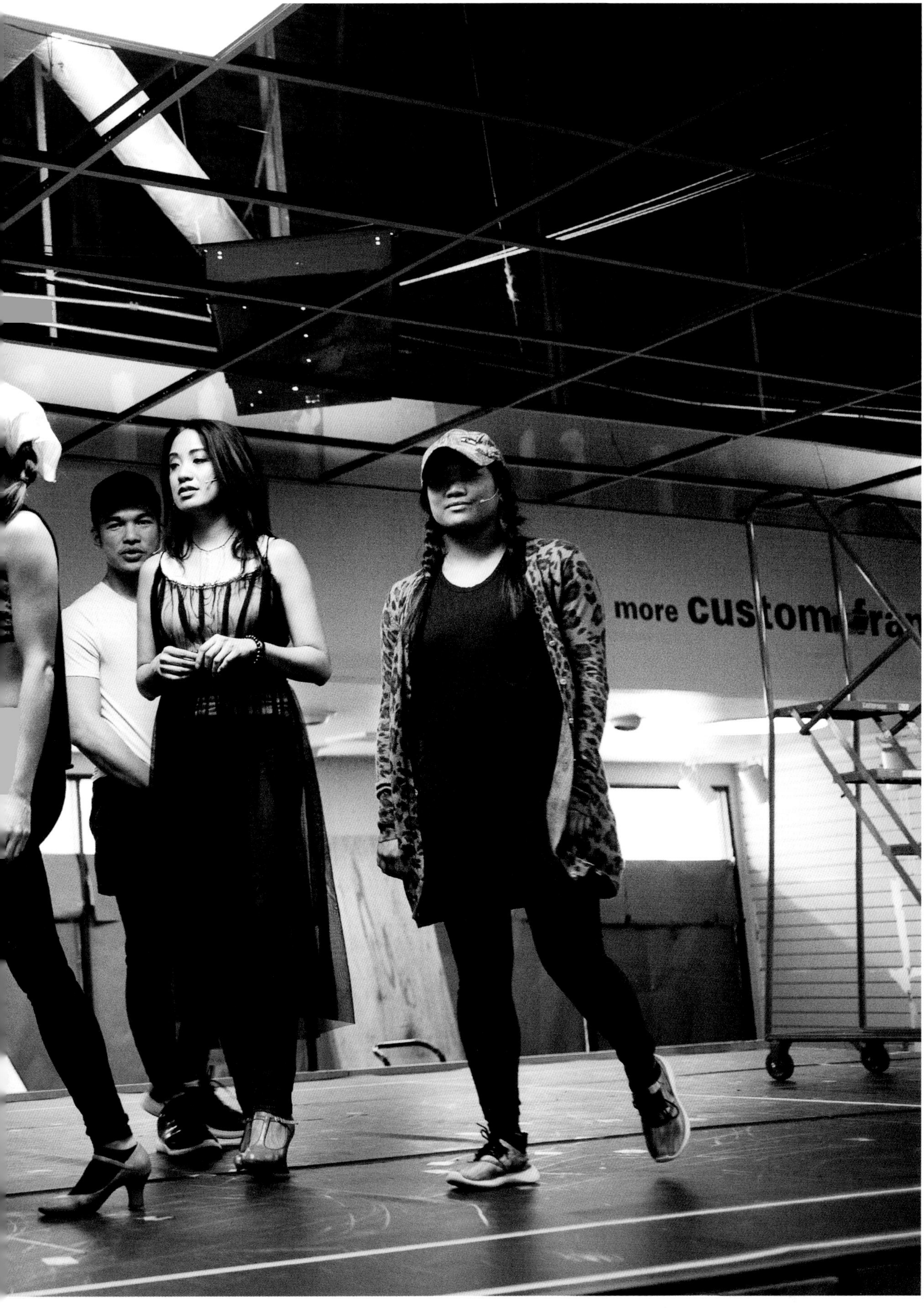
more

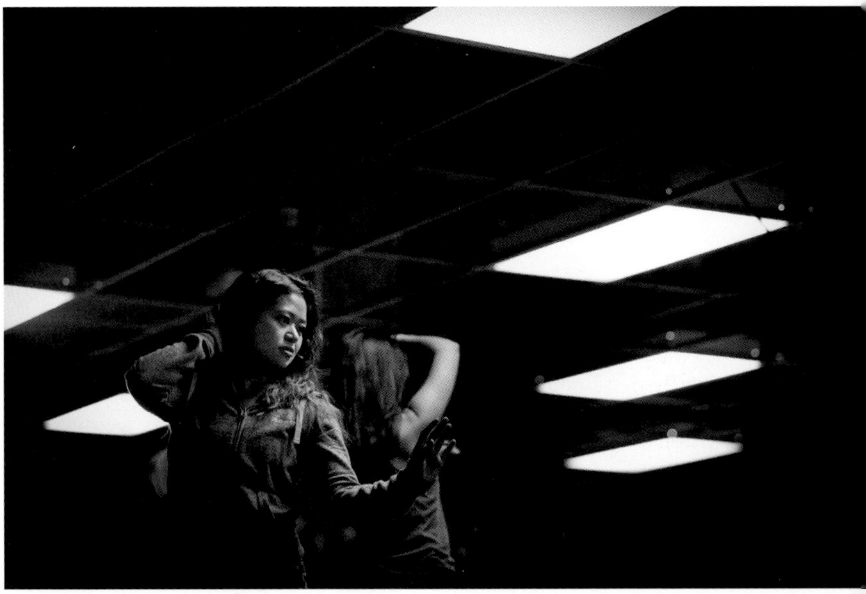

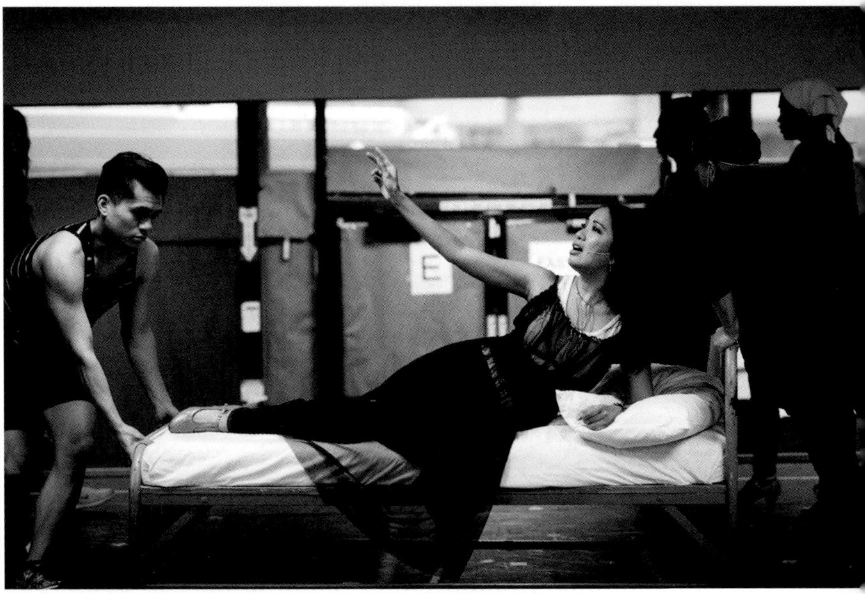
E

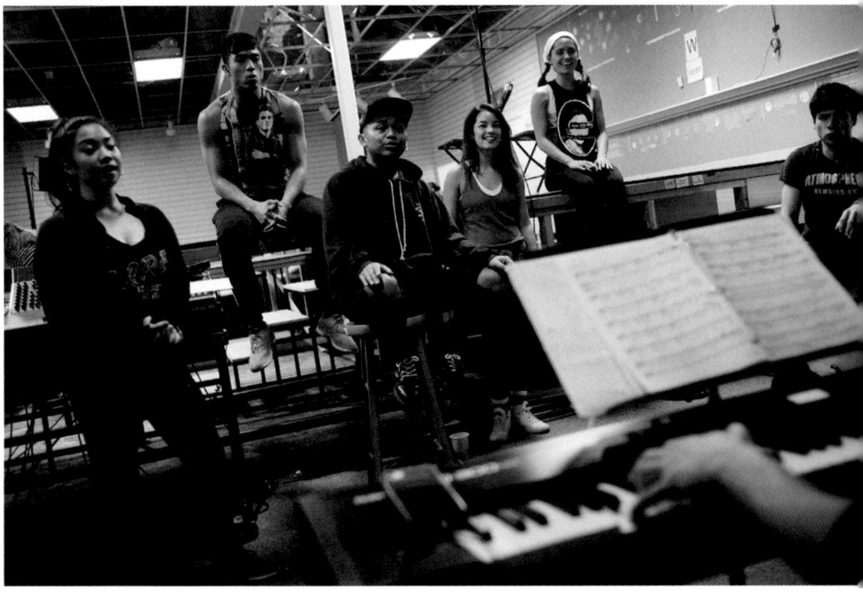
W

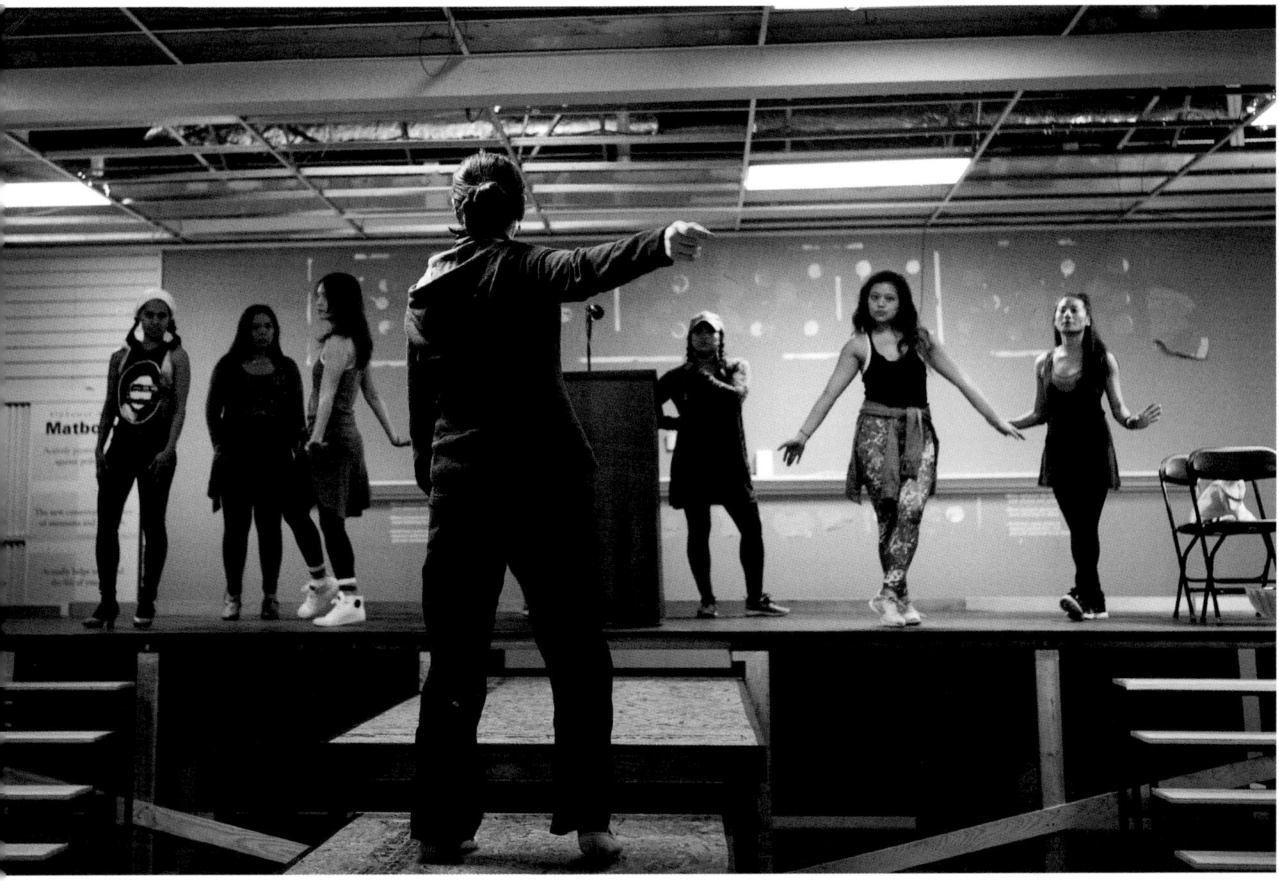

I FELT ABANDONED
I FELT CAST ASIDE
SO WHERE IS GOD
WHO NEVER SLEEPS?
I HEARD A VOICE SAY,
"WHY DO YOU CRY?"

THEN I FOUND MY INNER PEACE

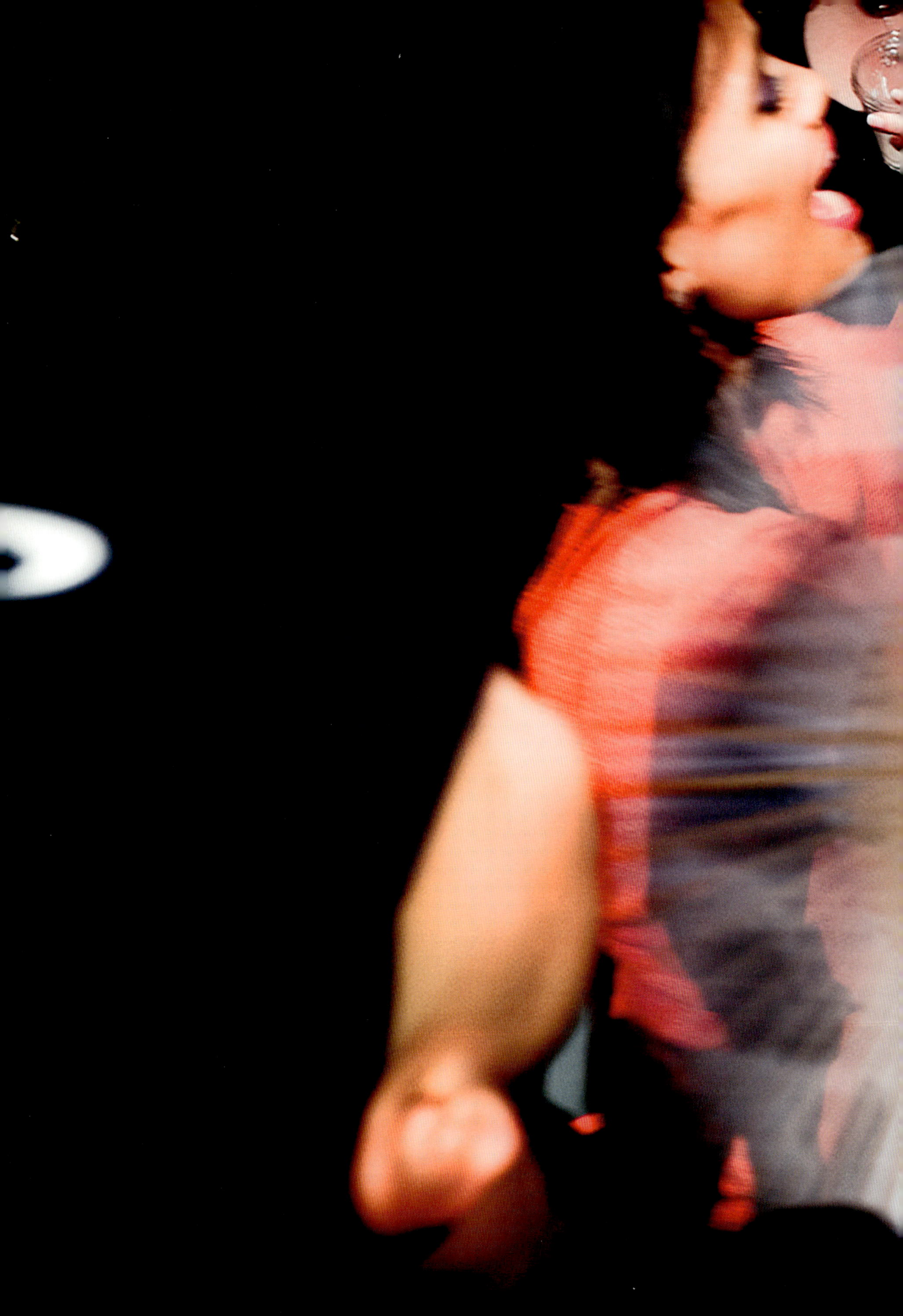

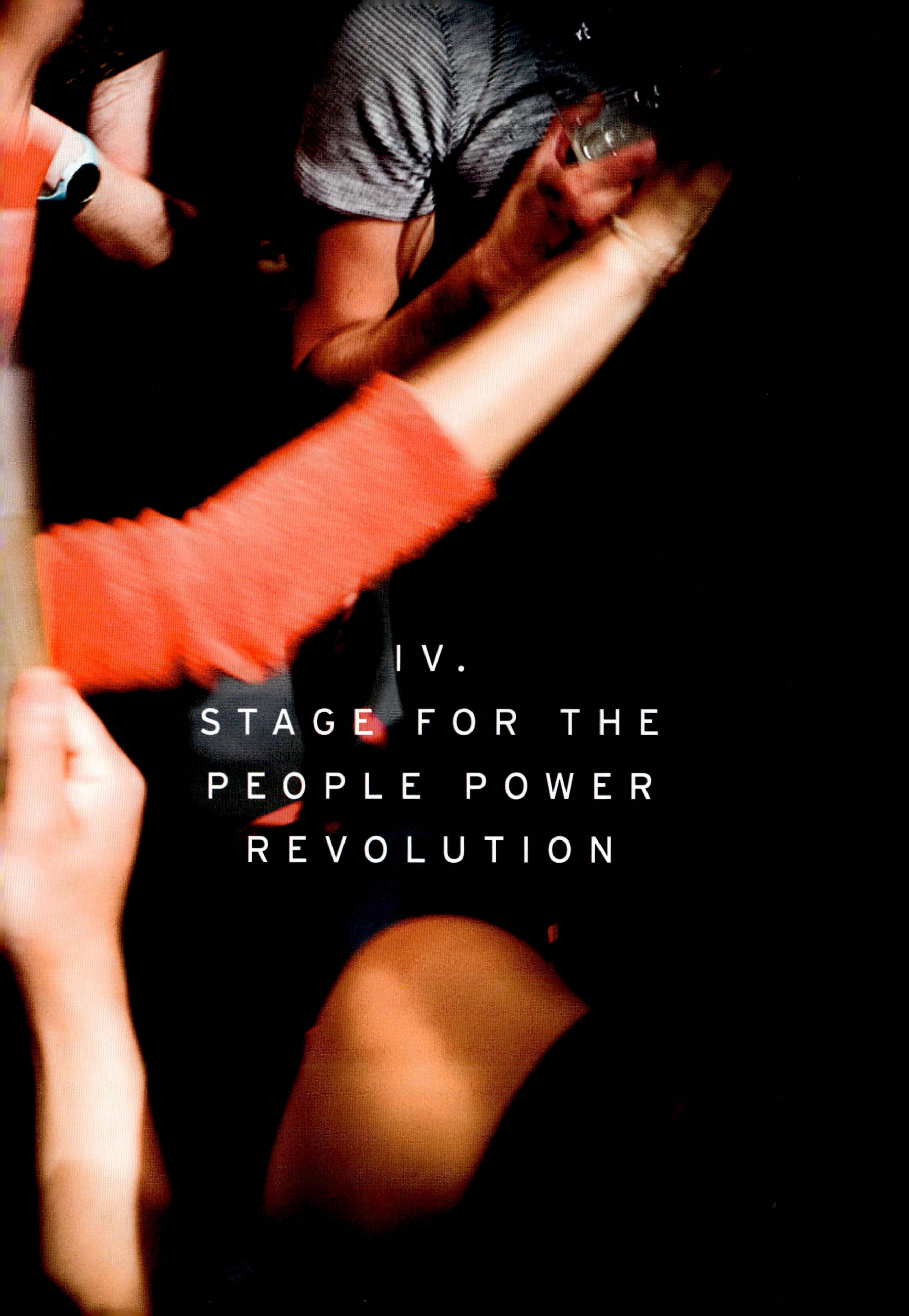

IV.
STAGE FOR THE PEOPLE POWER REVOLUTION

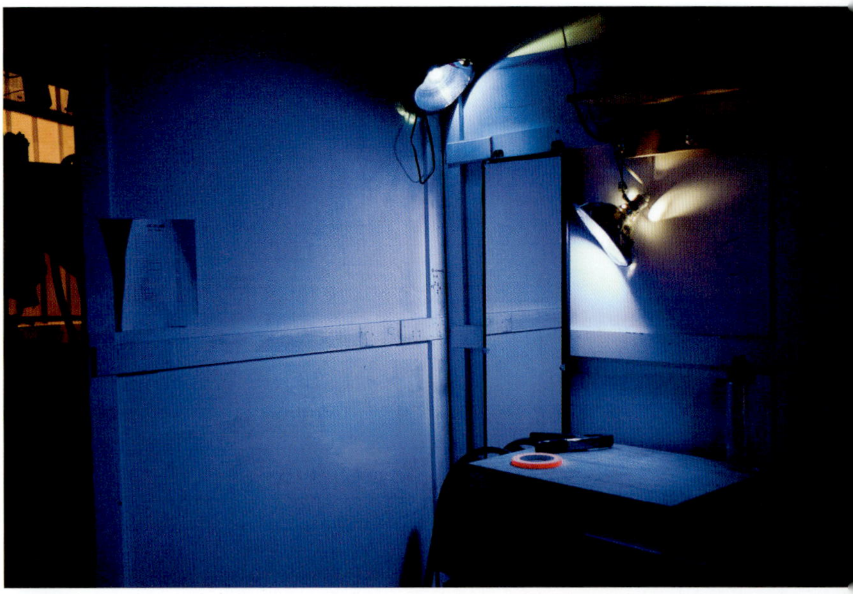

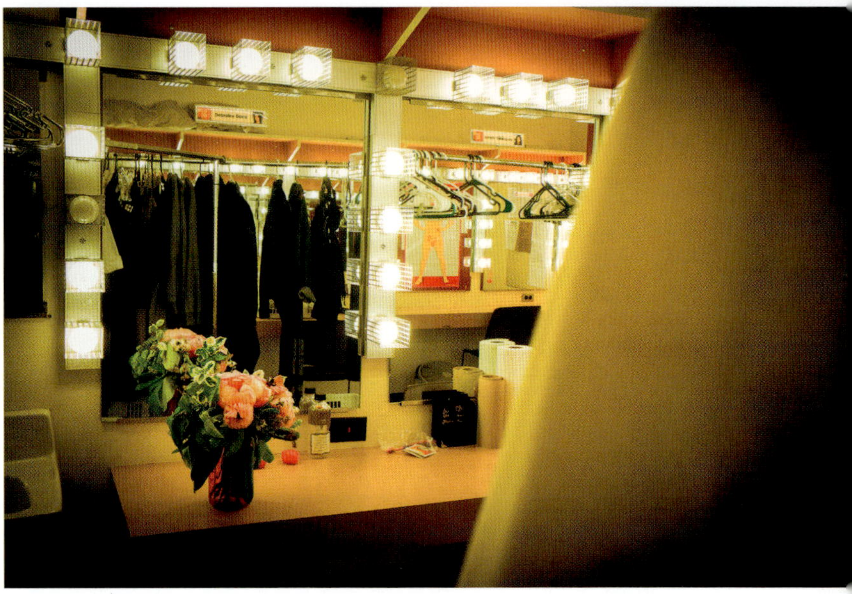

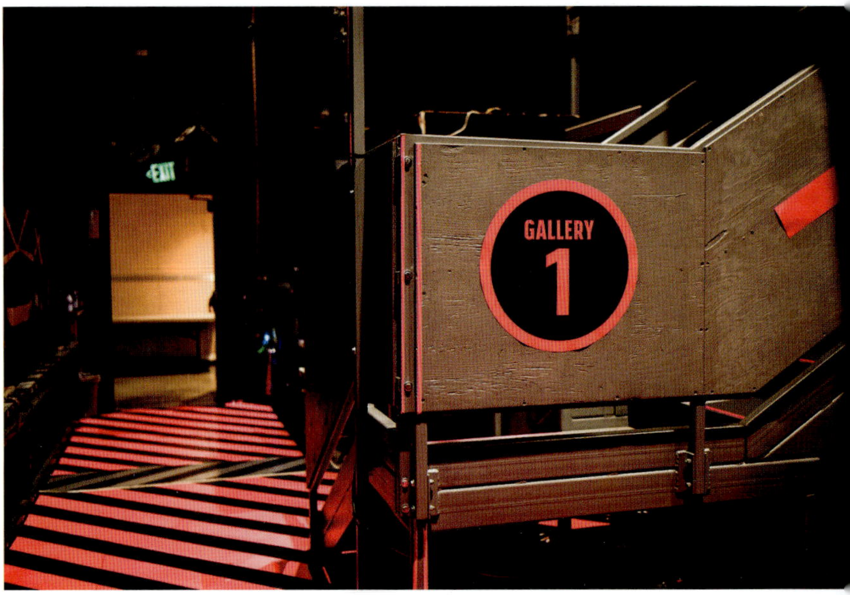
EXIT
GALLERY
1

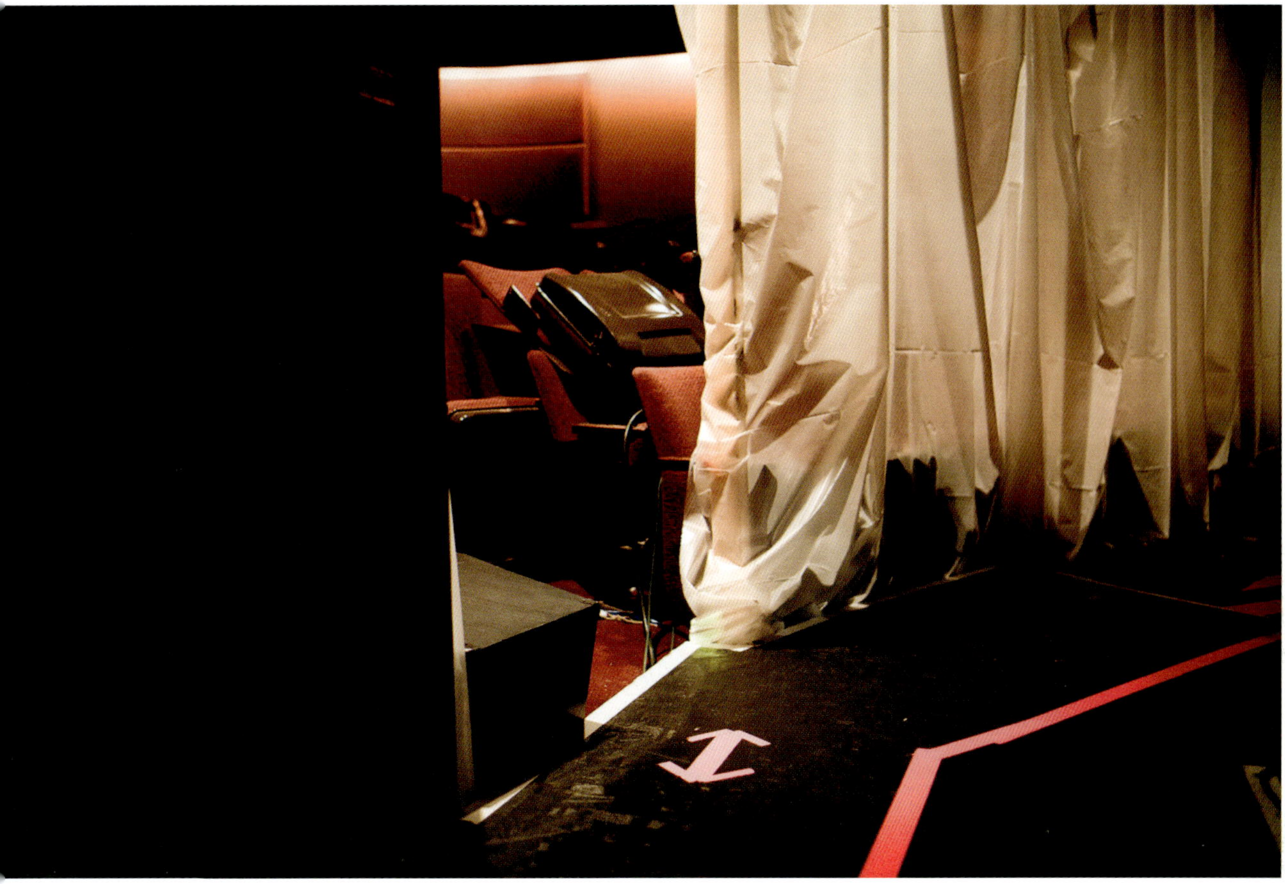

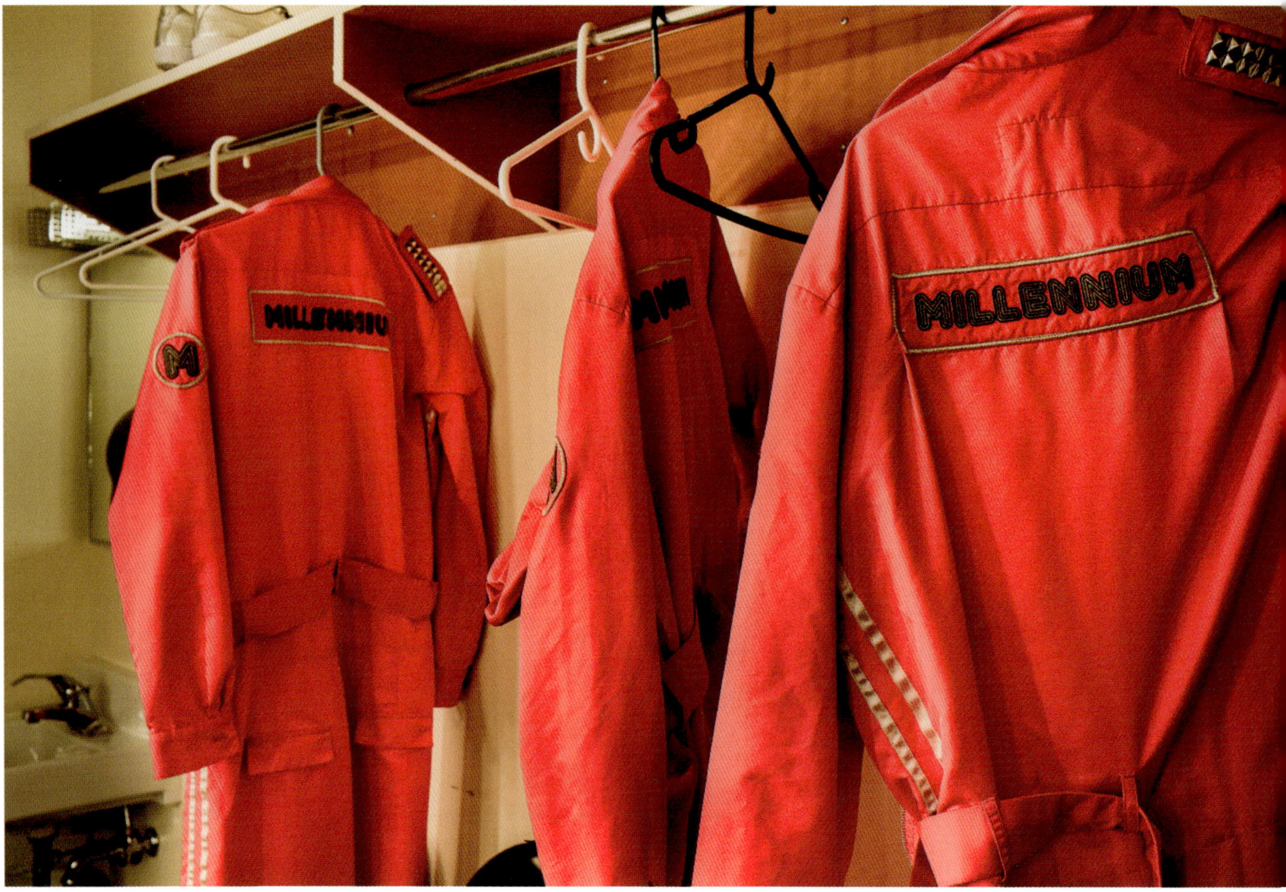
MILLENNIUM
MILLENNIUM

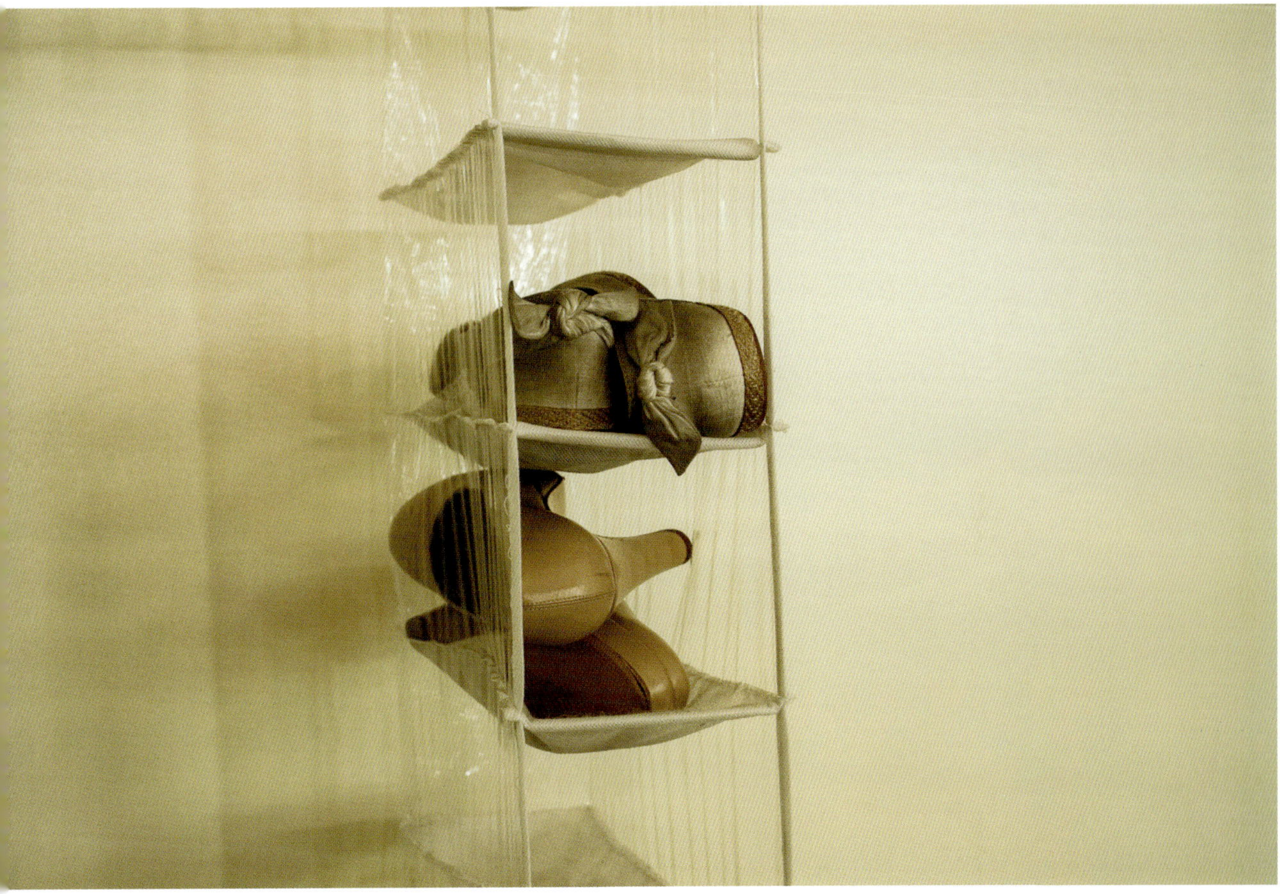

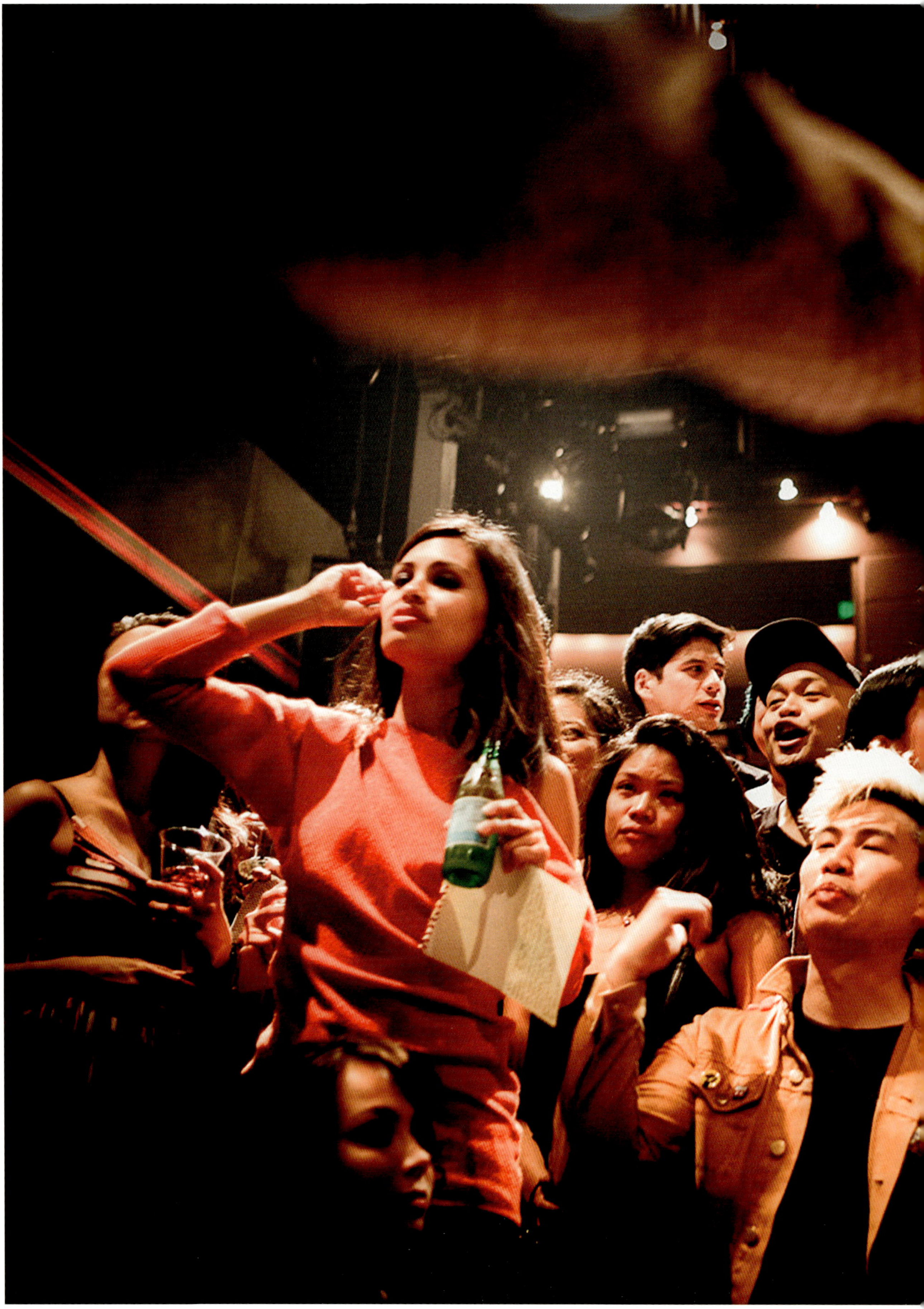

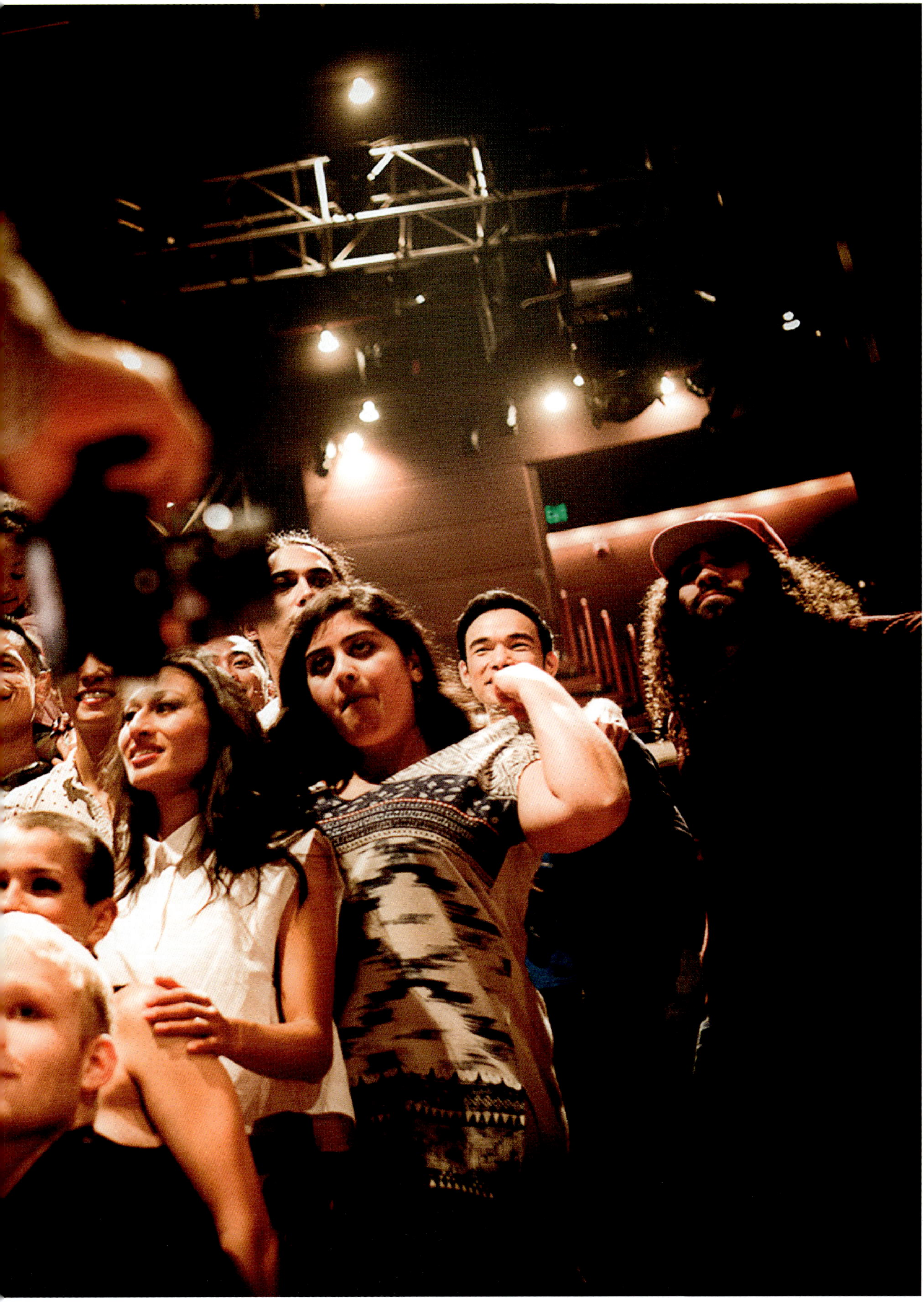

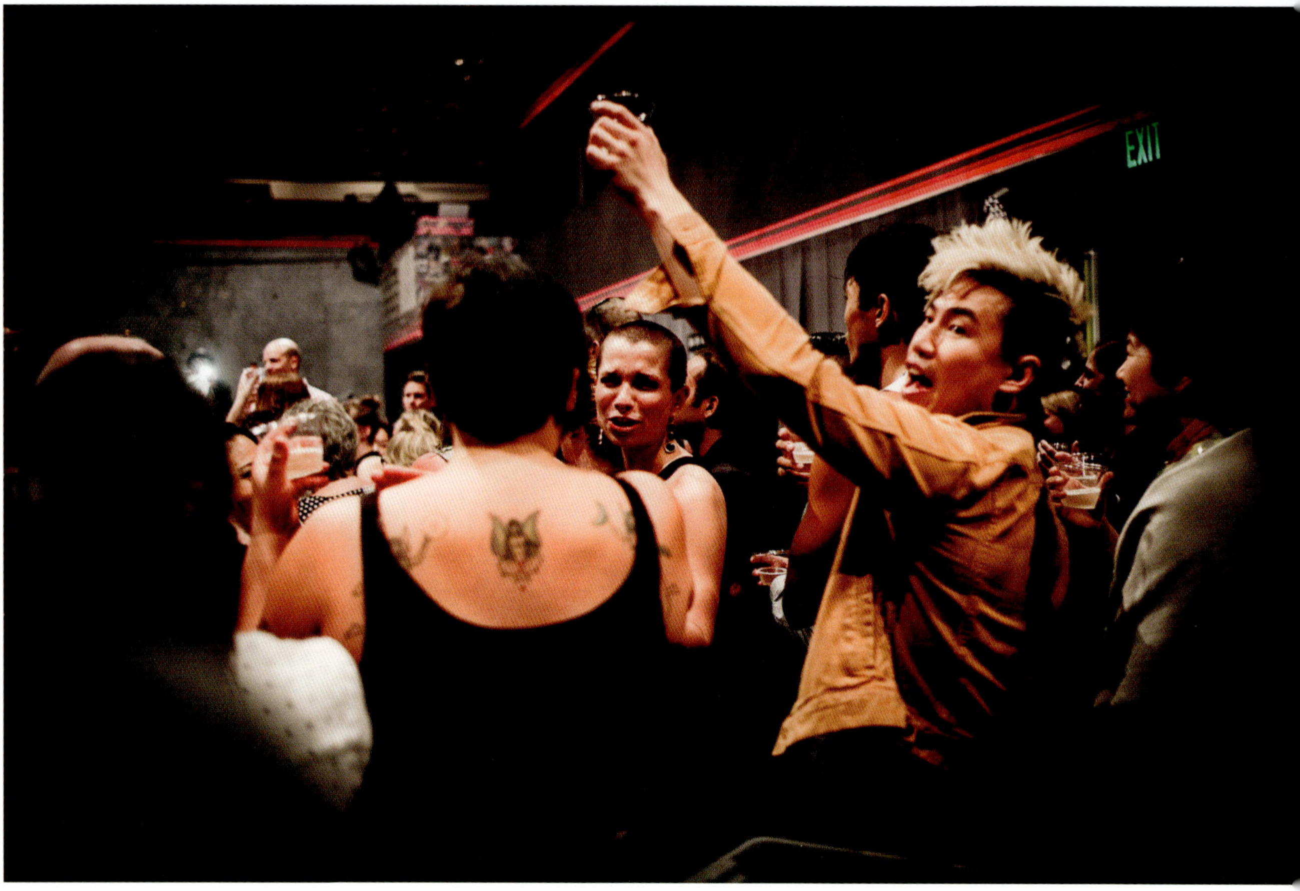
EXIT

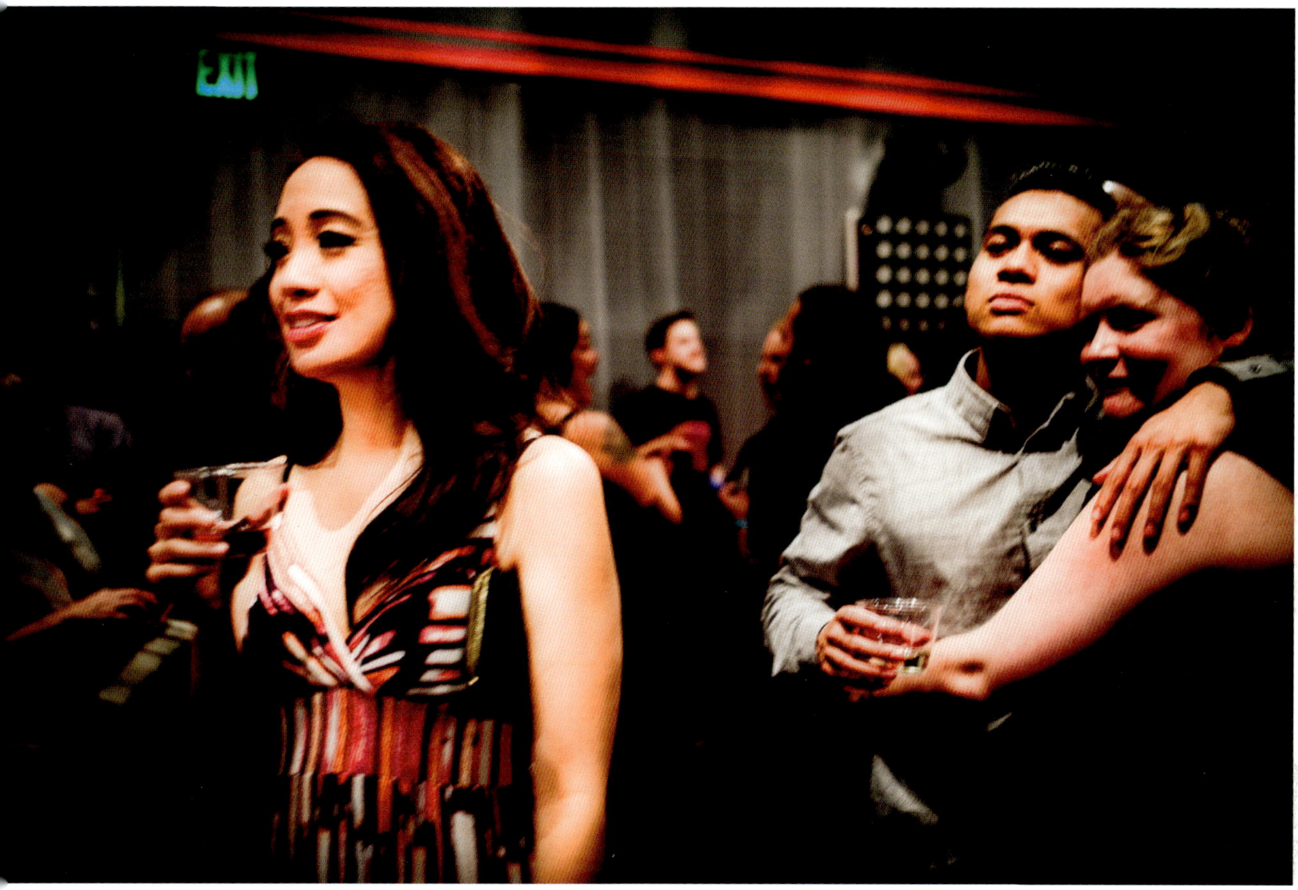

"I knew some of the music, but even after I flew to New York,
did the audition and got the part, I was like, What did I just get myself
into? I did this crazy monologue, I had not seen a script,
I knew some of the music, but I didn't know what the plan is.
I know David Byrne is awesome and Alex (Timbers) is reputable,
so OK. If you write it down, it's a disco musical about the
rise and fall of Imelda Marcos, *It sounds like a bad idea!*"

MELODY BUTIU

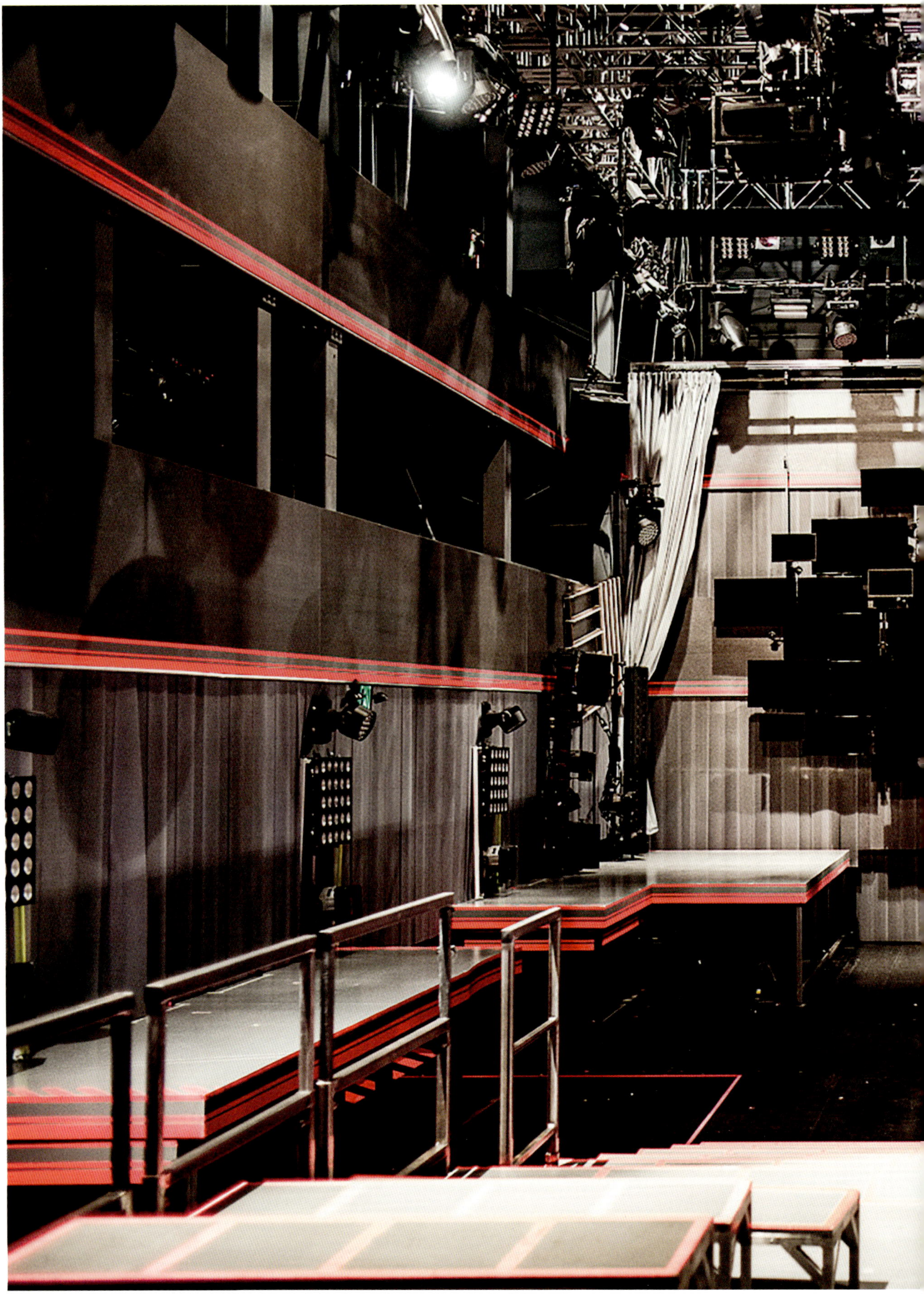

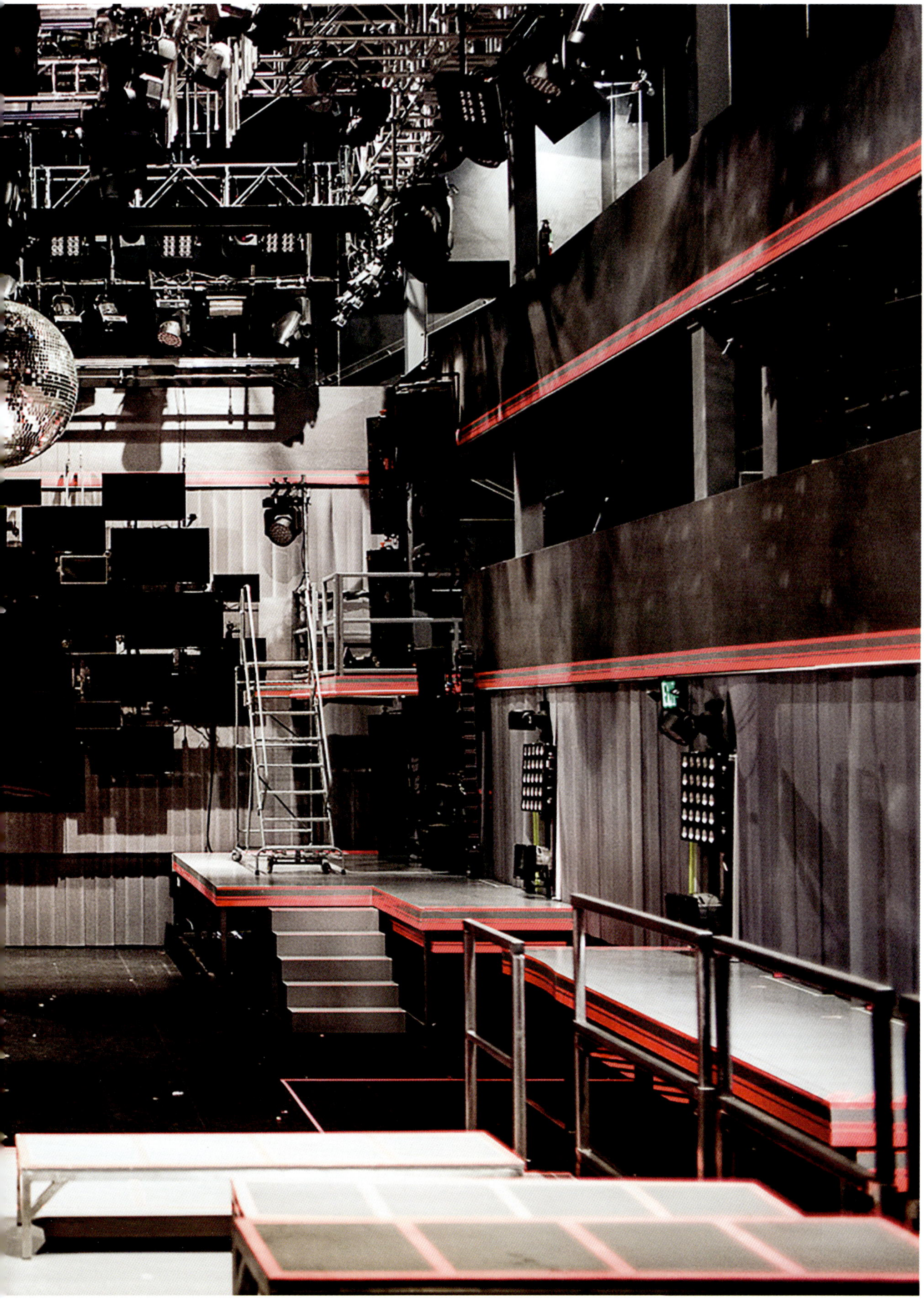

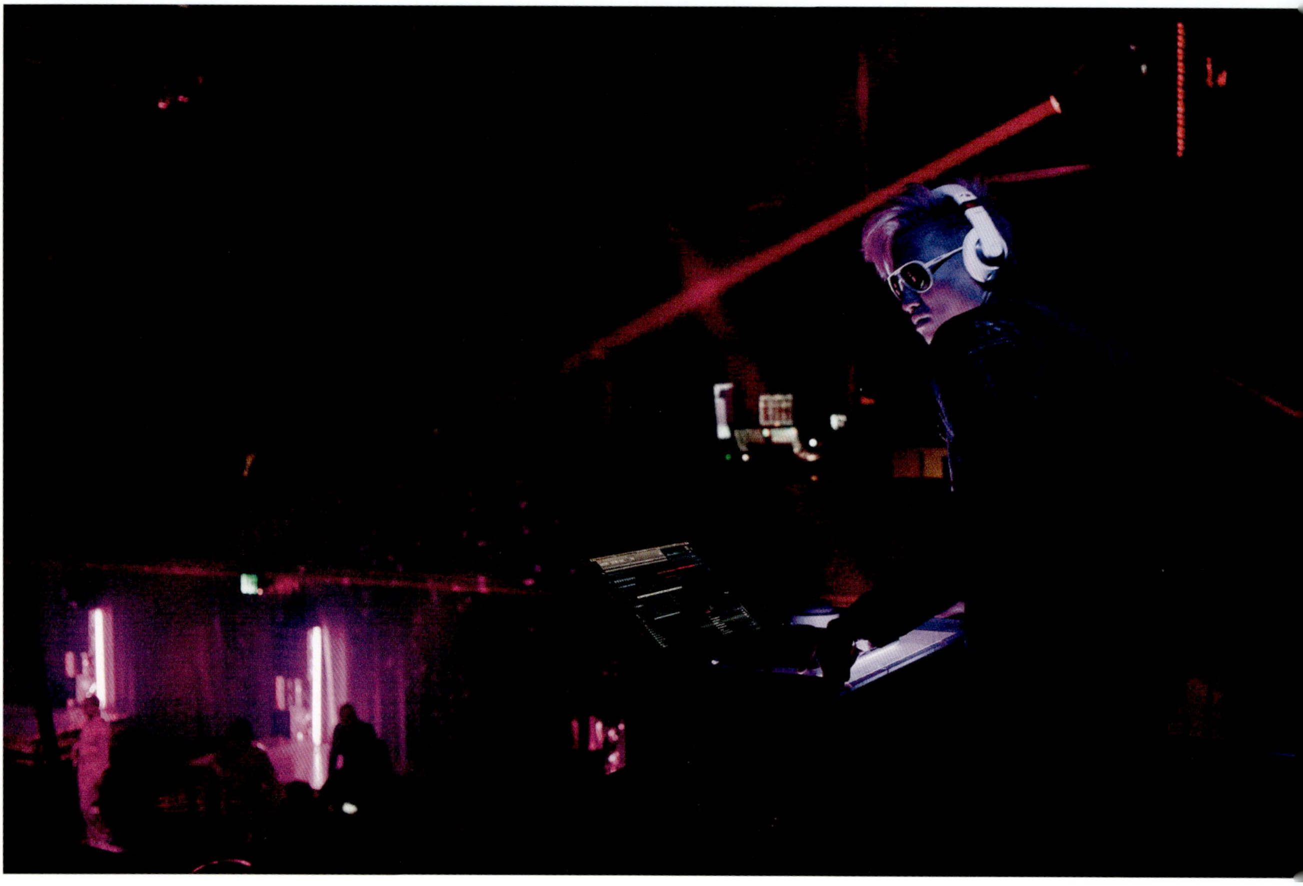

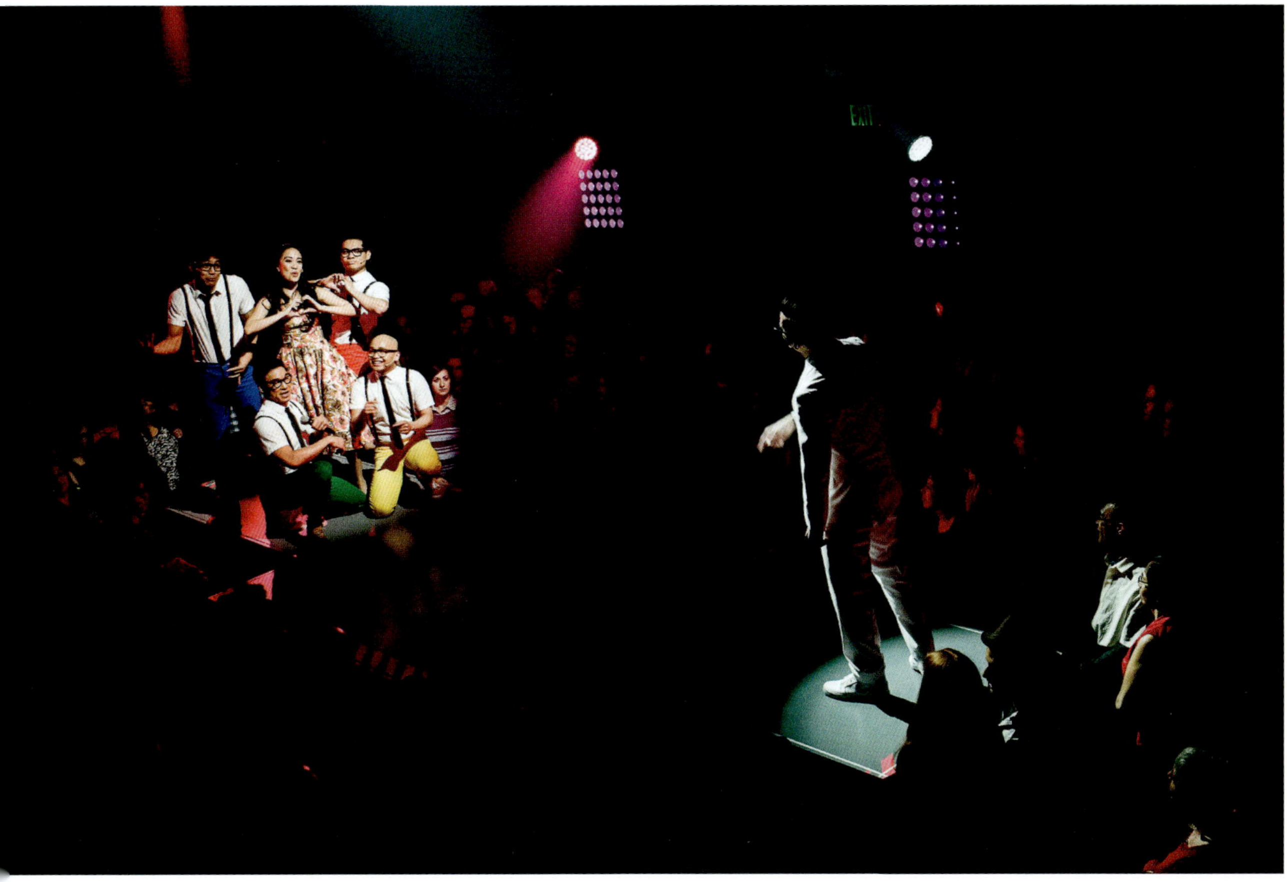

“The high schoolers were definitely moved by it. They’re teenagers, so they don’t want to seem too enthusiastic about anything. “

“If one kid starts to dance, the rest of them will.
You know they want to, but they don’t want to be that person.
But a lot of them have come back to the show.”

ENRICO RODRIGUEZ

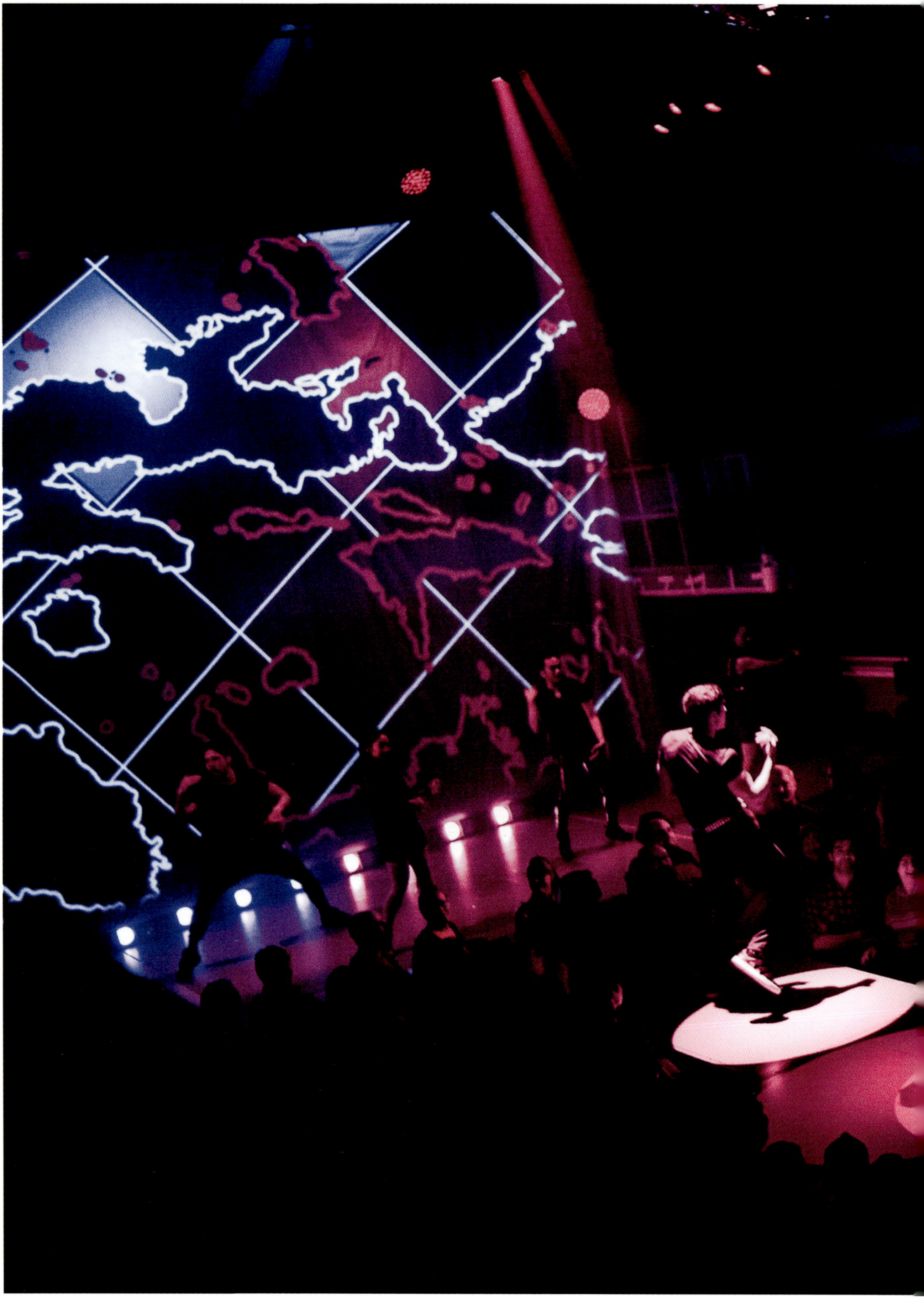

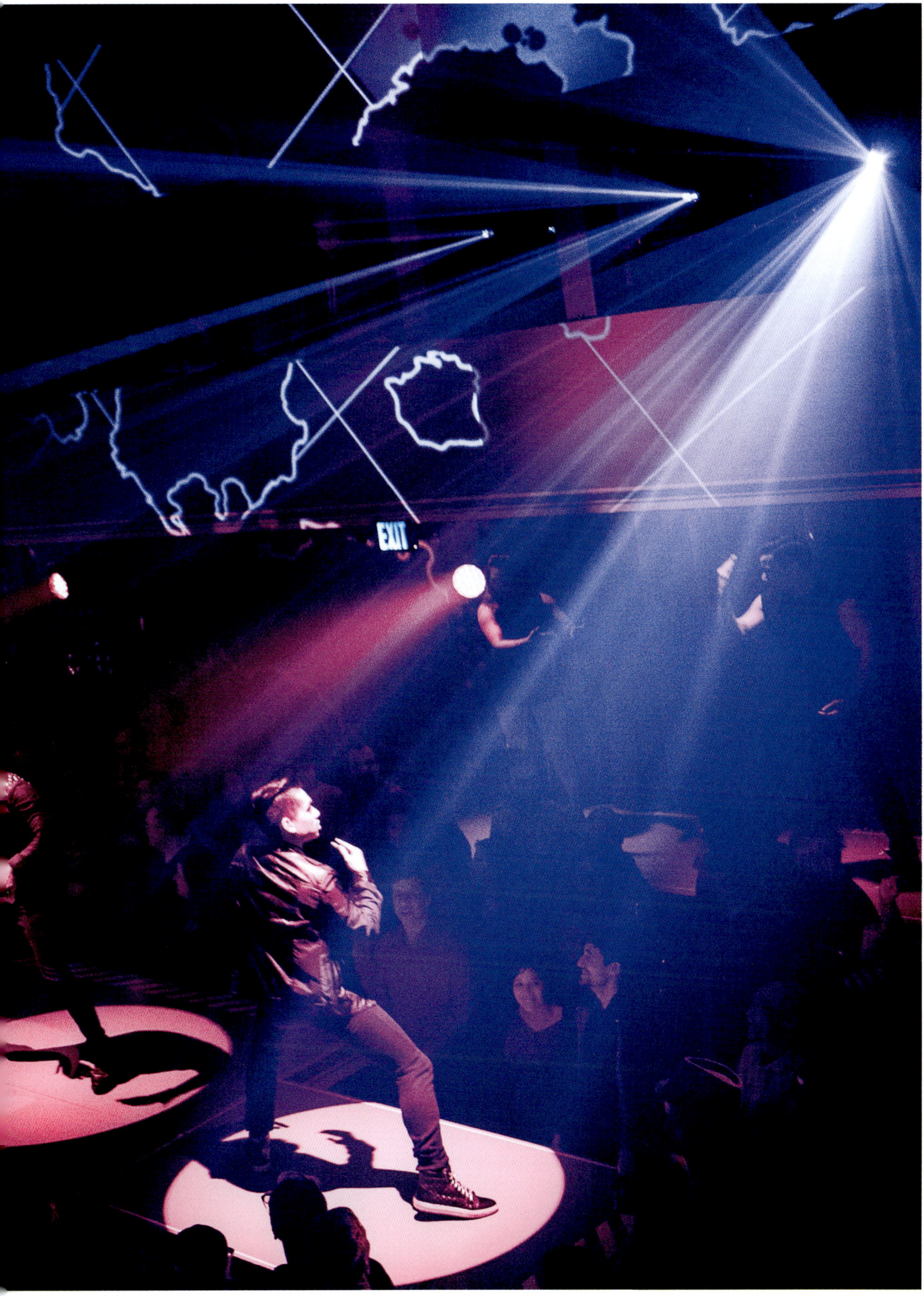
EXIT

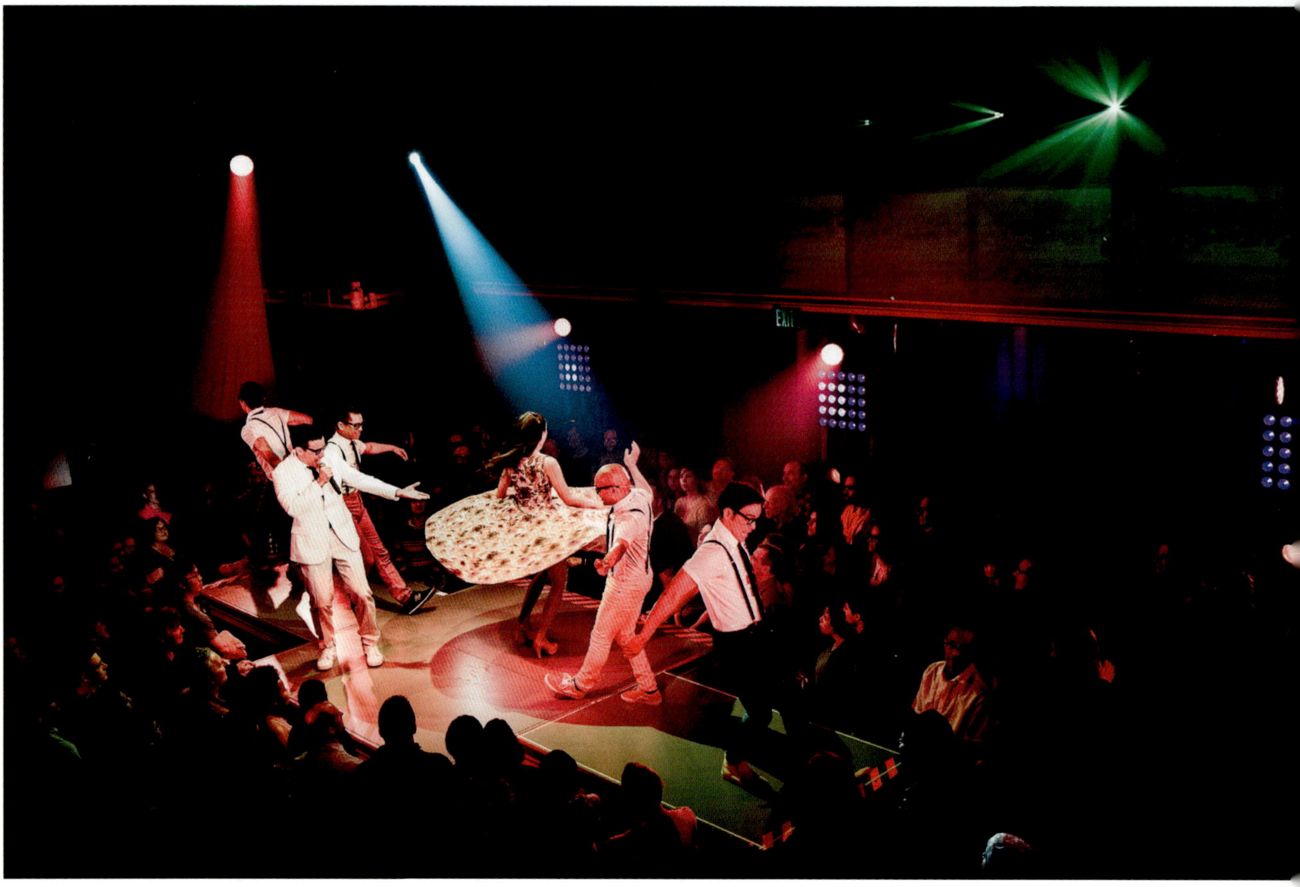

"A brother and sister come almost every night.
I think she's seen it maybe fifteen times.
I'll see them, and I'll wink at her, and she is like, Oh my gosh!
They know exactly where to be because they are regulars."

"A mother came up to me with her eight-year-old child.
She said, I just want to let you know that my child
was saying he sees himself in all of you guys on stage."

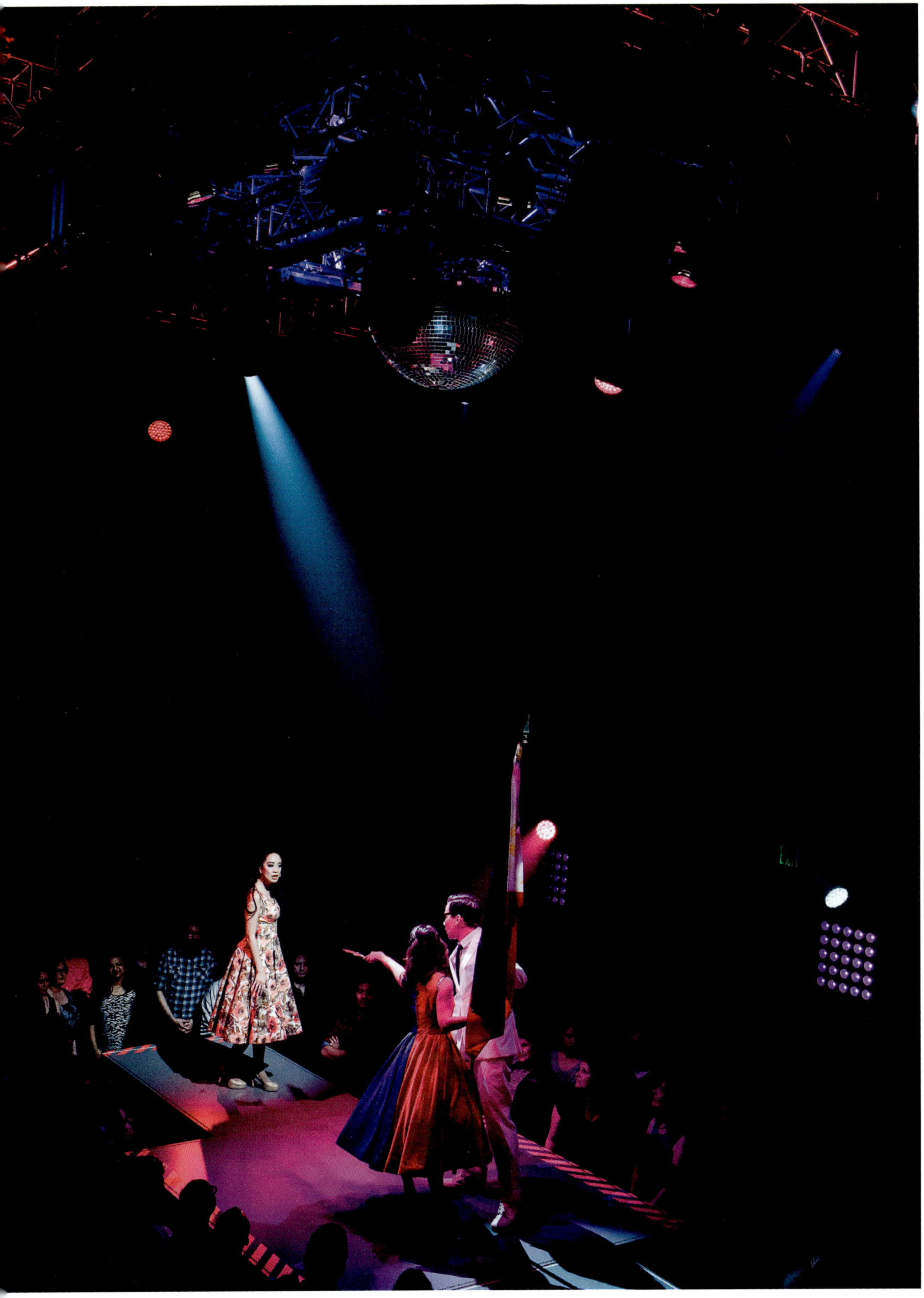

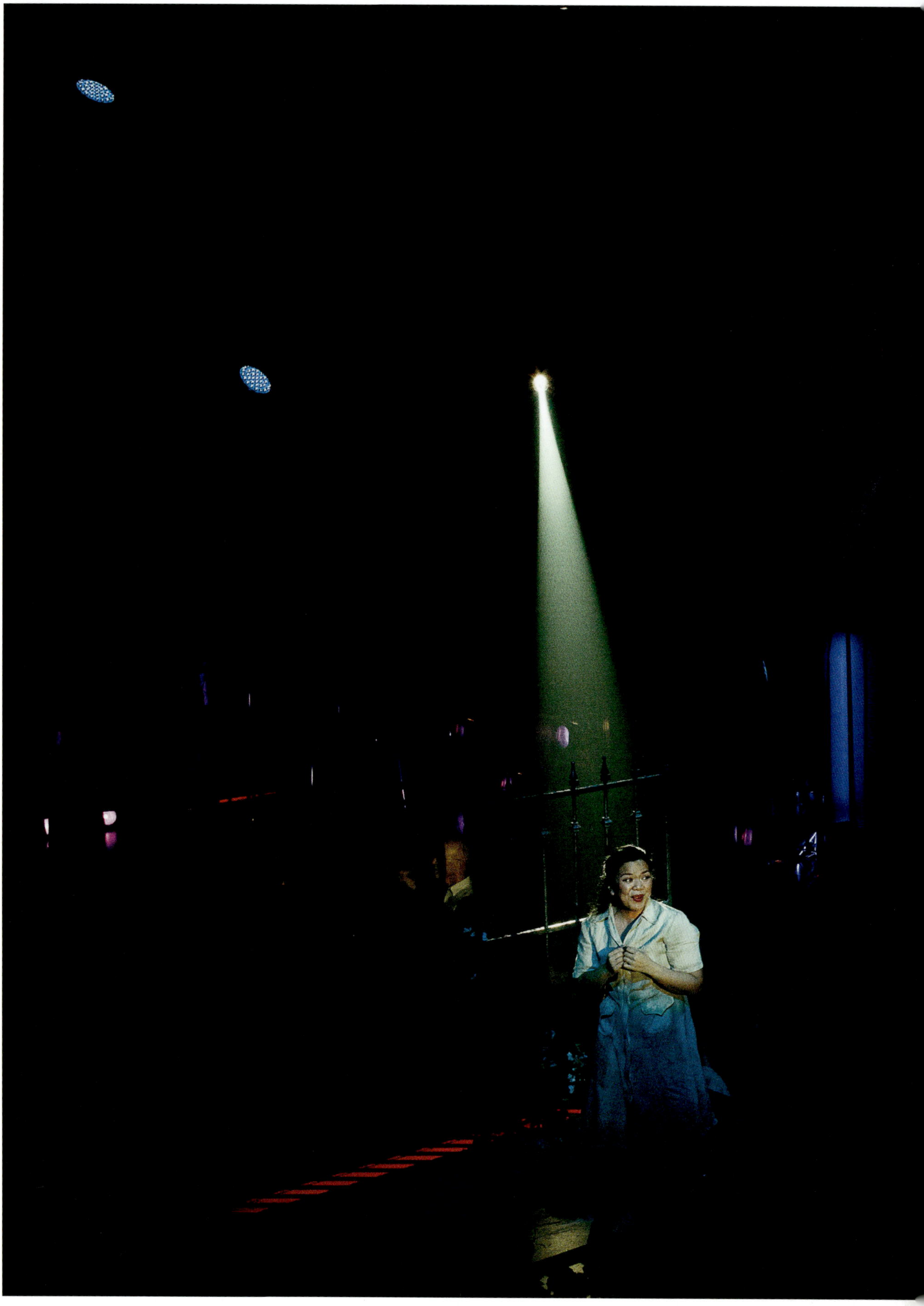

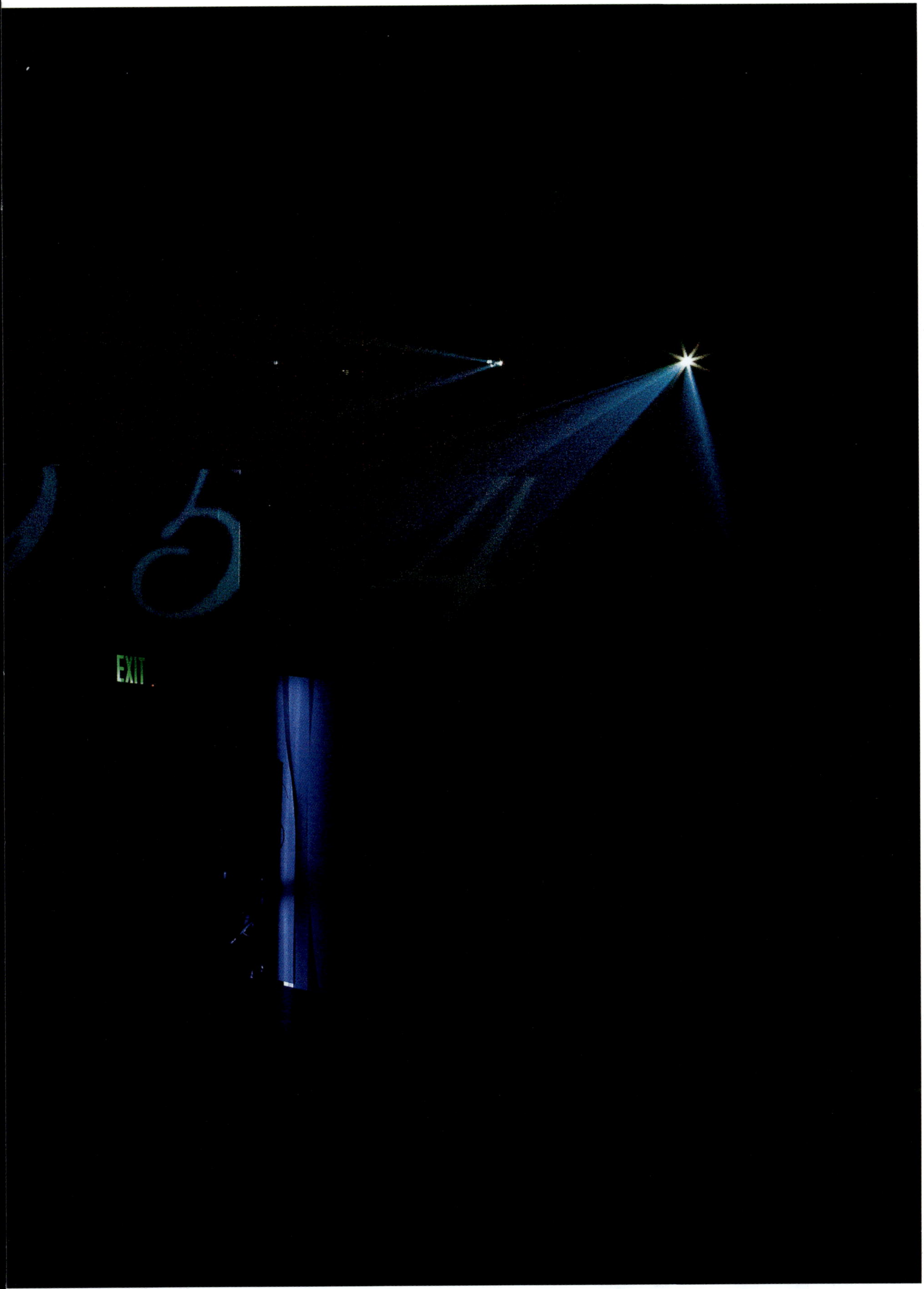
EXIT

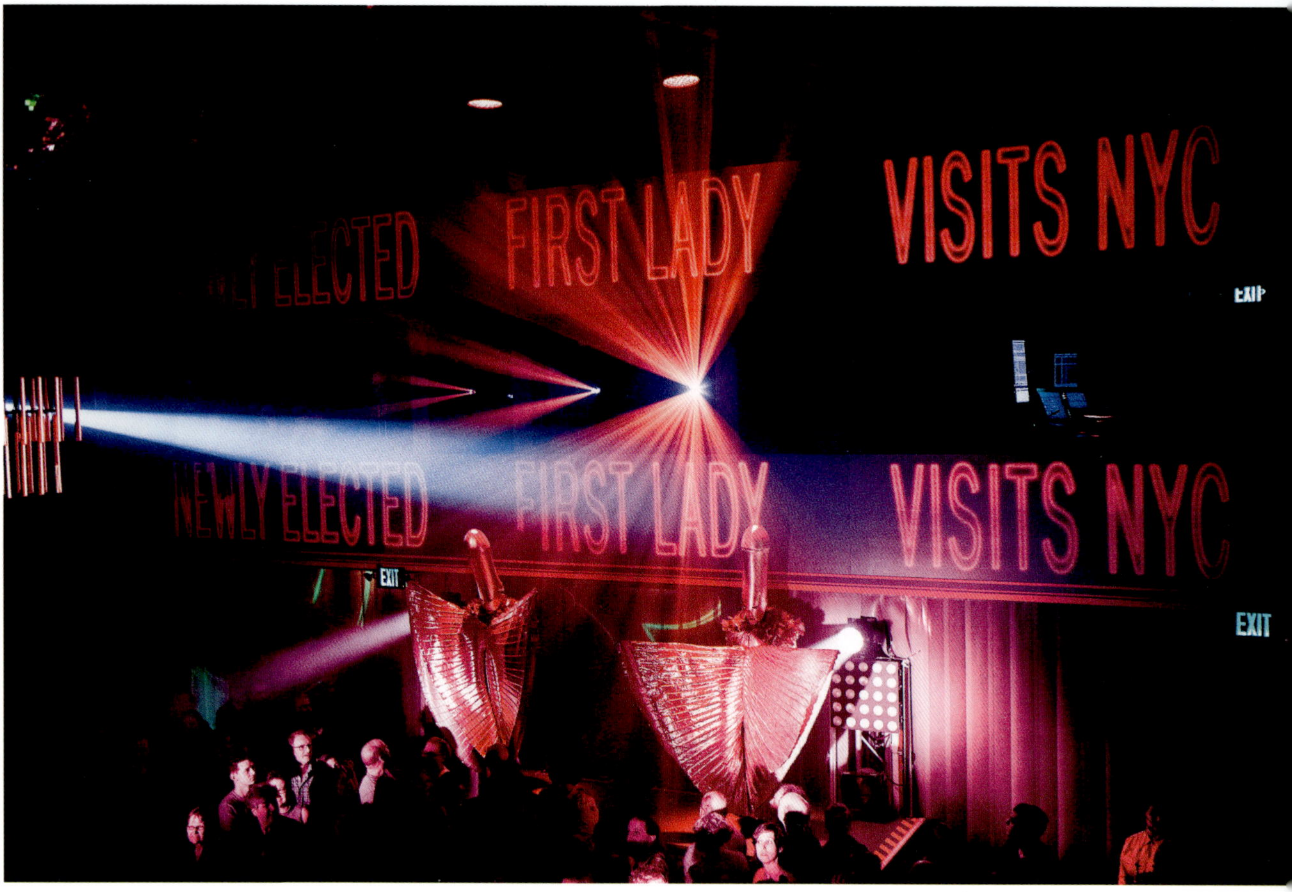
FIRST LADY
VISITS NYC
EXIT
NEWLY ELECTED
FIRST LADY
VISITS NYC
EXIT
EXIT

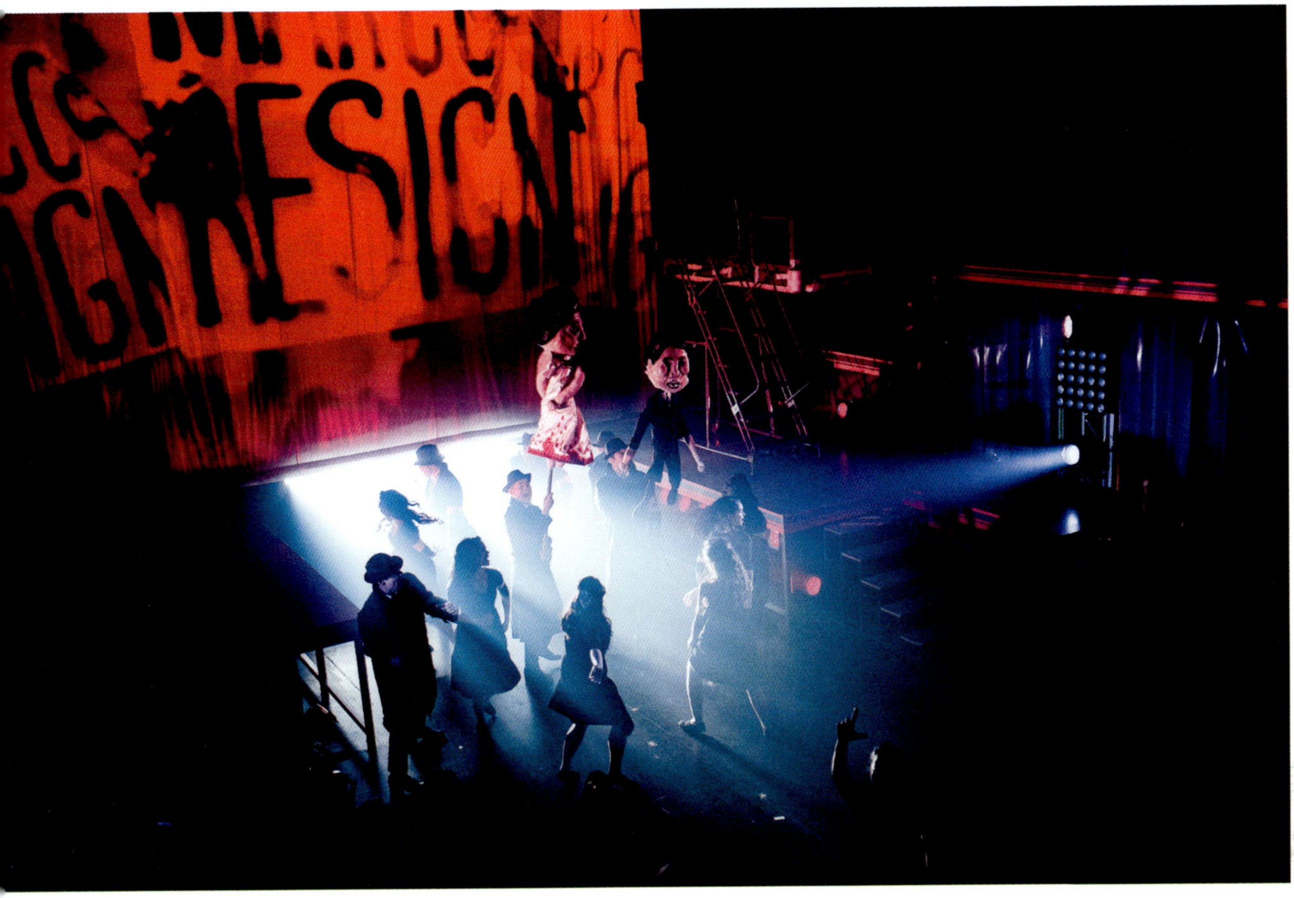

"The incredible thing about this show is that you're swept into the atmosphere, the rags to riches story, cheering for them. You're like, Yeah, they got elected! Even for people who do know the history, they know in the back of their minds, these are dictators who got ousted. If you don't know that, it's very easy to get swept up in the journey and the excitement and all of that. And then you get the rug pulled out from under you, which is very purposeful."

MELODY BUTIU

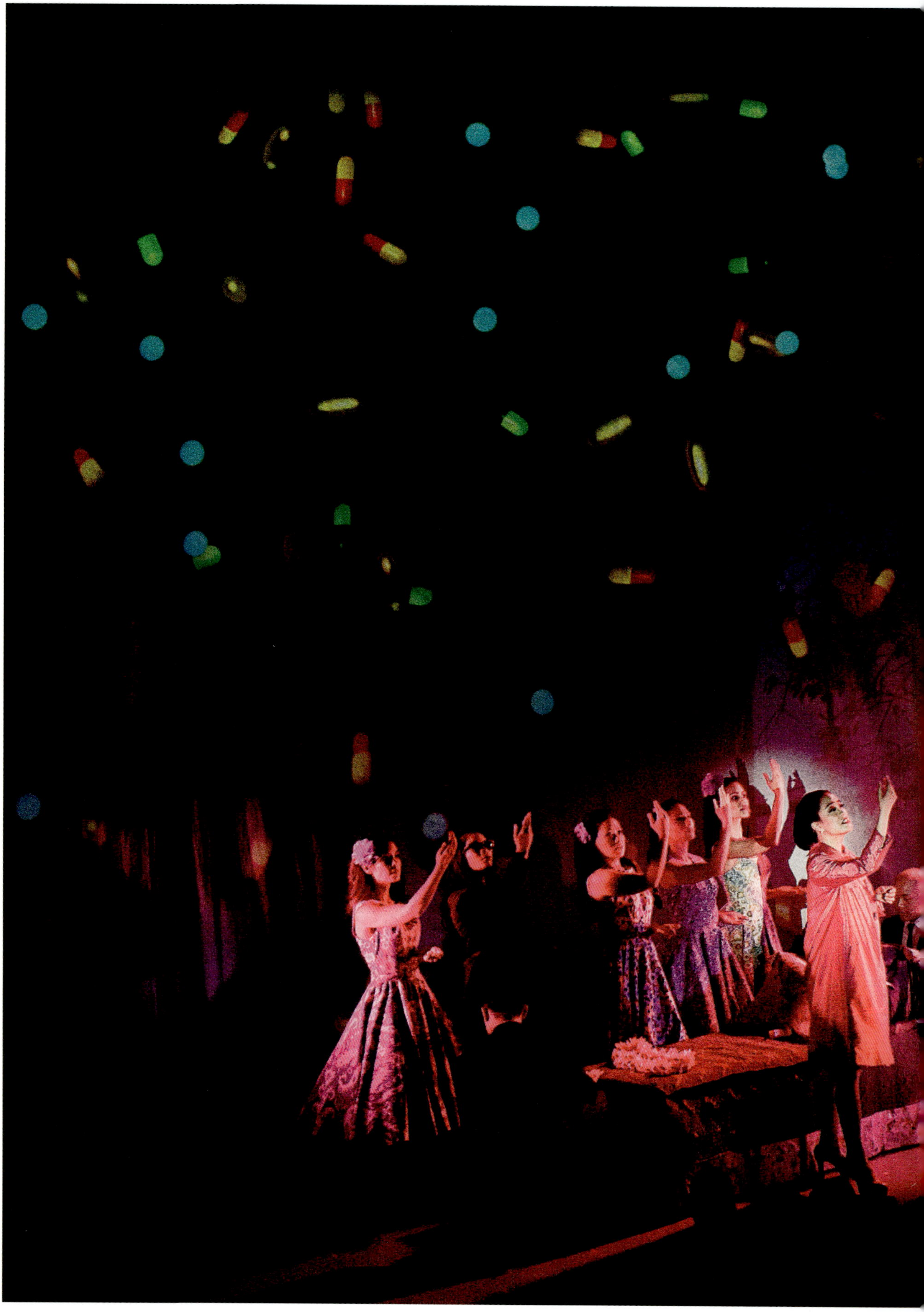

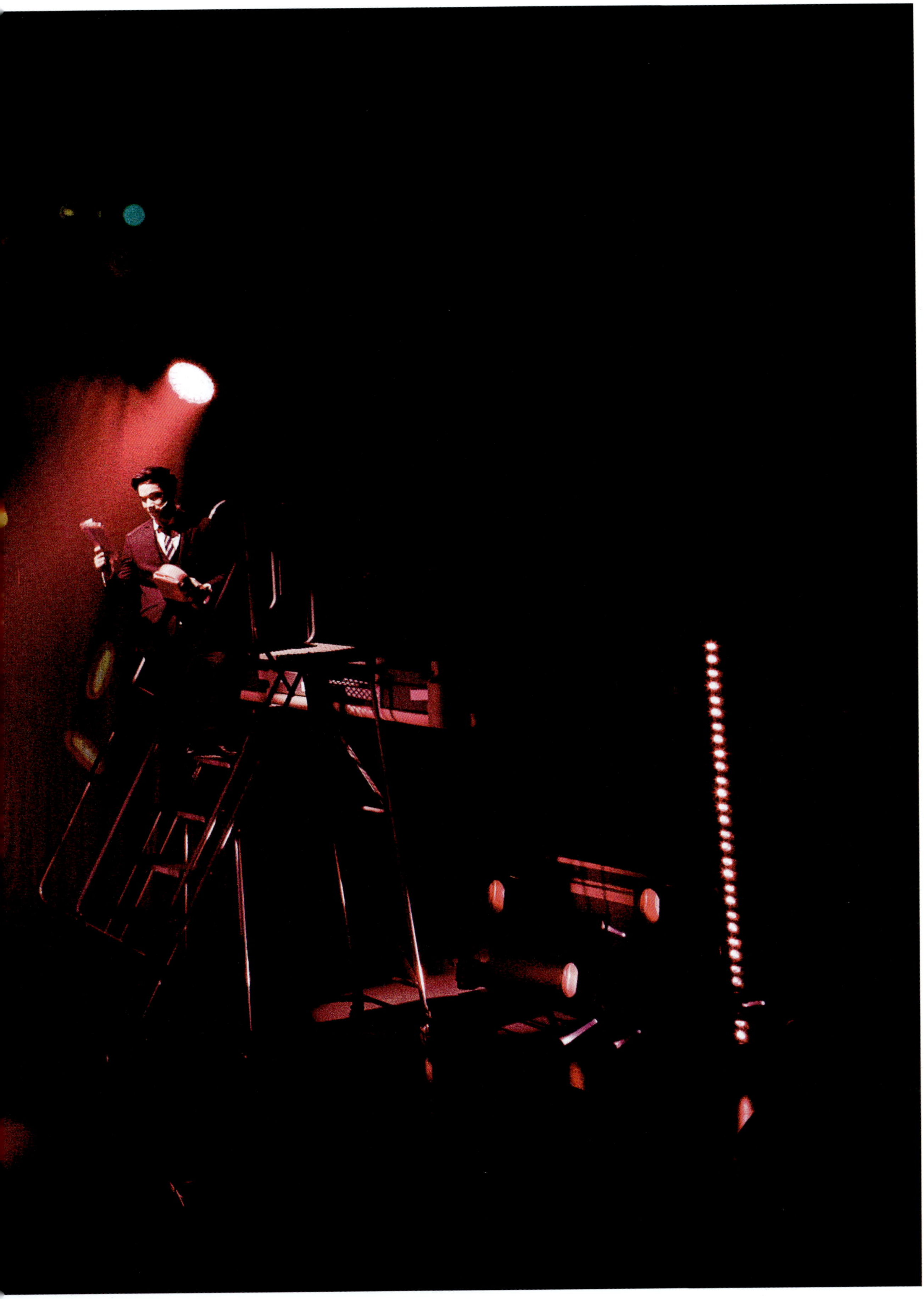

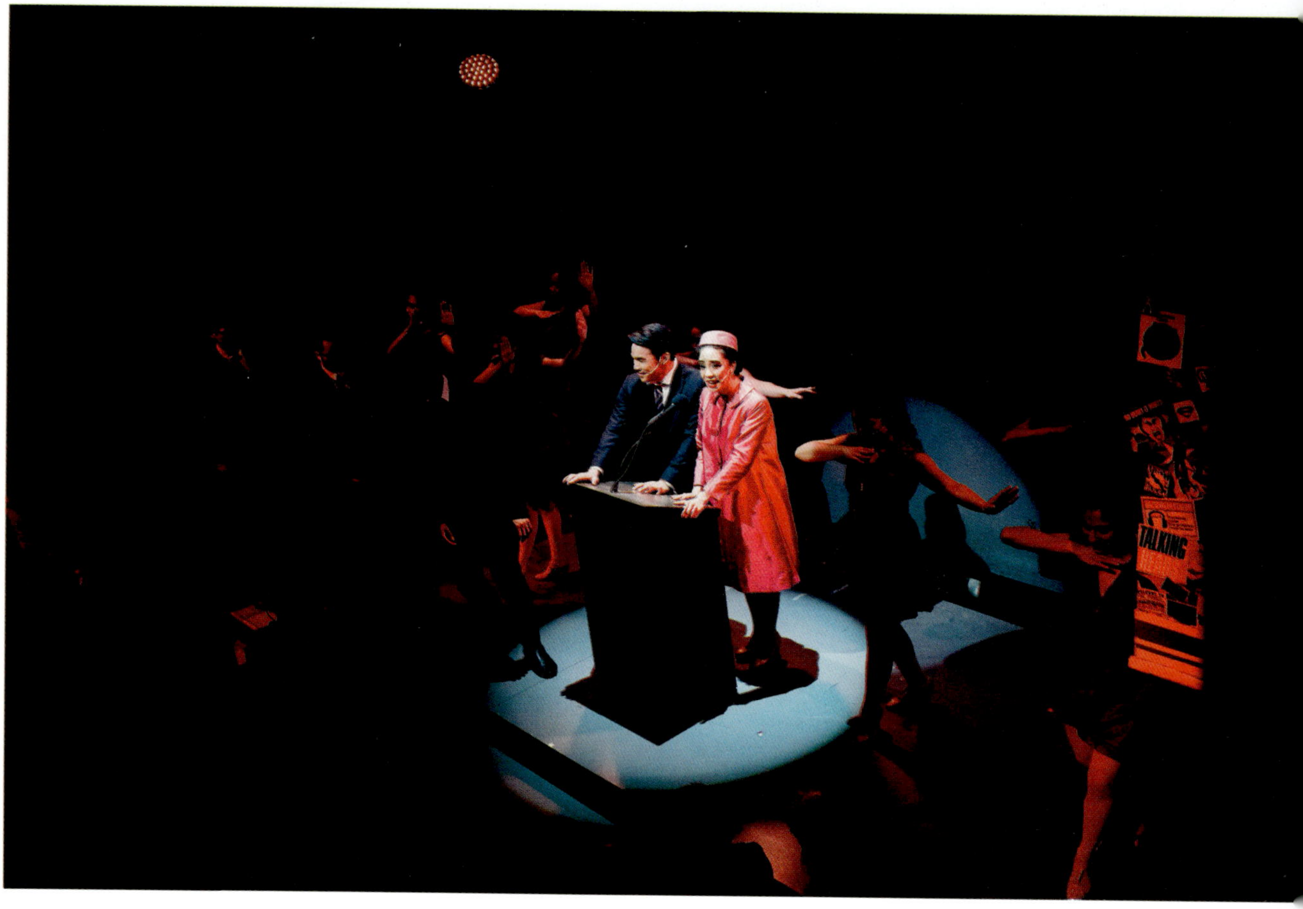
TALKING

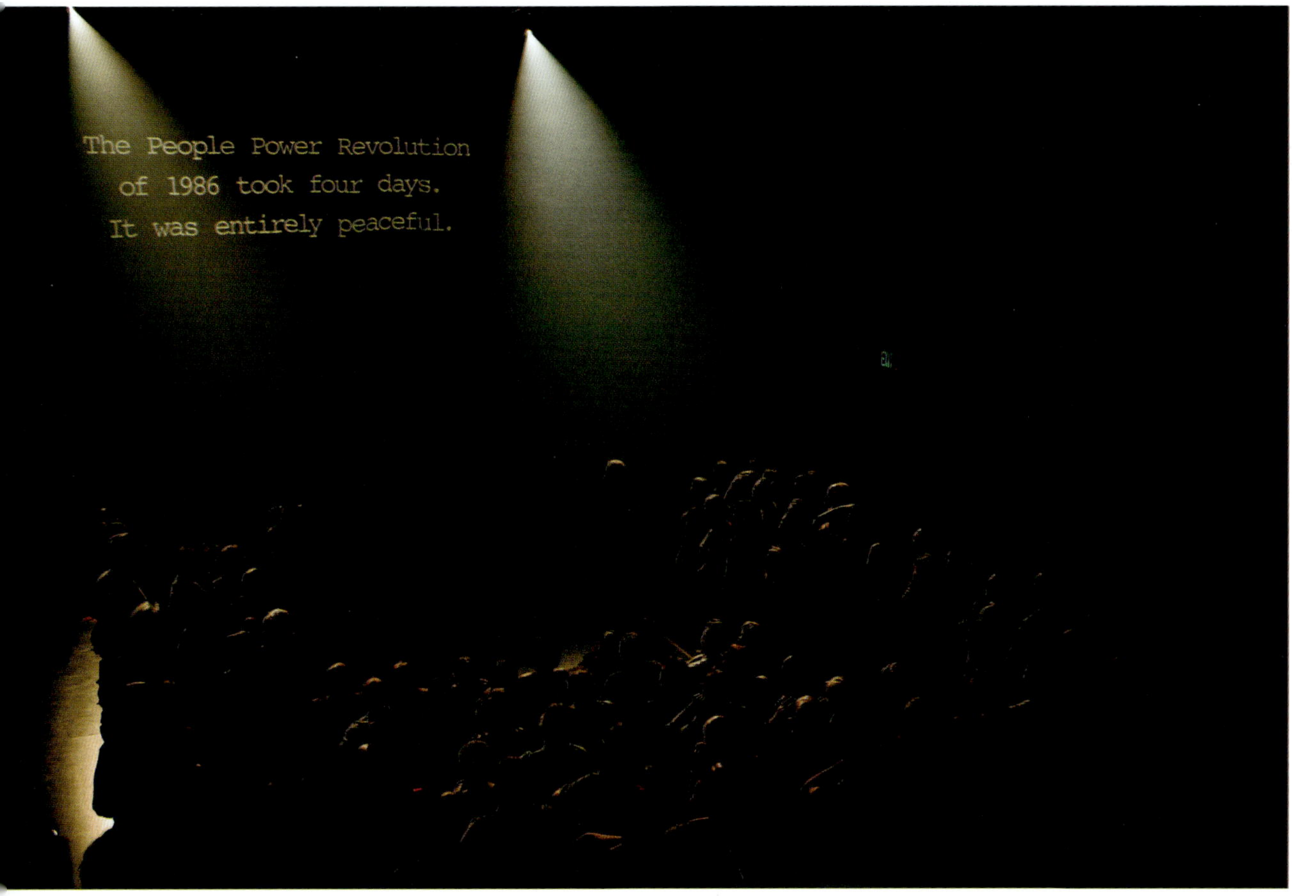

"(David Byrne) loves the show so much. He'll be in the audience, singing full out, jumping up and down and openly crying, and he knows where the story goes! There are no surprises! And yet he is moved every night! He's just a big, open heart."

MELODY BUTIU

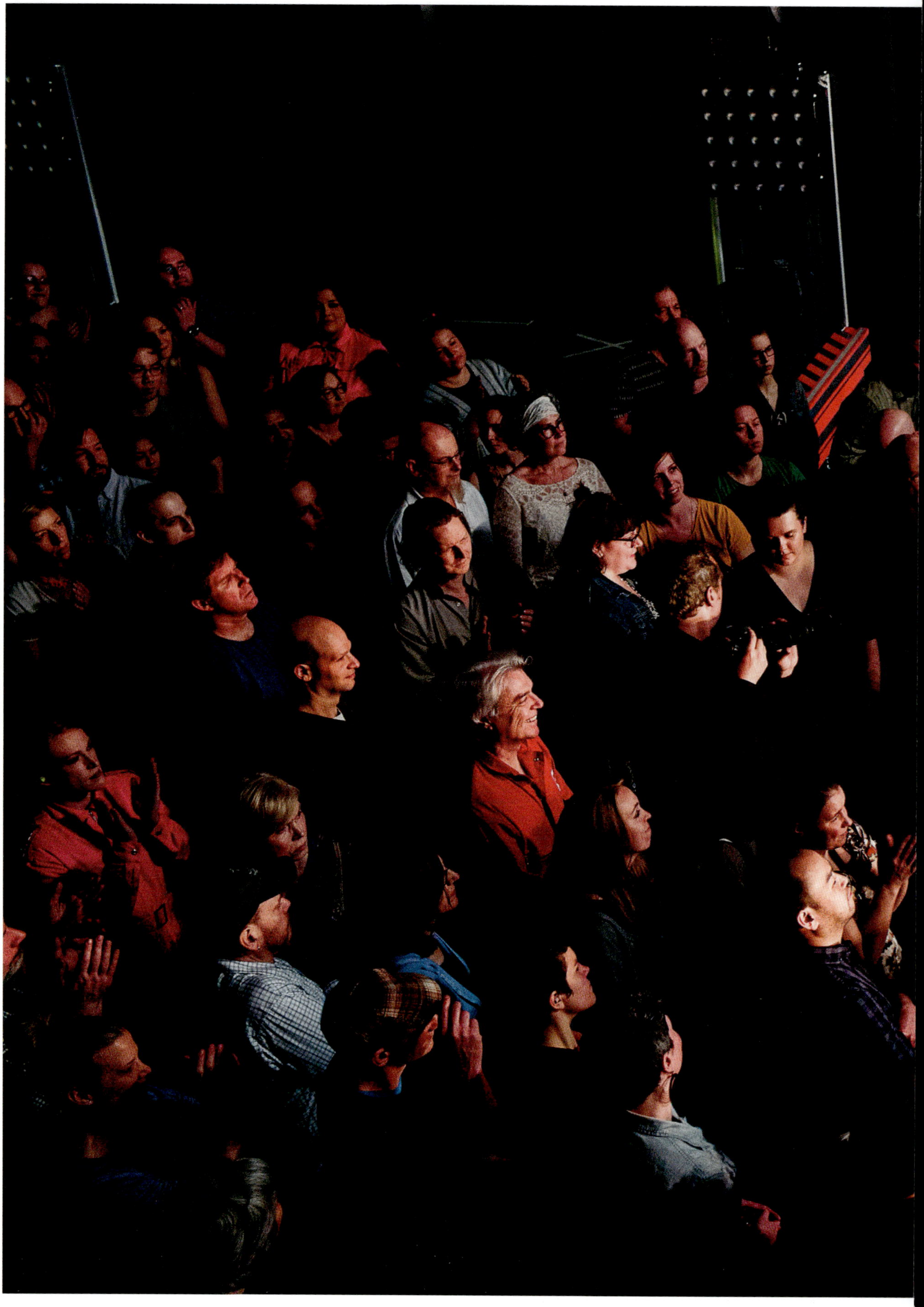

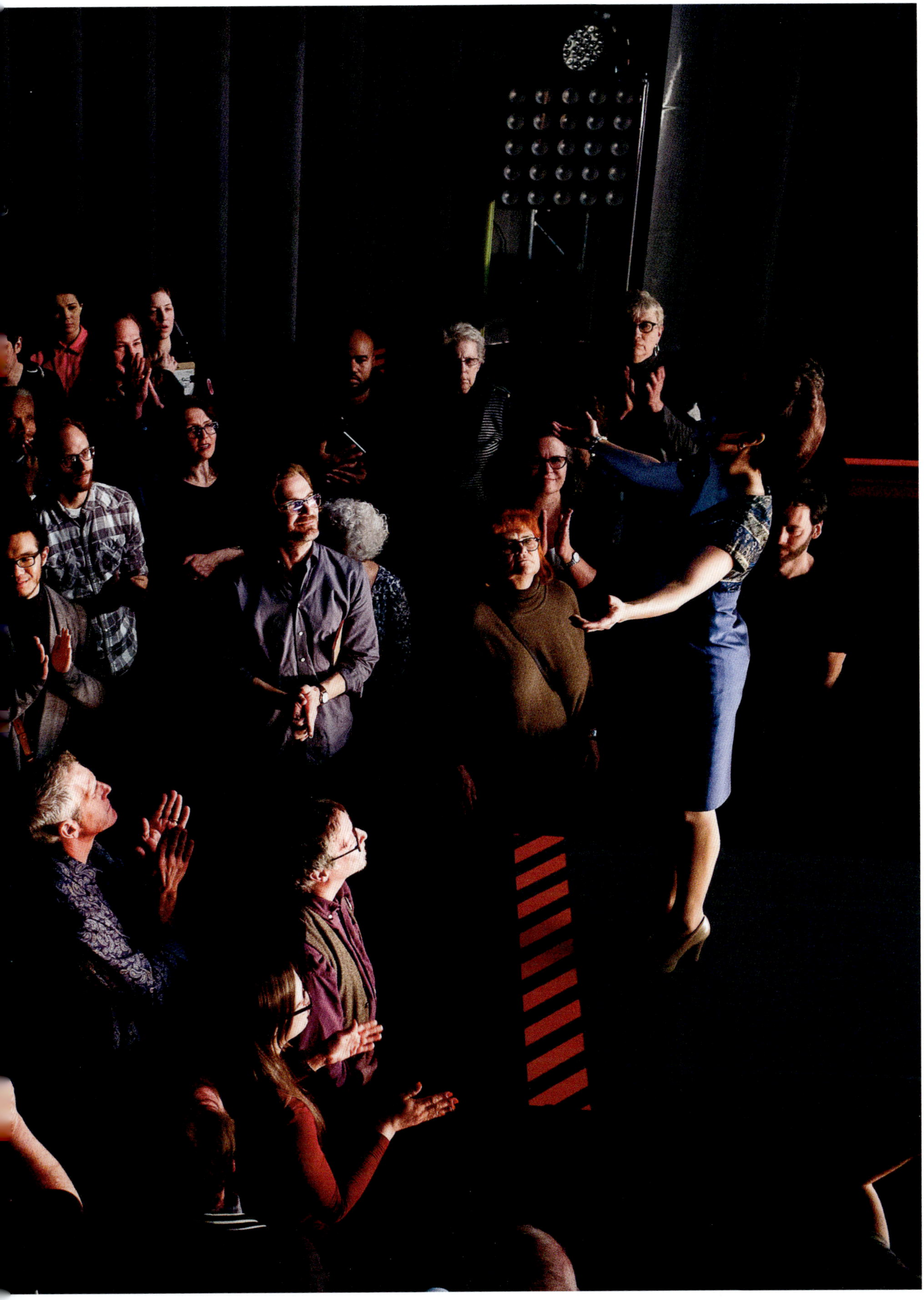

YOU MIGHT THINK YOU ARE LOST
BUT THEN YOU WILL FIND
THAT GOD DRAWS STRAIGHT
BUT WITH CROOKED LINES

CAPTIONS

P 2-3
David Byrne and Mark Bautista

P 6
David Byrne

P 8
Choreographer Annie-B Parson talks to her dancers

P 12
The cast at Seattle Rep Theater at the last performance's after-party

P 22
Alex Timbers

P 25
Jaygee Macapugay, Trevor Salter and cast at Seattle Rehearsals

P 39
Gerry Devost and Cam Hanrahan at F&D Calgary

P 40
Top left: F&D Welder. Top right: Devan Mackintosh and Nick James. Bottom left: Paul McKenna, Dean Baker and Mike Treutler

P 41
Top left: Finn McCornell. Top right: Paul McKeena. Bottom left: Nick James.

P 42-43
Gavin Kaposvary

P 44
Paul McKenna and Dean Baker

P 46
Pascale Lefebure

P 49
F&D crew at lunch break

P 50
Rick James, Drew Martson, Kevin Behrens and Jesse Allen

P 51
Cory Hummel

P 59
A set builder at Seattle Rep

P 74
Mark Bautista and cast at the Rep's technical rehearsal

P 75
Conrad Ricamora, Jaygee Macapugay and cast at the Rep's Technical rehearsal)

P 88
Shea Renne, Mark Bautista and Debralee Daco

P 89
Jordan Leon (with tray at left), Michael Feldman, Jaygee Macapugay, Mark Bautista and Trevor Salter (with tray at right)

PP 90-91
Jonelle Margallo, Michael Feldman, Renée Albulario, Debralee Daco, Mark Bautista, Jaygee Macapugay, Shea Renne

P 92
Top: Renée Albulario.
Middle: Jaygee Macapugay and ensemble.
Bottom: Geena Quintos, Trevor Salter, Jeigh Madjus, Janelle Velasquez, Debralee Daco and Michael Feldman

P 93
Debralee Daco, Melody Butiu, Janelle Velasquez, Annie-B Parson, Shea Renne, Renée Albulario and Jonelle Margallo

PP 96-97
Debralee Daco

P 104
Tobias Christian Wong at last performance's after-party

P 105
Jaygee Macapugay and cast at last performance's after-party

P 108
Tobias Christian Wong during performance

P 109
Cast and ensemble during performance

PP 110-111
Ensemble performance

PP 114-115
Melody Butiu

P 122-123
David Byrne, in pink. Jeff Herrmann, behind him, and Brandon Abraham in front row, with glasses

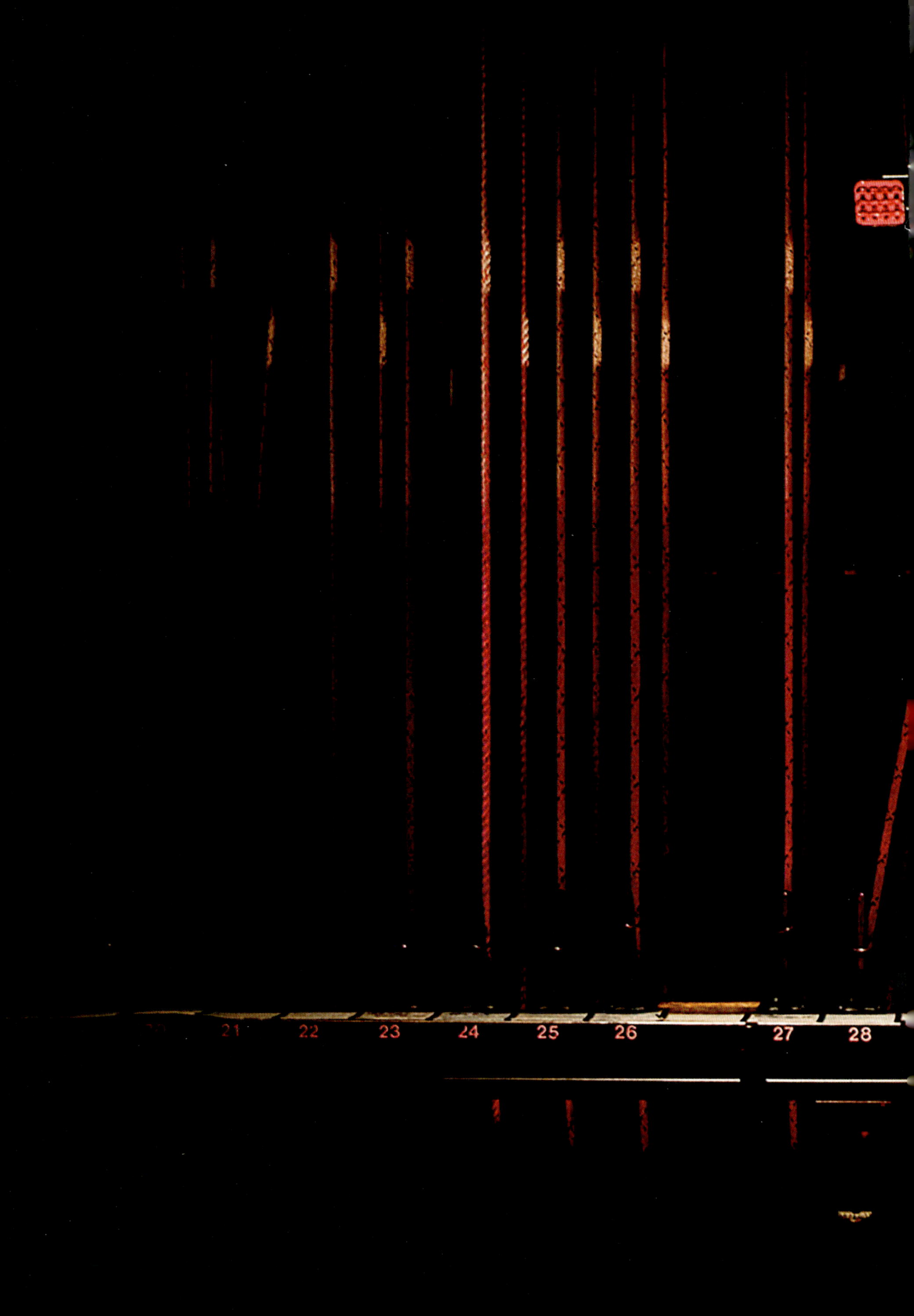
21
22
23
24
25
26
27
28

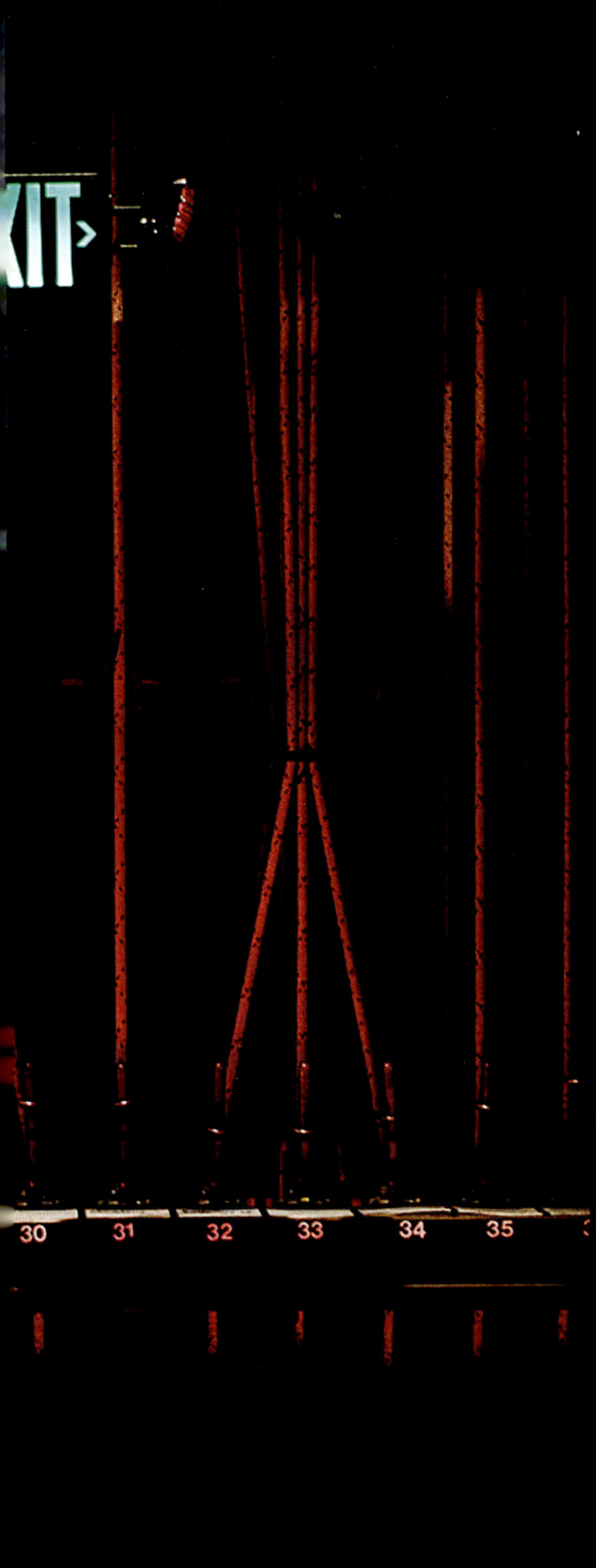
30
31
32
33
34
35

CREDITS (THE SHOW)

HERE LIES LOVE

was presented from April 7 to June 18 at Bagley Wright Theatre at Seattle Rep

Artistic Director	Braden Abraham
Managing Director	Jeffrey Herrmann
Production Director	Elisabeth Farwell-Moreland
Director of Marketing and Communications	Andrew Haines
Director of Development	Jamie Herlich
Director of Finance and Operations	Rachel Robert
Concept, music and Lyrics	David Byrne
Director	Alex Timbers
Additional Music	Fatboy Slim
Additional Music	J Pardo
Choreographer	Annie-B Parson
Music Director	Justin Levine
Scenic Designer	David Korins
Costume Designer	Clint Ramos
Lighting Designer	Justin Townsend
Sound Designer	Cody Spencer
Sound Designer	M.L. Dogg
Video Designer	Peter Nigrini
Wig and Hair Design	Dave Bova
Music Supervisor	Kin Grigsby
Production Stage Manager	Patty Grabb
Seattle Rep Production Stage Manager	Stina Lotti
Associate Director	Ricky Hinds
Associate Choreographer	Elizabeth Dement
Assistant Choreographer	Ricky Hinds
Associate Music Director	R.J. Tancioco
Music Programmer/Music Editor	Matt Stine
Associate Scenic Designer	Tony Gayle
New York Casting	Tara Rubin, CSA
New York Casting	Kaitlin Shaw, CSA
Seattle Casting	Kaytlin McIntire
Technical Director	Brian Fauska
Project Director	Steve Coulter
Resident Designer	L.B. Morse
Properties Director	Jolene Obertin
Costume Department Director	Denise Damico
Associate Lighting Designer	Robert J. Aguilar
Director of Artist Relations	Christy Bain
Audience Wranglers	Maggie Carrido Adams, Emily Blanche, Kirsten Deane, Tyler Dobies, Alannah O'Hagan, Grace Orr, Emma Pihl, Jacki Pomeroy, Jasmine Sim, Erik Siegling, Benjamin Wippel, and Fatima Wardick

CREDITS
(THE BOOK)

Published by:
Chin Music Press
1501 Pike Place #329
Seattle, WA 98101
www.chinmusicpress.com

First (1) edition
Photographs by Fernando Sancho
Book design by Guillermo Nagore

Printed in the United States

ISBN 978-1-63405-970-1

Library of Congress Cataloging in Publication data is available.